THE
WORLD
OF
DIAMONDS

THE
WORLD
OF
DIAMONDS

by
Timothy Green

WILLIAM MORROW AND COMPANY, INC.
New York   *1981*

Library of Congress Cataloging in Publication Data

Green, Timothy, 1936–
    The world of diamonds.

        Bibliography: p.
        Includes index.
        1. Diamonds. I. Title.
QE393.G73   553.8′2   80-26196
ISBN 0-688-03731-3

Printed in the United States of America

First Edition

1   2   3   4   5   6   7   8   9   10

BOOK DESIGN BY MICHAEL MAUCERI

To Snowball and Miranda,
my best friends

PREFACE

My interest in diamonds goes back over twenty years, ever since I investigated illicit diamond buying in West Africa for *Life* magazine. And I enjoyed my first real look inside the closed shop of the diamond community a decade ago for a chapter in my book *The Smugglers*. My approach in the present book is very much as a journalist, not a gemologist, looking at the intricate network of this fraternity to see who mines, who markets, who smuggles, who buys diamonds today.

At the outset I must express my thanks to countless *diamantaires*, not only in the main centers of London, New York, Antwerp, Tel Aviv and Bombay, but in many other cities from Bangkok to Rio de Janeiro, who gave up time to talk to me. In a trade that treasures its secrecy, many have asked not to be named. Obviously one cannot write about diamonds without writing about De Beers, and I must express my appreciation to countless people in that vast organization in London, Johannesburg, Kimberley and out on the mines of South Africa, Namibia and Botswana, who gave me endless help. In particular, I am most grateful to Richard Dickson in London, who coordinated all my travels around the De Beers empire.

Around the world I was also accorded much help by my old friend Madhusudan Daga in Bombay, by Tom de Graw at J. Walter Thompson in Tokyo and by Dale Wyatt, Betsy Irwin and Pat Tuck at N. W. Ayer in New York.

My research into the history of the diamond trade has been greatly assisted by the work I undertook for Dr. Henry Jarecki of Mocatta Metals in New York in writing the history of Mocatta and Goldsmid, the oldest members of the London gold and silver market, whose origins actually turned out to be in the London-Amsterdam diamond trade three hundred years ago.

The section "Buckets of Diamonds" originally appeared in a different form, in the Time-Life work, *The British Empire*, and I am grateful for permission to adapt it here.

My wife and daughter have, as always, put up courageously with my travels, and my wife has devoted her excellent skills as editor on the text. I am grateful to Janet Long for a great deal of help on the early research and, above all, to my secretary Carolyn Deuchars, who typed the manuscript time and again with exceptional speed and precision.

T.S.G.

Dulwich, August 1980

CONTENTS

THE
WORLD
OF
DIAMONDS

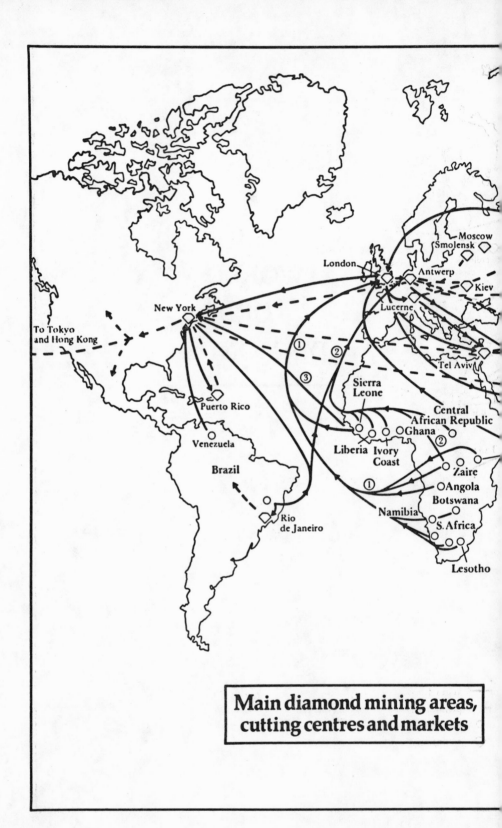

Main diamond mining areas,
cutting centres and markets

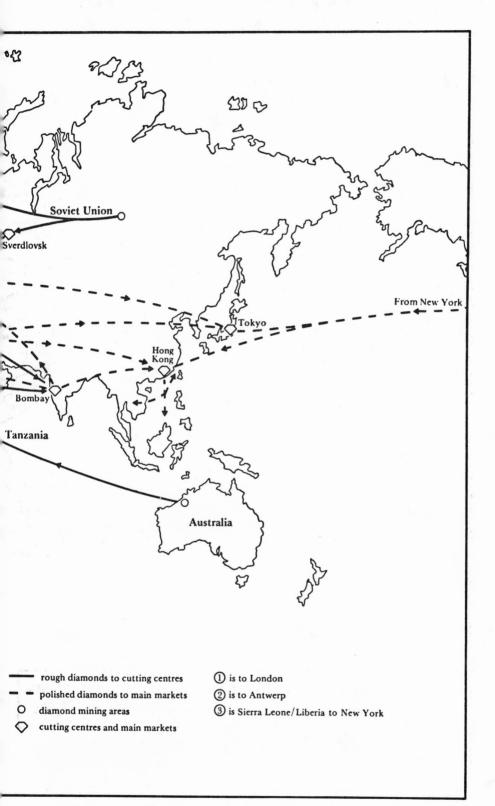

Soviet Union

Sverdlovsk

From New York

Tokyo

Hong
Kong

Bombay

Tanzania

Australia

— rough diamonds to cutting centres   ① is to London
– – polished diamonds to main markets   ② is to Antwerp
○   diamond mining areas   ③ is Sierra Leone/Liberia to New York
◇   cutting centres and main markets

INTRODUCTION

"The Goods"

> The true diamond is a hard, diaphonous perfectly transparent stone, which doth sparkle forth its glorie much like the twinckling of a glorious starre.
> —T. NICOLS, *The History of Precious Stones*, 1652

Diamonds, like the women so often reflected in them, are stunningly beautiful, rare and hard. And, unlike the women, they are virtually indestructible. They are the purest and toughest substance made by nature, formed when carbon is compressed into crystals under great heat and pressure deep within the earth's mantle. The phrases about diamonds that trip so readily off the tongue have to do, of course, with a rather different chemistry. A diamond is "forever," or is a "girl's best friend," and, as Ian Fleming once reminded us, "You can carry enough on your naked body to set you up for life." The image of the diamond has been carefully nourished to symbolize the purest love, but it also arouses the basest greed. Harry Oppenheimer, the chairman of De Beers, which has stage-managed the diamond trade for half a century, saw it slightly differently when he once observed, "The demand for diamonds is based on vanity." He cheerfully went on to give thanks that the fortunes of De Beers were so largely the result of such a durable human frailty.

The romantic vision that is conjured up by those glossy advertisements of dewy-eyed couples strolling hand in hand by the pounding surf, the new engagement ring sparkling in the sunlight, is a nice cloak for what is a ruthless, secretive and often illicit business. Everywhere from mine to jewelry store there is the temptation to steal or smuggle. Illicit diamond mining is a way of life in Sierra Leone or Zaire, with up to half the output passing along clandestine channels. Of the $4 billion of new diamonds mined each year, perhaps half a billion are smuggled at some stage on their journey to the eventual buyer. Not that a professional *diamantaire* would ever breathe the word "smuggled." The diamond trade has a language of its own, in which the stones themselves are invariably described as "the goods," and any goods that move along unorthodox routes are politely known as "outside goods," or, at best, "submarine goods." But do not confuse that with "a swimmer," which describes a fine diamond that fortuitously turns up amidst a parcel of poor quality goods and affords the dealer a nice surprise profit.

The *argot* of the diamond business helps to preserve an almost medieval sense of guild or community to which outsiders are rarely admitted. Probably no other profession in the late twentieth century is still run on such close-knit family lines. It remains almost exclusively a Jewish domain, except for the successful grafting on in the last twenty years of many Indians, who share similar respect for strong family and religious traditions. The family network, with a father in Antwerp, an uncle in Tel Aviv and cousins in Hong Kong or New York, is all-pervasive. Annie Marinower, the editor of the Belgian magazine *Diamant*, made me realize how one is born into the business when she told me, "My nephews, my nieces, my sister, my brothers, my father and my grandfather are all in diamonds." This creates a highly individual structure. "It's so personal," said Vivian Prins, a London broker, "that I've known somebody prefer to buy a diamond from Mr. X for ten percent more than he could have got it from Mr. Y." Tensions abound. "If you can't take jealousy, don't go into diamonds," advised another broker. "As for inquisitiveness, it's incredible. I often have to tell clients, 'Don't worry about someone else, concentrate on your own problems.'" Gossip thrives. "Tell one cutter and you've told the world," he went on.

Rather than a profession, it is a compulsive way of life. "Many of the older *diamantaires* knew nothing else," a dealer remarked, "nothing of sport or economics or probably even of sex." The new generation certainly has a broader view of life (and some love to conjure up a show business facade), but the intense feeling of concentration and secretiveness remains. The internal bonds of trust are strong. Each deal is still sealed (even among the Indians) with the traditional handshake and the murmured *mazel und broche* (luck and blessing). For a *diamantaire* to go back on his *mazel* is to invite oblivion.

With every deal agreed by handshake, and the goods passing around an endless international family circle, bookkeeping is usually regarded as irrelevant. *Diamantaires* everywhere fight a rearguard action against the tax authorities who seek to regularize their paperwork, threatening they will emigrate *en masse* to some more tolerant clime. The threat is not entirely empty; one reason Amsterdam is no longer a great diamond center, while Antwerp flourishes, is that the Dutch have smiled less kindly than the Belgians upon the diamond trade's wish to regulate and police itself through its own code of ethics imposed by an international framework of diamond dealers' clubs. The trouble is that their authority is not always rigorously applied. "The diamond business has its ugly side," complained a London broker, "and I'm heartbroken at the way some clubs do not always maintain integrity. There are proven cases of people who have not kept their word, who have not honored debts but have not been thrown out. If a fellow transgresses and gets away with it, the next fellow transgresses, too."

Yet it would be quite wrong to imagine the diamond business as all cloak-and-dagger, a world of dingy offices where you are not welcome in the next room. On the contrary, I found most *diamantaires*, despite some inbred caution at talking with a stranger, remarkably welcoming. Indeed, after I had traveled for a while, they were always eager to know what I had been finding out. A dozen leading Indian *diamantaires* entertained me at the pavilion of the cricket ground in Bombay to a long lunch, which turned into a barrage of questions fired by them out of genuine curiosity, rather than as a defense to block my own inquiries.

The starting point for the outsider is to realize that, just as you will never see two identical human faces or fingerprints, the same goes for diamonds. They can be sorted by shape, size, quality and color into two or even three thousand main categories, but no two are exactly alike. Many of the peculiarities of the diamond game stem from this fact. And the *diamantaire* is only as good as his knowledge of gemology. "I would say there is no other business where you must know your material so well," said Vivian Prins. "In gold you have only to be faithful to your chemistry and assaying, in insurance you know the terms and have reference books, in foreign exchange, if you get up late after a heavy night before, you have only to look at Reuters' monitor to know where you are. But in diamonds you don't deal in a known quantity; every single stone is different."

"In our trade you've never finished with learning," added P. N. Ferstenberg, the "dean" of Antwerp's *diamantaires*. "After fifty years I cannot say I know everything. Each day I see a diamond that's unlike any before."

The unique character of each stone means there cannot be a single diamond price, unlike gold or other precious commodities. One set of prices applies for rough goods (De Beers has 3,000 basic categories in its price book and negotiates individually for all large stones), and quite another for the diamonds once they have been cut and polished. The price range between two stones of identical weight can be immense. The wholesale price for one-carat polished diamonds of top quality clarity, color and cut (one carat is 0.20 gram) in the summer of 1980, for instance, was around $50,000, while the going rate for an inferior stone of the same weight was as little as $4,000. Moreover, one plus one does not necessarily make two; a couple of fine half-carat diamonds will not fetch as much as a one-carat stone of similar caliber, because the latter is rarer. (Only 1 percent of polished goods are over one carat.) Yet a really good half-carat stone could cost five times as much as a poor one-carat. The opportunity for chicanery in such a price patchwork is enormous.

Such hazards, however, cannot impair the glamour of the diamond. For the addicted, the flashing fire of a polished diamond is an irresistible beacon. "A great diamond should live, it should talk to you," Harry Winston, the prince of diamond salesmen, used to murmur as he turned a fine stone over and over in his hand. Famous stones could tell exotic tales. The 108.93-carat Koh-i-noor in the British Crown Jewels in the Tower of London has a pedigree that goes back at least to 1304, when it was owned by the Rajah of Malwa in India. Later it was taken as booty by the Mogul emperor Baber, then pillaged again by Nadir Shah of Persia when he raided Delhi in 1739. The legend has it that Nadir Shah could not find the stone until one of the women of the harem whispered that the conquered emperor had secreted it in his turban. Nadir Shah promptly invited his adversary to a feast, where, as a token of conciliation, he suggested they exchange turbans. The vanquished ruler could not refuse. After dinner Nadir Shah unwound his guest's turban. Out rolled the gem, ablaze with color. "Koh-i-noor—mountain of light," he exclaimed. He did not live long to enjoy its radiance. Four years later he was assassinated, and the Koh-i-noor was fought for regularly for a century until it ended up in Lahore, where the British took it as compensation for bloody battles with the Sikhs.[1]

Fine stones usually change hands more peacefully nowadays among a new breed of superrich. The battlefield is the auction room, where the bidders seek to establish that they are really winning the millionaire sweepstakes. When the Nizam of Hyderabad's diamonds came up for sale in 1978, the rivalry was between a Greek shipowner, Stavros Niarchos, and a business entrepreneur, Wahab Al Galadari, from Dubai in the Arabian Gulf. And the sale itself is likely to be prompted either by defeat at the hands of the taxman, or divorce. Richard Burton lavished over $1 million on a pear-shaped 62.42-carat stone for Elizabeth Taylor during their marriage; she sold it to a Texas oil millionaire for $2.8 million after the marriage went on the rocks.

Some buyers get quite carried away. A Chicago hotel owner, Potter Palmer, so lavished diamonds on his wife, the city's leading hostess, that she could scarcely stand upright at her

[1] *Notable Diamonds of the World* (published privately, De Beers Consolidated Mines, 1972), p. 20.

parties. And a fellow called Ned Green, whose mother had inherited a fortune made on Wall Street, cheerfully got rid of most of it for her on diamonds not only to adorn his girl friends, but also his chamber pot. Perhaps the prize for eccentricity goes to Herb Bales, a jeweler in Fairfield, Ohio, who has given sparkle to his smile with two diamonds set in his top front teeth. "I have a half-carat fine-cut round, VVSI, G color worth two thousand dollars in each tooth," Bales wrote to me, when I inquired about his fillings.[2] He was, he admitted, a "show-off," who enjoyed "holding little babies while mothers take pictures of us, chewing ice and biting college girls' fingers." Bales sent along pictures of himself being congratulated on finding a new use for diamonds by Moshe Schnitzer, the President of Israel's diamond exchange. "My teeth," Bales confided, "made a great impact on Mr. Schnitzer"—a remark that worried me until I called on Schnitzer myself a few months later and found him unscarred from his encounter with this Diamond Jaws. Bales signed off with a cheery "Put your money where your mouth is."

This motto is constantly adapted by anyone who wishes to transport assets discreetly from one country to another. "Diamonds are the currency of the refugee," noted a dealer, who did a brisk business in Lisbon in 1974 when more than a million Portuguese fled from Angola on overcrowded planes and ships, able to take with them virtually no possessions except hidden diamonds from the local diggings. And the lesson of the Vietnamese trying to scramble aboard the last helicopters out from the roof of the American embassy in Saigon in 1975, clutching briefcases overloaded with gold bars, did not pass unnoted. Diamonds suddenly came into fashion in Thailand among those who feared that one day they, too, might have to make a hasty exit. "You can carry only ten or fifteen kilos of gold," remarked a Bangkok dealer, doing a brisk business with goods smuggled in from Hong Kong, "but with diamonds you can carry a fortune in your top pocket." Modesty prevented him from mentioning that diamonds are often smuggled internally, wrapped in contraceptives, and that women have twice the internal capacity of men.

[2] VVSI means the diamonds have very slight flaws that are very difficult to find with 10xLens. G indicates the fourth category of color—D (or finest white) being the best.

* * *

The brilliance of a diamond in jewelry, or its versatility as international currency, should not obscure its prime virtue—hardness. Indeed, its original reputation was founded more on its toughness than its ability to dazzle; that appreciation came only much later when the art of cutting and polishing was fully mastered. The Greek origin of its name, *adamas*, means hardness. Pliny the Elder, writing in the first century A.D., regarded diamonds as "this invincible force." And "They resist blows to such an extent," he wrote in his *Historia Naturalis*, "that an iron hammer may be split in two and even the anvil itself may be displaced." A diamond resists acids, can penetrate steel and has the best thermal conductivity of any material. Modern industry would virtually halt without it. Diamonds are unequaled for etching, grinding, grooving, polishing and sharpening. They form the teeth of drilling bits for oil wells and the blades of knives that surgeons use to cut cataracts from eyes. They are even used for chopping spaghetti into neat lengths. When NASA needed a window for its space probe to Venus in 1978, they found that only a transparent diamond would do. "The diamond window had to keep the Venusian atmosphere out and let the light in," explained Max Drukker of the Amsterdam firm called in for the job. "The conditions included a four-month journey through the cold and vacuum of space, entry decelerations of five hundred sixty-five G, searing heat (the Venusian surface is red-hot), crushing pressure (one hundred times that of the earth's atmosphere) and a highly corrosive atmosphere containing carbon dioxide, sulphuric acid and other aggressive gases. There was no substitute for diamond."

Not that a diamond is indestructible; it is not forever. A diamond is brittle and, despite Pliny's remarks, can be shattered with a hard blow. One of the real arts in the shaping of a large rough diamond from the mine into the polished sparkler for a ring is cleaving the stone along its grain to split it, as if it were a log of wood. A tap in the wrong place will shatter it into a thousand pieces. And although a diamond is resistant to great temperatures, it will ultimately burn and convert into carbon monoxide and carbon dioxide at between 700 and 900 degrees centigrade. A diamond, after all, is only crystalized carbon and is composed of the same atoms as coal.

The diamond's nature as crystalized carbon has enabled modern alchemists to make synthetics, with exactly the same properties and qualities as the real thing, by subjecting carbon to high temperature and pressure. The technique was pioneered in Sweden in 1953 and actually patented by General Electric in the United States two years later. The catch is cost. Gem-quality diamonds can be manufactured, but at such expense that they offer, as yet, no competition to the natural ones. Synthetic industrial diamonds, however, are produced economically, and their output now exceeds that of industrial goods from the mines. The synthetics represent, of course, an immense challenge to the stability of the diamond market that has been so carefully cultivated by De Beers. Within a month of General Electric's announcement in 1955, De Beers, momentarily off balance, set up its own research team and was producing "industrials" commercially within four years. Synthetics, incidentally, should not be confused with diamond simulants such as cubic zirconia, yttrium aluminate or strontium titanate, which are crystals manufactured as diamond look-alikes. They can be cut to look sparkling (and are often used to make copies of famous gems), but they lack the hardness and luster of the real thing. The unscrupulous, however, can fool the unwary. An American diamond investment company was actually conned into paying $80,000 for cubic zirconia stones; neither they nor their clients were any the wiser until one investor took this "diamond" to a local jeweler for independent appraisal.

Judged by weight, the mass of diamonds end up in industry. Out of just over 46 million carats (10.5 metric tons) of diamonds mined each year, virtually 80 percent are either so small or of such inferior quality that they are of no use for jewelry. But that only puts a premium on the remaining 10 million carats that are worth cutting and polishing into gems. Gems account for scarcely 20 percent of output, but they bring in 80 percent of the return. The profit in gems explains why Zaire, actually the largest producer of diamonds, attracts much less interest than Namibia (South-West Africa). Zaire yields almost exclusively industrial goods, while Namibia's renowned "diamond coast" is a treasure trove of beautifully rounded gems. The whole economics of keeping some mines open is based on the gamble that exceptional stones turn up from time to time. The Premier Mine in South Africa, for instance, gives up a unique diamond every few years; it started with the 3,106-carat Cullinan, the largest diamond ever, back in 1904, and maintained its track record with the 353.90-carat Premier Rose in 1978.

Although just over 10 million carats of rough gem-quality goods are mined annually, less than half that amount ends up in the jewelry store. The rest vanishes in dust during cutting and polishing. An entire year's supply of polished gems is no more than 4 or 5 million carats (around 1 ton), which could easily be carried in a single pickup truck. The load would be worth, however, $15 billion, for a diamond's price mounts rapidly as it progresses from mines to lovers (or, increasingly, to investors). Not only is the cutter, the polisher, the wholesaler, the jewelry manufacturer, the jewelry wholesaler each taking his percentage, but the retailer regularly doubles—or keystones—the price he pays. The final markup is often 600 percent. The sole consolation for the buyer is that diamonds have appreciated steadily for half a century. Prices have moved up relentlessly since 1934, free from the volatility that afflicts most commodities. That progression is entirely the result of the guiding hand of De Beers, which stands like some colossus, astride the world of diamonds. "De Beers controls the market for diamonds to a degree which is completely unprecedented," wrote a mining analyst in 1980. "It is by far the most strictly controlled commodity market." Wherever you venture—to mines in Africa, to cutting centers in Belgium or Israel or India and to great markets for polished goods such as New York or Hong Kong or Tokyo—you feel their presence. In oil there are at least the "seven sisters" (as the great oil companies are known); in diamonds there is just the father figure of De Beers. All roads lead to and from the boardroom of De Beers Consolidated Mines in Kimberley, South Africa. As one market analyst put it, "Kimberley is to diamonds what Riyadh is to oil or Vienna to the classical symphony—the fountainhead and spiritual home."

PART
I

THE DIAMOND
IN HISTORY

1

Buckets of Diamonds

The legend has it that a glittering stone caught the eye of
fifteen-year-old Erasmus Jacobs as he strolled along the bank of
the Orange River in southern Africa one day in 1866. He
thought it was no more than *a mooi-klip*—a pretty pebble. But
he pocketed it, and, when he got back to De Kalk, his father's
farm near Hope Town in the north of Cape Colony, he gave the
pebble to his little sister to add to the collection she used to play
five stones. A few weeks later the children were playing with
the stones when Schalk van Niekerk, a local divisional council-
lor, came by. The bright pebble caught his eye, and, perhaps
suspecting it might be a diamond, van Niekerk asked if he might
keep it. Shortly afterwards he showed it to passing peddler John
O'Reilly, who also guessed it might be a diamond because he
could scratch his name on glass with it. He offered van Niekerk
a few pounds for it and dispatched it by ordinary mail to the
government mineralogist, Dr. Guybon Atherstone, at Grahams-
town, down near the coast. Dr. Atherstone promptly replied,
"It has blunted every jeweler's file here." Indeed, it was a diamond of 21.25 carats (about one-seventh of an ounce). The

diamond was sent to Cape Town, where Sir Philip Woodhouse, the Governor of Cape Colony, bought it for £500 and arranged for it to be displayed at the Paris Exhibition of 1867—a tantalizing foretaste of the riches that would transform not only South Africa from a poor neglected colony into one of the richest prizes of the British Empire, but usher in the modern world of diamonds.

Until the South African discoveries diamond production had been limited to India, which had been the traditional fountain of diamonds since before the birth of Christ, and to Brazil, where diamonds had been discovered in the early years of the eighteenth century. The entire perspective, however, was now altered; a completely new dimension was given to the trade as more diamonds were found in South Africa in the next ten years than had been mined in Brazil in the previous one hundred and forty and very probably more than in all history. The diamond business as we know it today unquestionably dates from the rush to what became Kimberley in the early 1870s.

Curiously, the first South African diamond aroused little excitement. A London firm did dispatch a geologist to the Orange River, but he reported there was no sign of diamondiferous gravel and concluded that the diamond must have arrived at the Orange River in the crop of an ostrich (he did not venture to add *where* the ostrich might have first eaten the diamond).

The ostrich theory was soon shot down; in 1869 Schalk van Niekerk came upon another diamond that had been found by a Griqua shepherd boy on a farm near the Orange River. The new find was a superb white diamond of eighty-five carats. In Cape Town, Colonial Secretary Sir Richard Southey proudly laid it on the table before the Cape Parliament, declaring, "Gentlemen, this is the rock on which the future of South Africa will be built." The diamond was named appropriately, "Star of South Africa."

Suddenly the whole of Cape Colony was talking about diamonds, for others were soon found, not only along the Orange River, but in even greater profusion by Vaal River a little further to the north. The new discoveries were just within the borders of the two independent Boer republics, the Transvaal and the Orange Free State, which had been created after the Great Trek of 1834. Within weeks everyone seemed headed for the fields, with highly romantic notions of what they would find. "They saw in their lively imaginings," said one contemporary, "diamond fields glittering with diamonds like dewdrops in the waving grass or branches of trees along the Vaal River, and covering the highways and by-ways like hoarfrost."

The reality was harsher. The first mining camps that mushroomed at Pniel and Klipdrift along the Vaal were reached only by a 700-mile hard slog on horseback, or by ox-drawn wagon from Cape Town, or by a 500-mile journey over mountains from Durban or Port Elizabeth in Natal. "The roads," one digger lamented, "were rough trampled tracks, changing after a rainfall to beds of mire. Their tortuous courses rambled from settlement to settlement, or from farmhouse to farmhouse over the veldt, and were often wholly lost in the shifting sands of the Karoo."

The mining communities of tents and corrugated iron huts were scorching dustbowls in summer and freezing morasses of mud in winter. Food was high-priced, and diggers who were smitten with malaria had to nurse each other as best they could. Most diggers had little notion of what rough diamonds really looked like, even less how to find them. They set up tents haphazardly and started groping around in the sand and gravel. They first sifted through the gravel with simple sieves on rockers, then spread the remaining pebbles on a bench and sorted through them with a wooden scraper. If nothing much turned up, they moved on after a few days. The names of the early mining communities —Cawood's Hope, Forlorn Hope, Good Hope and Last Hope— reflect their aspirations and disappointments. There were tales of remarkable good luck, including one of a young man who found a diamond on the earth floor of the church when he knelt down to pray.

But the frustrations were endless. "An English gentleman," reported one visitor to the diggings, "having worked a claim for six months and found nothing, went home disgusted, giving away his claim. The man who got it found on the same day a fine diamond of 29½ carats before he had gone six inches deeper than his predecessor. I believe he was offered £2,500 for it."

The eternal hope that beneath the next thin layer of gravel lay a fortune kept the diggers going through the worst privations. "Men who set out to work in the morning, not knowing where their dinner was to come from, became richer than any member of their family had ever been before it was time for an eleven o'clock snack," reported Charles Payton, a correspondent for *The Field*.

Important new discoveries kept up the excitement. In August 1870 diamonds were discovered on Jagersfontein Farm, to the south of the early Vaal diggings and about twenty miles from the river. A month later more were found on Dorstfontein Farm nearby. Scarcely were the diggers getting their shacks up there when Cornelius du Plooy, who owned Bultfontein Farm across the way, found a diamond in plaster he was using to do up his house. He promptly sold the farm for £2,000 as diggers came rushing in.

The real prize, however, was the Vooruitzigt estate of two Boer brothers, Johannes and Diedrich De Beer, a mile or so from Bultfontein. Diamonds were found there in May 1871 and then in even richer abundance at a little hillock on the farm known as Colesberg Kopje, a couple of months later. Presently a handful of diggers, who had no luck on the farm itself, moved a mile or two east where they found more diamonds in a shallow depression that was quickly christened "New Rush," but eventually became Kimberley Mine. During the next forty years the burrowings of diggers at the Kimberley Mine created the awesome Big Hole—the deepest open-pit mine ever dug by man, plunging down almost 1,300 feet into the depths of the earth.

The essential difference between these fresh finds and the earlier alluvial ones on the Orange and Vaal Rivers was that they were all diamond pipes, each no more than a few hundred feet square, thrust up from the bowels of the earth by volcanic activity. At first the ordinary diggers had little difficulty in sifting out the stones from the yellowish soil at the top of the pipe, just as they did on river diggings. A hundred feet down, however, they came upon a hard blue rock, which they christened kimberlite. Some assumed, unwisely, there were no more diamonds. Yet once the kimberlite was exposed to wind and rain, it too turned yellow and yielded diamonds in even greater profusion. The deep kimberlite pipes, however, meant that the days of the independent digger as king of his own small claim were numbered. Expensive and sophisticated mining techniques would ultimately be required, and the real future of diamond production in South Africa was to lie in great mining houses.

Still, for a few years the individual diggers reigned supreme. Like eager rabbits they burrowed into the top of the "pipes" on the De Beers' and neighboring farms. The De Beer brothers themselves did not join in. They promptly cashed in on the windfall; they sold the Vooruitzigt estate, which they had bought for a mere £50 in 1860, for £6,000 to a diggers' syndicate and went off to farm quietly elsewhere (although they were known to admit sorrowfully in later years they might have done better to settle for £6 million rather than £6,000). Their name, of course, has endured in the greatest of all diamond-mining houses.

Colesberg Kopje, on Vooruitzigt, the scene of the "New Rush," was renamed Kimberley, after the British Colonial Secretary of the day, who said he could not spell either of those names, nor was it dignified for any community in Queen Victoria's dominions to be known as De Beers New Rush.

Kimberley, with a population of over 10,000, took on the air of a boom town, with billiard halls and bars, cheap hotels and canteens, and even a racecourse of sorts. At Dodd's Bar, the whiskey and cigars were free for roulette and faro players. One crafty fellow named Champagne Charlie salted his claim with fake diamonds he had filed down from champagne bottle bottoms, sold out fast at a profit and vanished. And a prostitute up from Cape Town auctioned herself before a raucous crowd in a bar one night; a Dutch diamond buyer won her favors with a £25 bid. As they settled down in his tent, however, the lower bidders in the auction suddenly whisked away the canvas to watch what they had missed.

The Kimberley diamond pipes, combined with the Orange and Vaal River diggings, yielded diamonds in unheard-of quantities. By 1872 South African production was already over one million carats, or five times that of Brazil on the eve of the discoveries; it was over two million carats by 1879 and three million the following year. Remarkably, the international price for rough diamonds held up well to begin with, chiefly because the rapid industrial growth in Germany, France and the United States created an ever-widening wealthy clientele for stones. Throughout the next generation the diamond price became a close mirror of economic activity; during boom years the price was strong, in moments of recession it, too, slumped.

The flood of stones also brought a swift rejuvenation to the

cutting and polishing industry in Europe that had been stag-
nating during the 1860s because of the decline in output from
Brazil. This new lease of life was christened Kaapsche Tyd
(the Cape era) by the Dutch cutters, whose wages shot up
thirteen times, so great was the demand for their skills. New
cutting centers flourished. Antwerp, which had always run a
poor second to Amsterdam since the seventeenth century, became a boom town. Its rapid rise as the world's premier marketplace for the exchange of rough and polished diamonds began.
The Antwerp Diamond Club, the oldest of the city's four exchanges, was founded in 1893. By then there were already
forty factories for cutting and polishing stones. This new-found
prosperity attracted to Antwerp many Jewish emigrants from
Russia and Eastern Europe, thus providing a constant injection
of new dealers and craftsmen.

The diamond brokers from London, Antwerp, Amsterdam,
Hamburg and Paris all sent their agents on the first available
mail boats to Africa to open representative offices. The largest
advertisement in the first issue of the *Diamond News and Vaal
Advertiser*, published in Pniel in October 1870, boldly proclaimed that Mr. Wilhelm Schultz of Lippert & Co., with offices
in Hamburg, Germany, begged to inform the public that he had
opened a wholesale buying office. "Being in connection with
the above well known Firm," read the advertisement, "who have
their own Establishments in Europe, he ventures to say that he
will be able to DEFY ALL COMPETITION."

The diamond rush drew the attention not just of adventurers
seeking swift riches and of professional buyers from Europe, but
of politicians in Cape Town and London. Previously they had
paid scant attention to the two poverty-stricken Boer republics
of the Transvaal and Orange Free State, whence the Boers had
retreated in their Great Trek a generation earlier "to preserve
their purity." The discovery of diamonds, however, in territory
to which the Boers made some claim was a different matter.
Sir Richard Southey, the Colonial Secretary at Cape Colony,
regarded it as inconceivable that Britain should not have a stake
in the world's richest diamond fields. Moreover, the wealth from
the mines could change the balance of power in southern Africa.
Two penniless Boer republics were no threat to British rule;
two wealthy ones, on the other hand, could form a barrier right

across Africa to the Kalahari Desert, thwarting direct British access from the Cape to central Africa.

The British found an excuse to assert their authority because virtually all the diamond fields were in a region known as West Griqualand, inhabited by the Griquas, a tribe of mixed Hottentot and Boer blood. Although ostensibly this was in the Boer domain, no clear international agreement had been reached; it had been too insignificant to bother with before the diamond finds. The British, refusing international arbitration, set up their own commission to decide who should rule it. Not surprisingly, the commission came down in favor of British control. Thus in November 1871 the Union Jack was run up over the diamond fields. The Boers' protests were brushed aside. The Orange Free State later received a derisory £90,000 compensation; the Transvaal got nothing. This annexation of the diamond fields was never forgotten or forgiven by the Boers. It was one of the first bitter grievances to foment the Boer War thirty years later.

The very month that the Union Jack was hoisted, a tall auburn-haired young Englishman in baggy white cricket flannels came trekking over the veldt with a bucket and spade, a few volumes of the classics, a Greek lexicon and a box of cough lozenges piled on an ox wagon. His name was Cecil John Rhodes; he was just eighteen and many thousands of miles from the quiet vicarage at Bishops Stortford in Hertfordshire where he had been born in 1853, the third son of the Reverend Francis William Rhodes. He had been brought up in the strict, pious atmosphere of a Victorian family. His father was anxious that Cecil and all his brothers should enter the Church "as a preliminary step to becoming angels." That proposal, however, never matured, for Cecil caught tuberculosis. The doctor recommended a healthy open life to restore his health, and Cecil journeyed to South Africa in 1870 to join his eldest brother Herbert, who ran a cotton farm in Natal. Herbert Rhodes took off for the diamond fields soon after, but Cecil, with the dedication to succeed that marked his entire career, persevered and brought in a fine cotton crop. The cotton price, however, was poor. In disgust, Rhodes took off to join his brother at the diggings.

He set up his tent at De Beers' "New Rush," where he described the diggings in a letter to his mother as looking like "Stilton cheese." The diamonds were right on his doorstep. "I found a 17⅝ carat on Saturday," he wrote home; "it was very slightly off and I hope to get £100 for it. Does it not seem an absurd price? Yesterday, I found a three and a half perfect stone, but glassy, which I sold for £30 . . . I average £100 a week."

While the majority of diggers had no sense of organization and wandered aimlessly from claim to claim, Rhodes from the outset selected his claims carefully and worked them thoroughly.

After a while he went into partnership with another young Englishman, Charles Rudd, who had been a champion athlete at Harrow and Cambridge before deteriorating health had made him, too, seek an open-air life in Africa. Rudd proved an ideal partner for the restless Rhodes, who was determined to combine his diamond diggings with taking a degree at Oxford. Throughout the eight years from 1873 to 1881 that Rhodes spent commuting between Kimberley and Oriel College, Oxford, to complete his degree, Rudd worked on, quietly managing their claims.

As he traveled between the strangely contrasted worlds of Kimberley and Oxford, Rhodes was beginning to formulate his grand design for the future. He had already amassed a considerable fortune for a young man (he spent nearly five thousand dollars on fares alone during his Oxford days), but that was just the foundation stone of the wealth he wanted in order to fulfill an emerging dream of making not only Africa, but most of the world British. At Oxford one evening he invited some friends to dinner and during dessert made a little speech in which he explained that "he thought it right for every man, at the beginning of his life, to put an aim before him, and for his part he meant to work for the British Empire."

Henceforth, his whole life was dedicated to this purpose. "If there be a God," he said, "I think what He would like me to do is to paint as much of Africa British-red as possible." A fortune in diamonds was one way of underwriting that goal. "When I am in Kimberley," he once explained, "I often go and sit on the edge of the De Beers Mine, and I reckon up the value of the diamonds in the 'blue' and the power conferred by them. Every foot of the blue ground means so much power."

The discovery of the "blue" ground at Kimberley soon after Rhodes's arrival had changed the character of the diggings dramatically. At first, the diggers pitched into their small claims like fury, scooping out the soil without any regard for the danger. Soon pathways between claims were undermined and collapsed, while flooding was a permanent hazard. Organization and scientific techniques were badly needed, especially to hoist out and crush the lower layers of blue rock. But for a while the diggers still stuck to individual claims, which they reached, as the open pits got deeper and deeper, by buckets and trolleys slung from a web of cables over the diggings.

The novelist Anthony Trollope, viewing this chaotic scene at the Kimberley "Big Hole" in 1877, wrote, "It is as though you were looking down into a vast bowl, the sides of which are smooth as should be the sides of a bowl, while round the bottom are various marvellous incrustations among which ants are working with all the unusual energy of the ant-tribe." Trollope felt it "was as though some diabolically ingenious architect had contrived a house with 500 rooms, not one of which should be on the same floor, and to and from none of which there should be a pair of stairs or a door or a window."

Rhodes was determined to set his house in order. He already had a profitable sideline going in renting out steam pumps to get the water out of flooded claims. Now he told Charles Rudd, "The time is coming when the small man will have to go. These pits cannot be worked much deeper. We shall have to mine the ground on the largest possible scale. Now is the time to buy."

Rhodes and Rudd concentrated their buying on the De Beers Mine. They soon owned a major share of the claims and in 1880 formed the De Beers Mining Company Limited, with capital of $482,000.

Consolidation was taking place at all the mines. At the Kimberley Mine, at which 1,600 individual diggers had claims in 1871, just twelve companies shared the mine ten years later. By 1885 the four main mines, Kimberley, De Beers, Dorstfontein and Bultfontein, were controlled by forty-two companies (many of them with common directors) and a sprinkling of private holdings.

As the diamond business became more complex and costly, Rhodes and Rudd turned frequently for advice to Alfred Beit, a nervous little man who had first arrived in Kimberley as a diamond buyer for Lippert & Company of Hamburg and who later became a partner in Jules Porges & Company, one of the wealthiest French diamond houses. Beit was a financial wizard. He also enjoyed first-rate connections with major European dealers. Rhodes needed his skills to consolidate his diamond empire. When they had first met, Rhodes inquired, "What's your game?"

"I am going to control the whole diamond output before I am much older," replied Beit.

"That's funny," said Rhodes. "I have made up my mind to do the same. We had better join hands."

Beit's flair for diamonds, Rhodes soon discovered, was uncanny. Once, when a man tried to sell him some stolen diamonds, he identified them immediately as stones that had passed through his hands seven years earlier.

Rhodes, Rudd and Beit had to match their expertise, however, with other past masters in diamonds, who had also made their fortunes at Kimberley. There was Francis Baring Gould, who owned a major stake in the Kimberley Mine and was backed by excellent financial connections in the City of London; Joseph B. Robinson (known as The Buccaneer), a quarrelsome and aggressive man who was envious of Rhodes's success and spent much of his career trying to thwart every project Rhodes embarked on; and, above all, there was Barney Barnato, the irrepressible East End music-hall entertainer and boxer turned diamond magnate.

Barney Barnato was born Barnett Isaacs in Petticoat Lane, London, in 1852, the son of a small shopkeeper. He left school at fourteen and, aided by his Jewish-Cockney wit, got by on a host of odd jobs, including bouncer at the King of Prussia pub, selling discarded theater ticket stubs in the intervals and eventually doing a music-hall turn of his own. When diamonds were discovered in South Africa, several relatives joined the rush; inspired by their reports, Barney himself followed and headed for the diggings in 1873. His capital when he arrived consisted of forty boxes of cigars of doubtful quality, which he hoped to sell at a good profit to the diggers. No one wanted his cigars, so he turned his hand to any job going, including that of boxing champion at the local circus. Later he became a *kopje walloper*—an itinerant diamond buyer drifting around the fields, buying up diamonds. The legend goes that Barnato bought an aged pony from another *kopje walloper* to make his rounds; the pony knew the route so well it always stopped at claims where Barnato might be able to buy. His lack of diamond expertise was made up for by his genial nature, which encouraged the diggers to sell to him, even if they knew he was offering them a poor price. They felt he was one of their own.

Once he had a little money, Barnato bought four claims very near the center of the Kimberley "pipe." He and his brother worked like demons, digging ever deeper into the blue ground. "We soon found that the blue itself was the true home of the diamond," he once said. Soon he was making $5,000 a week and formed The Barnato Diamond Mining Company. Like Rhodes, Barnato kept on quietly buying up claims all around. His best coup was in 1884, when he persuaded a digger named Stewart to sell him six claims at the heart of the pipe for $430,000. The following year he merged his company with Francis Baring Gould's Kimberley Central Mining Company, thus giving him as strong a hold on the Kimberley Mine as Cecil Rhodes had at the De Beers Mine. The alliance with Baring Gould gave Barnato strong City backing, while his own income was easily $500,000 a year. He was by then the wealthiest diamond entrepreneur and a formidable rival to Cecil Rhodes.

Barnato had every reason to be content with his diamond empire. He controlled most of the Kimberley Mine, the richest in South Africa, and he felt there was plenty of room in the business for Rhodes and himself. Not so Rhodes, who saw his diamond empire merely as the springboard to launch him on his empire-building road. Control of the whole diamond business, now worth $12 million a year, was essential for this enterprise. His convictions on the benefits of monopoly were strengthened during the mid-1880s by wildly fluctuating diamond prices, as some firms gave up because of the increasing technical difficulties of diamond mining, while others tried to undercut the market to win a larger share. Rhodes was sure that if one company controlled all diamond production, the price could be stabilized by a steady sale of stones. Although a notorious woman-hater, Rhodes enjoyed pointing out that the whole foundation of the diamond's worth was based on the relationship between men and women; as long as they fell in love, the future of the diamond was assured. He had even calculated that four million diamonds were needed every year for engagement rings. He hoped to supply all four million.

Rhodes's ambition was checked by two companies—Barnato's Kimberley Central and the *Compagnie Française des Mines de Diamant de Cap de Bon Esperance* (known by everyone simply as The French Company), which held the other major share of the Kimberley Mine. Rhodes maneuvered first for control of The French Company. He traveled to London in July 1887 and approached N. M. Rothschild and Sons, that aristocrat of merchant banking houses, for financial support. Rothschilds offered him a loan of $2.4 million, whereupon Rhodes bid $3.4 million for control of The French Company. Back in Kimberley, Barnato received a cable warning of the deal and promptly raised the stakes with a bid of his own for $700,000 more. Rhodes was not unduly perturbed. "You can go on bidding *ad infinitum*," he told Barnato, "but we shall have it in the end."

He did. A compromise was worked out, whereby Rhodes bought The French Company for his original price and immediately sold it to Barnato for a one-fifth stake in Kimberley Central, plus $700,000 in cash.

That seemed to leave Barnato in an even stronger position, owning The French Company and retaining four-fifths of Kimberley Central, but Rhodes had outwitted him. His one-fifth share in Kimberley Central was the crucial toehold he needed in the Barnato diamond empire. Rhodes and his associates then began buying up all the other Kimberley Central shares they could corral. Barnato fought back, buying shares at absurd prices himself, so that the price soared from $33 to $118. In vain; some of his principal shareholders could not resist selling to Rhodes, who was offering them tempting holdings in the new giant company he proposed to form. Rhodes tackled Barnato himself by inviting him to lunch at the exclusive Kimberley Club which was housed, most unpretentiously, in a corrugated iron hut. Barney, with his East End background, had never been admitted as a member. Obviously this subtle maneuver did not win Barnato over, but after several lunches he began to see Rhodes in a new light. Previously Barnato had felt Rhodes, with his Oxford degree, looked down on his humble origins. Now he found Rhodes more sympathetic. He conceded, "The worst of Rhodes is that when you have been with him for half an hour, you not only agree with him, but you come to believe you have always held his opinion."

Sure enough, Rhodes's opinion prevailed. In return for promising to merge Kimberley Central with De Beers, Barnato was guaranteed the largest individual shareholding and a life governorship in the new De Beers Consolidated Mines, which was incorporated on March 13, 1888.

One final stumbling block then arose. A handful of Kimberley Central shareholders, unhappy at Barnato's selling out to Rhodes, challenged the merger in the courts.

This did not thwart Rhodes long. His advisers told him that if Barnato agreed to put Kimberley Central into voluntary liquidation, De Beers could simply buy its assets. So Cecil Rhodes wrote a check for £5,338,650 ($12.8 million) for the assets of Kimberley Central, the largest sum ever covered by one check at that time (the canceled check may still be seen in the De Beers boardroom in Kimberley). It gave Cecil Rhodes, at thirty-five, control of 90 percent of the world's diamond output and, with the resources of De Beers Consolidated Mines behind him, the financial power to proceed with his African ambitions.

By way of celebration, Rhodes is said to have turned to Barney Barnato: "I've always wanted to see a bucketful of diamonds."

Barnato obligingly had a bucket filled with gems. Rhodes plunged his arms in ecstatically and let the diamonds cascade through his fingers.

2

Building the Syndicate

Rhodes might have his hands on diamond production, but that was only half the goal. His conception was always that the supply of rough diamonds from the mines must be constantly adjusted to match the fluctuating world demand. That waterfall of diamonds from Barnato's bucket had, so to speak, to be regulated constantly by opening or closing the gap between his fingers. Such an aim could be realized only if De Beers brought under its wing any new producers that came along and at the same time channeled the sales of diamonds through carefully selected outlets. Production and sales must be allied. That was not all; in boom periods the producers must obtain the maximum prices (and profit) to enable them to weather lean times when it might be necessary to stockpile diamonds, or even curtail production.

The evolution of the diamond business in the forty or so years after Cecil Rhodes won the fight for De Beers in 1889 centers on the producers' search for a marketing structure to insure that control. The man who would ultimately fulfill Cecil Rhodes's dream was Sir Ernest Oppenheimer. As Rhodes towered over diamond mining in the last quarter of the nineteenth century, so Oppenheimer was gradually to dominate not only the mining, but the whole diamond scene during the first half of the twentieth. The world of diamonds today is his creation, more than of any other single man.

In the Kimberley of 1889, of course, that was still a distant prospect. Yet its image as a raucous diamond diggers' town was already waning. The growth of a mining giant like De Beers, with all the complexities of finance, machinery and technology that it would introduce, inevitably sobered the place. The day of the fast-living digger was over; he moved on in search of new horizons of adventure. The era of the corporate executive slowly dawned.

The immediate question, now that Rhodes controlled 90 percent of the world's diamond production of over 3 million carats a year, worth close to $12 million, was how best to dispose of them. Diamond dealers naturally were falling over themselves to do business with De Beers; to secure the right to sell their stones would be a unique catch. Shortly, Rhodes agreed to grant the sole marketing rights of De Beers rough diamonds to a syndicate formed by ten leading dealers. Each was assigned a quota. The three leaders were Wernher, Beit & Company (23 percent), in which Rhodes's long-standing ally Alfred Beit was a partner; Barnato Brothers (20 percent), run by Barney Barnato, his brother Harry and his nephews Woolf and Solly Joel; and Mosenthals (15 percent). All three firms were also important shareholders in De Beers. The fourth largest quota (10 percent) went to Anton Dunkelsbuehler, a young dealer who had originally started at Kimberley as a representative of Mosenthals but had then set up on his own. He already had a flourishing office in London, where very shortly two young German emigrants Louis and Ernest Oppenheimer, the sons of a middle-class Jewish cigar merchant in Hamburg, started work as diamond sorters, preparing Kimberley diamonds for monthly "sights." Both men were to play an essential role in the development of the diamond business over the next half century: Louis as a man with a rare flair, a sixth sense, some said, for being able to sift a parcel of rough diamonds through his hands and assess their worth; and Ernest as a business entrepreneur concerned to remold the entire industry.

This sales consortium was swiftly christened the Diamond
Syndicate. For a generation, with varying membership, it was to
prevail over the marketing of De Beers' and other producers'
diamonds. The essential difference between the syndicate and
the system that prevails today is that it was composed of independent dealers (even if, like Barnato, they had a close link
with De Beers); it was not controlled by the diamond producers.

The monopoly of De Beers and the Diamond Syndicate went
effectively unchallenged throughout the 1880s. Kimberley was
the home of diamonds. No rival was in sight. The only important
new diamond "pipe" found for a decade was Wesselton, and
that was just four miles out of town. But output was always
carefully tailored to match the needs of the market. The prosperous days of the late 1890s were immediately reflected in a
rise in production from 2.7 million carats in 1894 to 3.6 million
in 1898, which was achieved with scarcely a flicker in the price
of rough diamonds at 25 shillings per carat. The Boer War cut
rudely into that expansion. Kimberley was soon under siege, and
as diamond output fell to scarcely 2 million carats by 1900, the
price for rough rose to close on 39 shillings per carat by 1901.

With peace, the dilemma was how to hold the price high, for
De Beers was reluctant to see the price fall back to its prewar
level. Consequently, after an initial year of higher production in
1901, they cut back progressively on the output of the Kimberley
Mines. The issue, however, was no longer just what the market
could stand. Their comfortable monopoly was under fire. A
former bricklayer named Thomas Cullinan had located, on a
farm near Pretoria in the Transvaal, a little hill or *kopje* remarkably like those rising over the veldt around Kimberley three
hundred miles away. Sure enough, it was the top of another
kimberlite pipe, the richest in diamonds ever found. The mine,
Premier, has since yielded over 80 million carats (more than 15
tons), including many of the largest gemstones.

The discovery of Premier came just nine months after the
death of Cecil Rhodes in March 1902, which was by chance the
very year that the twenty-two-year-old Ernest Oppenheimer
moved from London to Kimberley to take charge of the local
office of Anton Dunkelsbuehler, the syndicate dealers. However,
even before Rhodes's death, his own preoccupation with politics

had allowed De Beers to become somewhat complacent about its hold on the diamond business. Rhodes himself had even remarked to his shareholders on one occasion, "The only trouble, with regard to the industry, is that it is becoming a matter of course and uninteresting. It goes like clockwork." [3]

Such boredom nearly caused disaster. When Premier was found, the new chairman of De Beers, Francis Oats, instead of responding swiftly to stake a strong claim for control, suggested the mine had been "salted" and was a "fake." The reverse was true. Within five years Premier was producing more diamonds than all the De Beers mines put together, touching over 2 million carats in 1908. Its superiority was driven home one evening in 1905 when the eye of the mine manager, Frederick Wells, was caught by a big stone gleaming in the low rays of the sun. He dug it out with his pocket knife, scarcely believing what he saw. The diamond was four inches long, two-and-a-half inches high and two inches broad; it weighed 3,106 carats, making it the largest ever found. This pear-sized stone was called the Cullinan. Ultimately, it was bought by the Transvaal government for $360,000 as a gift to Edward VII (while Wells received a bonus of $5,000 for his find). When the diamond was cut by Joseph Asscher of the great Amsterdam diamond house, it yielded nine major stones and ninety-six small brilliant-cuts. No better proof was required that the Premier was an unbeatable mine.

Francis Oats's initial dismissal of Premier as a fake cost De Beers dearly. Premier's directors were in no mood to join forces in marketing and instead set up their own sales organization, stepping up production. For a while the market was able to absorb the output of both groups without trouble; America, which took some 70 percent of all diamonds, was prosperous. But a stock market crash in 1907 wiped out that sponge. As the Diamond Syndicate found itself with over $7 million in unsold stock, an alliance with Premier was proposed. The Syndicate had succeeded in reaching a modest agreement with the new mine to take $450,000 of its output monthly (against $1.1 million from De Beers), but early in 1908, as the market slumped, it had to concede its "inability to continue purchasing fixed quantities." That was not good enough for Premier; its directors feared that

[3] Cecil Rhodes speaking at Eighth Annual General Meeting of De Beers, December 28, 1896.

the Syndicate, essentially a De Beers animal, was exaggerating the crisis. They declined further cooperation and went back to selling all production on their own, accepting a sharp decline in price. De Beers themselves had little option but to accept the Syndicate terms and were forced to cut back on mine production.

Everyone suffered. Premier got a miserable price, De Beers had to reduce output drastically, the Syndicate lost heavily and several firms withdrew. The lesson was clear. Rhodes's original principle of moderating the supply of rough diamonds to match the market mood had been violated because the outsider, Premier, refused to cooperate. De Beers and Premier were pulling in opposite directions. And although the immediate situation improved by 1909, as growth returned in America so that the Syndicate could finally shift some stocks, the outlook was bleak. For in April of 1908 a one-fourth-carat diamond was found by a young Cape boy, Zacharias Lewala, amidst the coastal sands of South-West Africa, then a German colony. Before long it was all too clear that diamonds were scattered like stardust all through the shifting sands of the great western desert. And unlike the deep pipes of Kimberley or Premier, these were alluvial deposits. Swiftly, prospectors had an army of African laborers literally crawling line-abreast through the sand, looking for diamonds. What they found were small gemstones of exceptional quality and color.

The surprising fact is that De Beers again initially misjudged the importance of the find. They decided that an *alluvial* deposit posed no real threat and, once reassured that there was no kimberlite pipe in South-West Africa, argued that all payable areas would soon be exhausted. They were wrong. The diamond desert surrendered over one million carats of diamonds in 1912, representing nearly 20 percent of all Africa's diamonds that year. Yet De Beers made no serious attempt to buy into one of the German mining syndicates exploiting the area. Moreover, the diamonds were all being marketed through a Berlin company, The Diamond Regie of South-West Africa, which won more favorable contracts from Antwerp dealers than the Syndicate in London was prepared to offer.

This was a serious threat to the preeminence of London as the world capital for rough diamonds, for the German outlet offered Antwerp, by now the premier cutting center and boasting four diamond exchanges, a direct source of first-rate stones. Both De Beers and the South African government soon had to admit that the discoveries in the German colony were not transient. Cooperation was essential. A conference of diamond producers, embracing all the major South African mining companies and the German Diamond Administration, met in 1914.

What they agreed amounted to the first international diamond cartel. They decided upon a diamond producers' pool, which would sell to the Diamond Syndicate, or Central Selling Agency as it was termed in the new agreement, $26 million worth of diamonds in 1915, rising to $30 million worth in subsequent years. Each member of the pool accepted fixed quotas; De Beers had 48.5 percent, the German Diamond Administration 21 percent, Premier 19.5 percent and the Jagersfontein Mine (another pipe near Kimberley in which De Beers were shareholders) 11 percent. The syndicate was to be composed of Barnato Brothers, A. Dunkelsbuehler, Mosenthals and L. Breitmeyer (which had taken over the diamond business of Wernher Beit in 1911).

The Great War, however, cut short these plans. The Syndicate canceled all contracts, fearing, quite rightly, a sharp drop in diamond demand during hostilities (wars are traditionally bad for luxuries). And the former German colony of South-West Africa was swiftly taken over by the British, who made it a mandate under the wing of the government of the Union of South Africa. That immediately posed the question of who was to take over the diamond mining interests of the former German Diamond Administration. One man, above all, had his eye on them—Ernest Oppenheimer.

Ever since his arrival in Kimberley in 1902 as the buyer for Anton Dunkelsbuehler, Ernest Oppenheimer had enjoyed an insider's view of the diamond business. His expertise was acknowledged by his appointment in 1912 as an alternative director of the Jagersfontein Mine, and shortly afterward he was one of three consultants asked by De Beers to visit the diamond fields of South-West Africa to make an appraisal of their long-term potential. He was closely involved, too, with gold and other mining interests in South Africa through Consolidated Mines Selection Company, in which Dunkelsbuehlers were major shareholders. Clearly, he could have carved out a remarkable career within the framework of one of the existing mining houses. He was eager, however, to create an organization that was, as he put it later, "a South African house," unlike the existing mining companies which were essentially of British or German origin. Consolidated Mines Selection, for instance, had four German directors, who all had to resign in 1914 when the company drew anti-German fire. Oppenheimer's aim was to create a South African company that might be a channel for American capital (not hitherto sizably invested in South Africa) to aid the growth of the mining industry.

He achieved his ambition at the age of thirty-seven, when, in 1917, he founded the Anglo-American Corporation of South Africa Limited, with the active support of the great American banking house, J. P. Morgan, and the Newmont Mining Corporation. The initial impetus behind the formation of Anglo-American was gold, not diamonds. Oppenheimer was eager to exploit a fresh generation of gold mines on a new field known as the Far West Rand. This was the first step in making Anglo-American the most important of the South African mining finance houses in gold. Even so, Ernest Oppenheimer's real love was diamonds. In a letter to his American associates soon after the formation of Anglo, he outlined his plans. The letter is worth quoting at length, because so much of the diamond business today is shaped by its consequences.

"From the very start," wrote Oppenheimer, "I expressed the hope that besides gold, we might create, step by step, a leading position in the diamond world, thus concentrating by degrees in the corporation's hands the position which the pioneers of the diamond industry (the late Cecil Rhodes, Wernher, Beit, etc.) formerly occupied. Such a position is most difficult to attain, requiring intimate knowledge of the diamond trade, pluck and a great deal of patience, but, above all, the support of powerful financial groups who would be prepared to play the part which Messrs. Rothschild played vis-a-vis the original leaders, at the time of the De Beers amalgamation. It is quite evident to my mind that eventually an amalgamation of the four big diamond producers (De Beers, Premier, Jagersfontein and Consolidated Diamonds) will be brought about, and I see no reason, if we continue our diamond policy, why we should not play a leading role in such an operation." [4]

It took him just twelve years from the formation of Anglo-American to secure that role. Relentlessly through the 1920s he went in pursuit of control of both the production and marketing of a predominant share of the world's diamonds. The first foothold was South-West Africa. Oppenheimer, with the aid of his bankers J. P. Morgan, succeeded in quietly arranging an amalgamation of the old German diamond companies to form his own Consolidated Diamond Mines of South-West Africa (CDM) in 1919. De Beers, who rather belatedly also began nosing around to make similar acquisitions, found themselves faced with a *fait accompli*. It was the initial step in what one South African historian called "the encirclement of De Beers."

Meanwhile the diamond market, which had already improved by 1917, was going through a postwar boom, so that the Syndicate was happy to make new contracts with all the major producers. Five-year agreements were signed with all leading groups; De Beers still enjoyed the lion's quota of 51 percent, but Oppenheimer's Consolidated Diamond Mines of South-West Africa was awarded a substantial 21 percent slice (compared with Premier at 18 percent and Jagersfontein at 10 percent). Oppenheimer also enjoyed a roundabout entrée into the Syndicate itself through his old firm of Anton Dunkelsbuehler, which had a 12.5 percent participation on the selling side. His elder brother Louis, by now a partner in Dunkelsbuehler, was always his confidant and closest ally in London, so that the rapport between Anglo-American and the diamond house was exceptionally close. Yet Sir Ernest (he was knighted in 1921 in recognition for war service) was not satisfied; he wanted his own direct stake in the Syndicate. Production and marketing, he always argued, must go hand in hand.

His strategy was to establish discreet but close ties with mining houses which had recently discovered important diamond deposits in Angola, the Belgian Congo and West Africa. Previously, South and South-West Africa produced over 90 percent of the world's diamonds; by 1923 that share was down to 76 percent.

[4] Correspondence of Sir Ernest Oppenheimer, November 1, 1921, quoted in Gregory, op. cit., pp. 96–97.

Oppenheimer realized that this swift growth in diamond output outside the joint umbrellas of the producers' pool in South Africa and the Syndicate could upset the delicate balance of the market, especially as the postwar boom in diamond demand soon petered out. So, through Anglo-American, he began signing contracts to buy up these diamonds, which he then sold to the Syndicate through Dunkelsbuehler and Barnato Brothers. The tactic to involve Barnato Brothers (now run by descendants of the legendary Barney Barnato) was deliberate. They were the most powerful members of the Syndicate. Their aid was essential to his long-term plan. Together Anglo-American and Barnato Brothers concluded a contract with the Belgian company *Societé Internationale Forestière et Minière du Congo* for their production and acquired significant shareholdings in the *Companhia de Diamantes de Angola*, of which Sir Ernest became a director, while also contracting for their diamonds.

Sir Ernest could then play his card. He agreed to hand over the Angola contract to the London Diamond Syndicate in return for acquiring an 8 percent participation for Anglo-American in its overall affairs. Thus, by 1923, he had a firm foothold, not only as a producer in South-West Africa, the Congo and Angola, but also a direct role in diamond marketing with Anglo as a full Syndicate member. Battle was now joined for control of the Syndicate. The existing five-year contracts with the producers were about to end. Bitter arguments broke out between the mining houses on the new quotas each would provide to the Syndicate, and the old contracts expired at the end of December 1924 without renewal being agreed.

Sir Ernest's careful cultivation of Barnato Brothers in his ventures to the Congo and Angola now paid off. He had a good relationship with Solly Joel, a nephew of the late Barney Barnato, who ran the firm. Joel's approval was the key to his whole plan. For besides being the most important single member of the Syndicate, Solly Joel was a major shareholder in both De Beers and Jagersfontein mines. His support, therefore, for an "Oppenheimer" Syndicate to replace the old one would prove crucial in persuading these two producers to offer it their diamonds. Ultimately it was his pressure on the board of De Beers that tipped the balance in Oppenheimer's favor. And when they hesitated at the last moment, he openly threw in his lot with Oppenheimer.

De Beers were then faced with a cable from Sir Ernest bidding "on behalf of Barnato Brothers and friends, Anglo-American Corporation and friends . . . for your and Premier Diamond Mining Company's production." They gave way. On October 22, 1925, Oppenheimer cabled joyfully to one of his colleagues, "Pleased to inform you that we have bought out old Syndicate as from today." The "new" Syndicate was made up of Anglo-American and Dunkelsbuehler (where Louis Oppenheimer was partner) with a joint 45 percent share, Barnato Brothers also with 45 percent and Johannesburg Consolidated Investment (in which Barnato Brothers were also large shareholders) with 10 percent. Under five-year contracts with the producers, the Syndicate agreed to De Beers having 51 percent of sales, Consolidated Diamond Mines 21 percent, Premier 18 percent and Jagersfontein 10 percent.

With the Syndicate under his wing, the only real mountain left for Sir Ernest Oppenheimer to scale was De Beers itself. Here again the liaison with Solly Joel of Barnato Brothers proved vital. Joel's agreement to join the Oppenheimer Syndicate was in itself an indication that he was not happy with the existing management of De Beers. Within a matter of months he secured Oppenheimer's election to the De Beers board. Just three years later, at the end of 1929, Sir Ernest became chairman.

In the meantime, however, the world of diamonds suffered two severe shocks: the discovery of important new alluvial diamond fields in South Africa, and the Wall Street crash of 1929. The one sent diamond supplies soaring, the other, ushering in the Depression, virtually eliminated demand.

The new diamond deposits were at Lichtenburg in the western Transvaal, and near the mouth of the Orange River in Namaqualand on the west coast of South Africa. Both were alluvial, thus precipitating a rush of ordinary diggers over which the mining houses had little control. These independent diggers ferreted out the stones at such a rate that by October 1926 the Lichtenburg field alone was producing more diamonds than all the mines in the De Beers group. World diamond output shot up from 4.7 million carats in 1925 to almost 8 million carats by 1927. Virtually all the diamonds from the new fields were snapped up by independent buyers and thus bypassed the Syndicate in London. Fortuitously this diamond rush coincided with the heydey of demand in the United States, in the years of euphoria leading up to the 1929 crash. American diamond imports hit a record $64 million in 1926 for rough and cut stones, a level not achieved again until 1943.

American buying at least gave the big producers and the Syndicate some breathing space. From the outset the Syndicate was active bidding for diamonds in Lichtenburg, and it tried also to persuade the main importers of alluvial diamonds in London and Antwerp to channel their diamonds through them. Meanwhile, both De Beers and Anglo-American pressed a reluctant South African government to exert strict control on licenses and production of the new diggings, but without much initial success. Popular sentiment demanded that the little digger should have his stake, too; the great mining companies must not rule all.

The lesson, Oppenheimer soon realized, was that the mining houses must not rest on their laurels but become more active in seeking new deposits like Lichtenburg. Through geological detective work they must locate potential diamond fields and swiftly buy up the surrounding land. "A new era of scientific diamond prospecting has been inaugurated," Sir Ernest told Anglo-American shareholders in 1929, "and if the big producers are vigilant, the chances of surprise discoveries will be very materially decreased." What worried him was not new discoveries as such, but what he called their "irrational exploitation" by outsiders with no interest in a stable market.

That long-term aim, however, could not solve the immediate problems presented by the flood of stones from the Lichtenburg and Namaqualand fields, nor deal with the growing output of diamonds elsewhere in Africa. Despite the boost given to South Africa's share of world output by the new alluvial fields, the outlook was that her paramount position as number-one producer would be eroded. The answer had to be a permanent reorganization and strengthening of the Syndicate. Its original purpose as the selling arm for South African diamonds was becoming outdated; it had to become the marketing conduit for the world's diamonds. But that called for much more capital than

the Syndicate itself possessed to enable it to buy up outside production and finance stocks. The solution had to be producers'
participation. The outcome was the Diamond Corporation, created in February 1930, in which De Beers, Consolidated Diamond
Mines, Premier and other leading producers took an equal 50
percent share with the Syndicate. The Diamond Corporation was
to market not only the output of the participating mines, but
was also provided with the financial resources to buy up all
possible outside production to insure stable prices. The chairman, not surprisingly, was Sir Ernest Oppenheimer.

Thus, at the age of fifty, this slight, shy man who had started
his career as a $3-a-week diamond sorter for Anton Dunkels-
buehler in London in 1896 commanded not only De Beers and
Consolidated Diamond Mines, the foremost producers, but controlled the marketing of a major part of the world's diamonds.
Yet he was not satisfied.

He believed that the diamond trade could only be properly
managed if a paramount producer presided over it. "In my opinion," he wrote, "the problem facing the trade can only be solved
by a single institution tackling the various problems instead of
several as at present. De Beers is to my mind the one institution
that should take the lead." [5] His first task, therefore, as chairman
of De Beers was to bring all South African producers firmly
under the De Beers wing. He authorized the sale to De Beers by
his own Anglo-American group of a 20 percent holding in Consolidated Diamond Mines of South-West Africa and persuaded
Solly Joel of Barnato Brothers to let De Beers take over 370,000
of their shares in Jagersfontein. Since Premier had already been
brought into the De Beers stable in the early 1920s, that knit together all the major diamond producers in southern Africa. True,
each mine still had its own independent board and many other
shareholders, but the strings from De Beers were strong. (In
much the same way Oppenheimer let his other great enterprise,
Anglo-American, of which he was also chairman, forge ahead
with a specialty in gold. Over the years Anglo has moved into
many other areas of mining, too, but has always kept out of the
diamond arena.)

With De Beers molded to his satisfaction, Sir Ernest could

[5] Sir Ernest Oppenheimer in a letter to the Secretary, De Beers,
Kimberley, May 5, 1927.

turn to honing the new Diamond Corporation in the same way. The Corporation had a dismal inheritance. The "Oppenheimer" Syndicate, which it replaced, had built up $25 million in stocks by the end of 1929, and these had to be taken over gradually. As his brother Louis Oppenheimer constantly reminded him in letters and cables from London, the prospect for sales was bleak. In the aftermath of the Wall Street crash, the American appetite for diamonds, the mainstay of the trade for almost fifty years, virtually vanished. Imports of diamonds into the United States slumped from $52 million in 1929 to $29 million in 1930, and were scarcely $9 million by 1932, as the Depression bit deeper. So it was not just the headache of outstanding stocks but the continuing day-to-day production that was threatened. The Diamond Corporation could not shift what it held, let alone absorb new output. The price of rough diamonds weakened rapidly. The Diamond Corporation's price fell from £3.15 per carat in 1930 to £1.74 two years later—the lowest level in price since 1912, an admission, in fact, that in the extremities of a depression, the cartel could not hold the price.

The sole option, Oppenheimer soon realized, to "prevent a complete collapse of the diamond trade" was to cut back drastically on mine production. In a confidential memorandum to De Beers directors in the summer of 1931 he warned them that for two years there was little likelihood of any diamonds from their mines being sold. That meant one thing—close the mines. Thus a bleak De Beers statement in February 1932 announced, "It has been generally known that since the latter part of 1929 the world's demand for diamonds has been far below normal . . . as conditions today are worse than they have ever been, and there is no indication whatever of a revival of the world's demand for diamonds, the directors of De Beers Consolidated Mines Limited regret to have to announce that the company's mines will be closed down on 31 March 1932." And Oppenheimer sadly told his shareholders, "With the exception of the State diggings and the alluvial production, all production of diamonds in South Africa and South-West Africa has ceased." Five years would pass before proper resumption.

The need for closure is confirmed by a glance at the Diamond Corporation's stocks. In 1931 its sales out of a stock of $34 million were a scant $5.3 million; the following year sales were a mere $3.6 million, and the stock value rose to $36.2 million. Sir Ernest himself often tried to persuade diamond cutters to take up at least a few stones. Lazare Kaplan, the famous New York cutter, recalled many years later that Sir Ernest never mentioned payment. "If you asked him about payment," Kaplan remembered, "he would say, 'Who said anything about that?' " The priority was to keep some stones moving down the cutting pipeline. Even so, business was so slack that the Corporation's staff spent their days patiently sorting rough diamonds into the customary piles but every evening mixed them all together again just to give themselves something to do the following day. They also sifted out the round stones and used them to play "marbles" on the sorting benches to while away the hours. "It was," recalled a contemporary broker, "a desperate moment."

Only the decision to shut the mines, thus reducing South African and South-West African production from 4.2 million carats in 1929 to a mere 0.4 million by 1934, enabled the Diamond Corporation to weather the crisis. Diamond output elsewhere was not so severely curtailed, although other producers with long-term contracts with the Corporation agreed to limit supplies and to take only enough payment to cover their basic working costs. And as world production fell from 7.2 million carats in 1929 to 4 million carats by 1933, the flow of fresh stones became manageable.

The lesson, however, was to achieve even better coordination between all diamond producers, not just those of southern Africa. Thus Sir Ernest Oppenheimer came up with a further expansion to the structure of the diamond industry—The Diamond Producers Association, which was created in 1933. This embraced not only the leading South African mines and Consolidated Diamond Mines of South-West Africa, but also the governments of South Africa and South-West Africa, together with the Diamond Corporation itself wearing two "hats"—as the holder of large stocks and representing diamond producers elsewhere with whom it had long-term contracts. Each member accepted quotas; De Beers initially had 30 percent and CDM 14 percent, while the Diamond Corporation was granted 15 percent for its stocks and 16 percent for outside contracts, with smaller allocations for the South African government, Premier and other mines.

An additional refinement was the birth of the Diamond Trading Company (DTC), as a daughter company of the Diamond Corporation. The DTC was charged with the exclusive task of selling at "sights" the rough diamonds originating both from the mines belonging to the Diamond Producers Association and from the Diamond Corporation's stocks and outside contracts. Over the years this overall setup has become known as the Central Selling Organization. Despite some subtle retouching, there have been few changes since then (the most important extension to the CSO was the establishment of a separate marketing company for industrial diamonds, Industrial Distributors Limited in 1946). Otherwise, the establishment of the DTC in 1934 ushered in the recent era. The DTC became the conduit through which up to 80 percent of the world's gem diamonds reach the marketplace.

With its creation, Sir Ernest Oppenheimer felt he had imposed the right structure upon the diamond industry. Producers, on the one hand, were ready to tailor their output to match the mood of the market, while the buying and selling of rough diamonds had, as far as was possible, been completely centralized. It was clearly a monopoly, but in Sir Ernest Oppenheimer's eyes a necessary and benevolent one. And almost half a century later this monopoly that grew out of the worst years of the Depression outlives him.

PART
II

THE MINERS

1

Genesis of a Diamond
Mine

"Think of a soufflé," said the lanky, white-haired geologist, putting his feet up on the desk of his office on the second floor of De Beers' Johannesburg office, "and then you'll get some idea of how a diamond mine is born." The analogy is apt, for diamonds, which were originally crystalized from carbon amidst reservoirs of molten magma a hundred miles below the earth's crust, were thrust upward with the swiftness of a rising soufflé when volcanic activity weakened the mantle above. Liquid kimberlite, the igneous rock which plays host to the diamond, punched its way through the earth's surface in an explosion of rock, gases and water. "This mixture blows a neat hole," the geologist explained, "and then, like a soufflé, collapses quickly as the gases escape. The liquid rock sinks back into the hole. That is the origin of a kimberlite pipe."

The essential difference from the birth of a volcano is that the kimberlite does not flow like lava. A little spills around the top of the pipe through the force of the initial explosive break-out, but most slides back, swiftly cools and solidifies into a soft flaky core of rock. Sealed off from air or water, the kimberlite is usually a blue-black color, but once exposed on the surface it soon turns yellow and crumbles. The diamonds, ranging in size from fine gems to tiny specks useful only to industry, are embedded in the kimberlite like small chips of ice. Not every pipe contains diamonds; many either encase no diamonds at all or have too few to be worth mining. And although kimberlite pipes exist on every continent, they are found in such profusion only in Africa; among them a dozen African countries produce 75 percent of the world's diamonds.* Zaire is the league leader judged in terms of carats, but most of her diamonds are only of industrial quality. The real wealth is in South Africa, Botswana and Namibia which between them produce over half of all gemstones. Even there, only a handful of diamond pipes are actually payable. In South Africa itself scarcely one pipe in two hundred is worth mining; in Botswana, which is rapidly becoming a prime source of diamonds in the 1980s, the odds are rather shorter—three out of forty-five pipes so far discovered are rich in diamonds.

The narrowness of this chimney from the center of the earth means that the technique of diamond mining is unique. The miner in search of coal or gold digs out a whole reef that may be spread like layers of a sandwich over many miles underground. The diamond miner, on the contrary, is focusing his energy on a single core covering only a few acres. The largest diamond pipe, at the Mwadui (or Williamson) mine in Tanzania, is only a mile and a half long and a mile wide. Small pipes, such as those in Sierra Leone, are scarcely a hundred yards across. Sometimes there is no proper pipe, but rather a long, narrow fissure up which the kimberlite has been squeezed like toothpaste leaking from the side of a tube. Mining simply starts at the top with an open pit and proceeds downward. After a few hundred feet the depth and steepness of the sides make it more practical to sink a shaft a little way off in the country rock and then tunnel into the pipe from the side to mine and haul the ore out from below. It is like eating ice cream in a cone; it is easy to lick at the wide top but much trickier to get at the ice cream lower down.

* Angola, Botswana, Central African Republic, Ghana, Guinea, Lesotho, Liberia, Namibia, Sierra Leone, South Africa, Tanzania and Zaire.

The eruptions that created the kimberlite pipes took place millions of years ago. The best estimates are that the Premier pipe in South Africa, which has produced more large gem diamonds than any other, dates back 1,700 million years; the pipes in Sierra Leone and Ghana may be around 1,100 million years old; the Mir pipe in the Soviet Union is perhaps 400 million years old; while those around Kimberley in South Africa are relative newcomers, aged only about 100 million years. Through the millenia all these pipes have been eroded slowly by wind and rain. Originally, they stood up like a volcano above the surrounding countryside. Today, not only have most pipe mouths been weathered flat, so that they blend totally into their surroundings, but often many hundreds of feet of the surrounding land may have been washed away, too. "We've lost almost 6,000 feet of surface everywhere round here in the last ninety million years," remarked a geologist in Kimberley, "and so the diamonds must be scattered all over southern Africa."

A third of the world's diamonds, therefore, are found not by excavating pipes, but in far-flung alluvial fields. Close to Kimberley itself, alluvial deposits of diamonds lie along the banks of the Vaal River or buried deep in the potholes of its bed. In Namaqualand on South Africa's southwest coast and just to the north in Namibia, a treasure trove of diamonds, washed down long ago from the interior along the Orange, the Buffels and other ancient rivers, is hidden beneath the beaches and the ocean floor. In Angola there are rich alluvial pickings some fifty miles downstream from weathered kimberlite pipes; in Sierra Leone the diamonds from three small pipes have been spread, over the ages, through the surrounding forests by the meandering river system; and in Zaire diamonds are dispersed through 150,000 square miles of jungle. The location of the pipes from which some alluvial diamonds originally spewed is not even known. In Brazil, more than two hundred and fifty years after alluvial diamonds were first discovered, no one has yet found any diamond-bearing kimberlite pipes.

Diamonds defy the best geological detectives. "We've been trying for years to put together a coherent philosophy on which to base our prospecting, but we've failed," conceded a leading De Beers geologist. Meanwhile, it is a matter of playing hunches and good old-fashioned legwork Divining exactly where a diamond pipe covering only a few acres may lie amidst hundreds of square miles of open bush country or desert calls for infinite patience.

"Look at this map of Tanzania," said the geologist, pulling out a detailed chart covered with hundreds of tiny black dots. "Each of those dots represents a sample we took after the discovery of the Williamson mine there. We took one hundred eighty thousand samples, each a mile apart over three hundred thousand square miles, and found nothing."

They had better luck in Botswana, although even then the hunt lasted twelve years. Three telltale alluvial diamonds found in a stream in eastern Botswana in 1955 were the first clues that eventually led to the discovery over a hundred miles away in 1967 of the great Orapa diamond pipe, almost a mile in diameter, on the fringes of the Kalahari desert. The intriguing thing about Orapa (as with the Williamson mine in Tanzania) is that much less erosion has taken place than at Kimberley. Orapa is still the top of the ice-cream cone, while the Kimberley mines were not discovered until half was long gone. Yet the Kimberley pipes have already been mined for over a hundred years, so the life of Orapa, which only came into production in 1971, must be judged in centuries.

Although a diamond pipe plunges deep into the heart of the earth and, in theory, could be mined down for many miles because diamonds do not peter out, there are practical constraints. Usually the cone narrows after two or three thousand feet, and the cost of getting out the kimberlite is not justified, at present diamond prices, by the return in stones. The single pipe may also give way to a series of fissures which are much more difficult to excavate. "It's like getting to the root of a tooth," said Kidger Hartley, the general manager of De Beers' Kimberley division where several of the oldest mines are in the final years of their life. "A diamond mine is not forever."

2

South Africa: The View
from Kimberley

Four times each year the eighteen directors of De Beers Consolidated Mines Limited gather around a long leather-topped
teak table on the ground-floor boardroom of 36 Stockdale Street
in Kimberley. It is a light, airy room, with large windows and
French doors giving out onto a sunlit courtyard filled with trees
and flowering shrubs; around the walls are portraits of Cecil
Rhodes, Sir Ernest Oppenheimer and other diamond magnates
from the heydey of Kimberley as the world's greatest diamond-
mining center. Harry Oppenheimer, a small, modest, shy man in
his early seventies, presides as chairman. Two other members of
his family, his son Nicholas, a cheerful fellow in his thirties, and
his cousin Sir Philip Oppenheimer, who runs the London end
of the De Beers empire, are beside him. Close at hand, too, are
Julian Ogilvie Thompson, the chief executive who handles the
day-to-day running of affairs in Africa, and Monty Charles, the
managing director of the Diamond Trading Company in London, which markets De Beers (and most other) diamonds. And

with them are geologists, engineers and technicians—all mining
men with long practical experience. The group is rounded out
by two bankers, Baron Elie de Rothschild from Paris and Evelyn
de Rothschild from London, a reminder that the De Beers fortunes have been closely entwined with the great banking family
for a century. There is another reminder, too. On the wall behind Harry Oppenheimer is a framed check, the original payment for £5,338,650 sterling by De Beers Consolidated Mines
to the liquidators of the Kimberley Central Diamond Mining
Company in 1888 that gave Cecil Rhodes his control of the diamond-mining industry. The policies emanating from the boardroom in Kimberley almost a hundred years later are still directed
at maintaining that pre-eminent position. The men seated around
the table run one of the world's real—and longest-lasting—mo-
nopolies.

The seventeen mines in the De Beers group still control 90
percent of South African diamond output and 100 percent in
Namibia, Botswana and Lesotho.* Their combined contribution
to world production was around 25 percent in 1980, but, more
significantly, they produced over 40 percent of gem diamonds,
including the exceptional high quality ones from Consolidated
Diamond Mines in Namibia. And the real money in diamonds
is in gems; if a mine produces 20 percent gem and 80 percent
industrial, the contribution to profits is usually inverse. Gems
are the cream. And if all goes well with a massive expansion
program that will virtually double group production by the mid-
1980s, the De Beers mines will shortly be yielding nearly 20
million carats annually, a third of global supply, including 7
million carats of gem quality. Besides this, De Beers' Central
Selling Organization, the syndicate so successfully put together
by Harry Oppenheimer's father in the early 1930s, still handles

---

* The group's mines are:

SOUTH AFRICA—De Beers, Dutoitspan, Bultfontein, Wesselton, Finsch
(92 percent share) and Koffiefontein, all controlled by
the Kimberley division; Premier, Annex Kleinzee,
Dreyers Pan, Koingnaas, Langhoogte and Tweepad,
controlled by the Namaqualand division.
NAMIBIA—Consolidated Diamond Mines of South-West Africa (CDM).
LESOTHO—Letseng-la-Terai (75 percent share).
BOTSWANA—Orapa, Letlhakane, Jwaneng (developing), all three 50 percent share with Botswana government.

the marketing of diamonds from many other countries; Angola, Russia, Sierra Leone, Tanzania and Zaire all rely, to a greater or lesser extent as we shall observe later, on the CSO Thus, at some stage en route from mine to customer, 80–85 percent of the world's diamonds pass through De Beers' hands. The resulting revenues are immense. Diamond sales by the CSO earned almost $3 billion in 1980, contributing to the group's total net profit of almost $800 million. It would rate among the top ten industrial and mining companies of the *Fortune 500* in the United States if it were U.S. based (and could trade there). The catch for De Beers is that American antitrust authorities have long viewed it as a cartel, and it can do no business at all on U.S. shores. The eagle-eyed trustbusters have even raided the offices of the New York advertising agency that handles diamond promotion for De Beers, hoping (without success) to nail them that way.

No one tries to deny that it is a cartel, but in De Beers' eyes, at least, it is a benevolent one. As Harry Oppenheimer has declared, in an oft-repeated explanation, "Whether this measure of control amounts to a monopoly, I would not know. But if it does it is certainly a monopoly of a most unusual kind. There is no one concerned with diamonds, whether as producer, dealer, cutter, jeweler or customer, who does not benefit from it. It protects not only shareholders in the big diamond companies, but also the miners they employ and the communities that are dependent on their operations. The well-being of tens of thousands of individual diamond diggers of all races is dependent on its maintenance."

The well-being of De Beers is not neglected either. "Benevolence begins at home," remarked an international civil servant, who has helped several African nations negotiate contracts with The Diamond Corporation, the De Beers affiliate which handles negotiations with producers outside South Africa and Namibia. "When it comes to the fine print in contracts, De Beers are the past masters." They are masters, too, at the drafting of their annual accounts. They do not give clear statements of the profits of individual mines, nor of The Diamond Corporation or the CSO companies. There is no clear-cut explanation either of the real value of the diamonds in their inventory, beyond the statement that it is assessed on the average cost of production. So no one can gauge precisely the exact size of the stockpile, which is shrewdly built up at the mines themselves, at The Diamond Corporation and in the Central Selling Organization. "De Beers presents almost unique problems for investment analysts," remarked a special report prepared by a Johannesburg stockbroking firm for the confidential advice of its clients. "De Beers is the analysts' Nemesis, and few, if any, have escaped the pitfalls strewn in their path by that superb but ambiguous work of modern art, the De Beers financial statement."

The subtle drafting of annual reports, and the way in which the faces of senior De Beers executives become inscrutable when asked a detailed question about the real working cost or profit of this or that mine, cannot mask the fact that the ground rules are changing in the 1980s. One has only to step outside the boardroom in Kimberley. It is not just that the famous Big Hole, a stone's throw from the doorway of 36 Stockdale Street, is long closed and is now merely a tourist attraction (second in South Africa to the Kruger National Park). Most of the other famous mines from the days of the Kimberley rush are closed or are long past their peak. Jagersfontein shut down in 1971, a century after its discovery. The remaining four mines around the town, De Beers, Dutoitspan, Bultfontein and Wesselton, have only a few years to run, and their life is being eked out by recycling the mountainous waste dumps that contain small diamonds overlooked by less sophisticated earlier separation techniques. The recycling will delay the final denouement, but Kimberley is a shadow of its former self, contributing scarcely 10 percent of South African output from the four neighborhood mines.

The sole consolation is a new skyscraper called Harry Oppenheimer House, where the rough diamonds from mines all over South Africa and Namibia come for sorting, prior to "sights" for the Central Selling Organization's local customers or to shipment to the Diamond Trading Company at 17 Charterhouse Street in London. Otherwise, the De Beers umbrella, under which Kimberley has prospered for more than a century, is gradually closing. The city is suffering withdrawal symptoms and is desperately searching for a new role. "I sometimes feel Kimberley stopped in the 1930s and has been living a legend ever since," said one young lady working in the De Beers office.

The eclipse of Kimberley, where most production will probably phase out inside thirty years, underlines De Beers' dilemma in the 1980s. The real strength of its hand has long been that South Africa itself was the major mining center. (Zaire, of course, is the largest producer of diamonds, but virtually all of industrial quality.) A mining house with a firm base in domestic output was much better able to dictate to others; the wide margin of profit on its own mines—often 70–80 percent—provided financial flexibility in offering highly competitive prices to outsiders. Until the early 1970s virtually 80 percent of the group's own production came from their mines in South Africa itself, and the rest were from Consolidated Diamond Mines in South-West Africa (CDM), which was then firmly under South African control. A decade later the balance was shifting rapidly. Not only was South-West Africa achieving independence as Namibia, but the De Beers mines in South Africa yielded under 60 percent of the group's total of 14.5 million carats, because two new mines in Botswana, Orapa and Letlhakane, in which De Beers has a 50–50 share with the Botswana government, turned in close to 5 million carats. The prospect ahead is that Botswana's output will rise still faster when a new mine at Jwaneng in the Kalahari desert comes on stream in 1982.* Thereafter, the De Beers mines in South Africa alone will account for only 40 percent of the group's diamond production, while Botswana, riding the diamond tiger, will certainly press for more and more favorable terms.

That is not necessarily cause for alarm. De Beers enjoys remarkably good, pragmatic relationships with many black African nations. "We stride across Africa in a very satisfactory way in all sorts of very strange places," said Peter Leyden, a senior executive. "Part of the secret is that we respect confidences. We don't talk much. And we have been able to convince governments that the system works, and that it is in their interest and ours that it continue to work." He conceded, however, that they were faced with a new situation. "A large domestic base in South Africa seems *a priori* for control of the diamond industry, but even if our output does decline, I don't believe this will necessarily endanger the structure." Then he added, wagging a finger sternly, "Remember, we are here through good times and

---

* See Part II: 4. Botswana. The New Champions.

bad. In good times lots of sharks are around, but when times are bad the system is vindicated."

One way to keep the sharks at bay is to squeeze the most out of South Africa's own potential. The rapid growth of mines in Botswana often steals the limelight, obscuring a determined De Beers push for new production in South Africa. It may be the dog days for the famous old mines around Kimberley, but elsewhere the watchword is expansion. Major capital expenditure is going forward to extend existing mines, like Finsch, Premier and Koffiefontein (which was reopened in 1971 after being closed for forty years, ever since the shutdown of almost the entire South African diamond-mining industry in the early 1930s). The alluvial deposits beneath the beaches of the Namaqualand on the western shores of South Africa are being excavated apace and treated in new plants at Koingnaas and Tweepad. By 1980 the diamond yield of these Namaqualand marine terraces actually exceeded that garnered from the famous deposits of the "diamond coast" north of the Orange River in Namibia, where production by De Beers Consolidated Diamond Mines of South-West Africa (CDM) has peaked. "Namaqualand and CDM will be neck and neck in the early eighties," said Peter Leyden. "The production is very similar, especially at Kleinzee, which is fully competitive with CDM. We are getting some beautiful stones."

This investment initiative has also prompted De Beers to spend over $40 million in a joint project with the government of Lesotho, the small independent African nation in the heart of South Africa, to develop the Letseng-la-Terai mine almost 10,000 feet up on the Maluti plateau. The mine, the highest in the world, on the very "roof of Africa," had long been known as a small pipe, which occasionally produced a stunning large stone —the 601 carats Lesotho Brown found there in 1967 was the eleventh-largest diamond ever found—but it was basically uneconomic, with a terrible winter climate and almost impossible access. The last company to try to make a go of it, Rio Tinto Zinc, gave up in 1972. The trouble is that the average grade at Letseng-la-Terai is a mere 3.09 carats (i.e., 0.62 gram) for every 100 tons of kimberlite mined; this compares with 10.31 carats at CDM in Namibia, 27.62 carats at Premier mine and 73.42 carats at the Finsch mine. The saving grace, as Harry

Oppenheimer himself noted when he opened the mine in 1977, was that its "profitability will depend on a small number of exceptionally beautiful diamonds, which has always seemed to me a very romantic circumstance about Letseng." The production on this mountain-top is a tiny 50,000 carats a year, but in the first few years of its new lease of life it performed admirably, yielding well over a hundred diamonds in excess of 20 carats, and two over 200 carats.

Letseng-la-Terai is just one sign of a new lease for old mines. Many abandoned pipes around Kimberley are being surveyed to determine if they are worth reopening at today's higher prices and if their dumps are also worth recycling. Long-forgotten pipes from diamond-rush days, such as Otto's Kopje, Taylor's Kopje, Kamfers Dam and Lace, are all being reviewed. And a relentless search is on for new mines. De Beers' prospecting team, Stockdale Prospecting, which had a strength of five or six geologists a few years ago, now musters over fifty. No one is complacent; there are too many unanswered questions. Where, for instance, is the kimberlite pipe—or pipes—from which the alluvial diamonds mined at Lichtenburg in the Western Transvaal since 1927 were eroded? And no one forgets that the Finsch mine, the last great diamond pipe to be found in South Africa itself in 1961, was located quite by accident by a man named Allister Thornton Fincham, who was really prospecting for asbestos deposits in Cape province about 130 miles west of Kimberley. The finding of Finsch, which has since become the largest mine in South Africa with production of 3.5 million carats a year, took geologists by surprise. "The feeling before Finsch was that the prospectors at the turn of the century had covered all of South Africa," said a De Beers geologist. "Certainly no one saw the possibility of something scarcely a hundred miles from Kimberley—that had been gone over with a fine toothcomb. Finsch suddenly showed that the old-time prospecting had not been so thorough, after all. We've been looking hard ever since."

This determination to leave, almost literally, no stone unturned in an effort not just to sustain, but to raise South African diamond production to the highest possible level reflects De Beers' confidence on the brink of the 1980s. They see no rival in sight to snatch away their superior position. Russia, where diamond production has grown apace in the last twenty years, seems to pose no real threat. Australia, Brazil and even China have some prospects, but nothing so far to undermine the De Beers supremacy. "We've said our group production will go up to 19 million carats by 1983," said Peter Leyden, "and it is implicit that we've taken a view the market will expand, and that our competition will not be of such devastating proportions that the decision will be invalidated."

Harry Oppenheimer put the question bluntly to Monty Charles of the Diamond Trading Company at a board meeting in Kimberley a few years ago. If De Beers expanded production, could he guarantee to sell the diamonds? Charles replied quietly, but confidently, that he could. The clearest evidence today of the action initiated by that reply is to be found just north of Johannesburg at the most famous of all mines—Premier.

Journey to the Center of the Earth

Fifteen hundred feet below ground a Toyota Landcruiser barrels down a precipitous whitewashed tunnel that leads straight to the center of the earth. "We go down for about a kilometer before we come to the mining area," shouts Colin Shaw, the shift boss, negotiating the vehicle around a tight curve with the dexterity of a driver in the Monte Carlo Rally. As we plunge on downwards the heat and humidity rise. A fierce growling ahead heralds the arrival of a monster dump truck laden with crumbled rock. We are on a collision course, but Shaw ducks the landcruiser into a side shaft, and, like a dragon disturbed in its lair, the truck grumbles past. We proceed deeper. Presently Shaw turns down a small tunnel leading off the main drive and stops. He flashes the beam from his miner's lamp on the wall. "We're now leaving the country rock and going into the kimberlite," he says. The contrast between the lighter country rock and the blue-black kimberlite is stark, as if wallpaper pattern was changed halfway down a passage. We are inside the diamond pipe.

A hundred yards further on is a blur of dust and lights. We get out of the landcruiser and walk forward. An electronic drill, known to miners as a road-heading machine, is biting through the kimberlite as if it were no tougher than cream cheese, pushing the tunnel forward three feet at a gulp. The red beam of a

laser keeps it on a straight track. Clouds of dust obscure everything. "The kimberlite is too flaky for us to spray with water,"
says Shaw. Behind the road header, black mine workers fit rock
bolts in the roof and sides of the tunnel to help hold the kimberlite together. On particularly crumbly sections they stretch
what looks like a giant hair net over the tunnel roof and spray
it with liquid cement—a process known as garnetting. "What
you are seeing here is a new lease of life for Premier," says Shaw.
"De Beers is spending three years on this development work to
open up a completely new area of the pipe below what we call
the gabbro sill. By 1990 all the mining at Premier will be below
the sill, and its life will be extended at least to 2038."

The gabbro sill, a seal of barren rock stuck across the pipe
about twelve hundred feet down, is a unique feature of what is
already an exceptional mine. The diamond pipe at Premier,
thirty miles northeast of Pretoria, is one of the oldest ever found;
it is 1,700 million years old, compared with the Kimberley pipes,
which are scarcely 100 million. Volcanic eruptions took place
here on several occasions, spewing up three different types of
kimberlite that contain a richer crop of large diamonds than any
other pipe ever located. Premier has yielded over 80 million
carats of diamonds (more than 15 tons) since it was discovered
in 1902, including the great 3,106-carat Cullinan, the 726-carat
Jonker, the 426-carat Niarchos, the 354-carat Premier Rose and
nearly three hundred other gems weighing over 100 carats. More
than one-quarter of all known large diamonds have been found
in this pipe, shaped like a giant egg, that covers twenty-eight
acres. Not only that, they include the exceptionally rare icy-blue
2B diamonds beloved by jewelers and the rare nitrogen-free 2A
diamonds that are supreme conductors of heat and thus of high
value in sensitive electronic equipment for space satellites.

Originally Premier was worked as an open pit, but, after being
closed in 1932 like so many other diamond mines, it was redevel-
oped in the 1940s as a proper mine, with a shaft sunk through the
surrounding country rock from which tunnels radiated into the
pipe itself. All went well until, at around twelve hundred feet,
the kimberlite gave way to a thick strata of ordinary rock blocking the pipe, rather like a faulty cork that had gotten pushed
down into a wine bottle. This was christened the gabbro sill.
Test drilling showed it to be over two hundred feet thick, yet,

below, the pipe continued with diamondiferous kimberlite. What to do with this useless mass of rock weighing 55 million tons?

Mining it out directly would have been prohibitively expensive. The alternative, De Beers decided, was to bypass the sill with a deeper shaft through the country rock and then cut into the kimberlite pipe again from below. Even more ingeniously, the kimberlite will initially be mined out directly beneath the sill, leaving cathedral-like caverns almost three hundred feet high, in which pillars of kimberlite will remain at strategic intervals to hold up the roof. Ultimately the pillars themselves will be hacked away. The sill will then gradually collapse and be left to "float" on top of the ore body as mining goes on below. Thus diamonds can be mined without digging out the sill. Even so, the project is a mammoth one. It will cost at least $350 million and take almost ten years to bring into full production what is effectively a new mine below the sill. The extension is possible only because the South African government has granted De Beers special tax concessions that will allow them to write off the capital costs against group profits and escape some export duty on Premier's diamonds.

"We've got a good tax break on Premier," conceded a De Beers executive, "but it's in the government's interest, too. They had received a ludicrous cut of the profits for years, but the costs had become so high it was a marginal operation to continue. Now they've given us a deal. We'll extend the life of the mine by up to half a century, and they'll get taxes for much longer."

Even so, the extension is a gamble that the kimberlite beneath the gabbro sill will hide as many large diamonds as that above. "It's those two or three large stones a year that make all the difference to Premier," the De Beers man allowed. "One would hate to think that the big ones have petered out."

For the next few years there is no immediate worry. Premier is really two mines in a single pipe: the old mine above the sill that is still turning in well over 2 million carats annually; and the new one being drilled out below, which will produce only a handful of diamonds as a by-product of development until the mid-1980s.

Our journey in the landcruiser had been along the new tunnels spiraling down below the sill. But after a couple of hours' driving around in this subterranean world, complete with its own workshops hacked out of the living rock, Colin Shaw parked and led the way back through double airlock doors to the bottom of the mine shaft. Ten of us packed into a tiny lift not much bigger than a crate and were hoisted slowly up to the main working level, a thousand feet below the rim of Premier's open crater. Here the miners get at the kimberlite through a warren of tunnels cut through the country rock into the pipe. What they are really doing is making Premier's "big hole" deeper and deeper all the time.

They achieve this in two ways. Either by "block caving" or open-bench mining. Block caving, as the name implies, involves undermining huge chunks of kimberlite that gradually collapse. The crumbled ore is then extracted through a series of tunnels leading to cone-shaped pits down which it is dropped to the main haulage level far below, where it is crushed, conveyed back to the main shaft and hauled to the surface.

Open-bench mining, on the other hand, involves cutting back a series of steps down the side of the crater from the inside. Tunnels a hundred feet apart are driven right through the kimberlite until they give out onto the open hole itself. Going down one is quite a trek, for it may be several hundred yards, and there is no transport. The tunnel is narrow and low; the blue-black kimberlite presses in on all sides. The sole light comes from miners' lamps. Eventually a speck of daylight appears ahead, and we emerge, as from the back of a cave, with the whole of the Premier pit open before and above us. Peering cautiously out at the cliffs of country rock towering up to the small circle of bright blue sky far above, you know what it is like to look up and out of the mouth of a volcano.

Conversation is impossible because a black miner is boring into kimberlite with a long needlelike drill. Twenty-nine drill holes have been marked out in red paint around the sides and top of the tunnel. A new series of holes is drilled every ten feet as the miners work back. This is a retreating game that gradually collapses the tunnel into the pit outside. Explosive charges will be placed in each drill hole. Then every afternoon, after the morning shift has clocked off and before the next shift goes down, the blasting takes place. The kimberlite at the pit end of the tunnel is ripped apart and goes tumbling down the crater into a series of cone-shaped shafts that direct it towards the haulage level. As it drops down the shafts through force of gravity, the pieces of kimberlite are further broken up by steel bars, known as grizzlies, that act as a giant sieve. A chunk of kimberlite that is too big to get through a grizzly's "jaws" is broken up with explosives.

Down a dead-end tunnel we came upon a white miner and three black assistants getting ready to blast several blocks of kimberlite stuck above a grizzly. They used an explosive known as Anfex, which looks like polystyrene foam. They piled Anfex on one rock just by the grizzly and packed it around with mud. "The mud prevents the force of the blast being dissipated," explained the miner. He then reached out for a long pole with a sack tied on one end. "This is a bomb," he said cheerfully. "If you lean out over the grizzly and look up the shaft above you'll see some more chunks of kimberlite stuck up there. We aren't allowed to climb up the shaft because of the danger of rocks being dislodged, so we push this bomb up on the pole and place it against the rock we want to break." The mud pies complete and the bomb in place, he hooked detonator wires to a central wire running down the tunnel, and we all retreated. Back in the main tunnel, he checked that everyone was out, unlocked a red detonator junction box to which he alone had the key and set off the blast. A sharp thump cracked through the mine. "We wait ten minutes and then go in," he said. "All that rock should be broken up and have fallen through the grizzly."

Far below ground with drills chattering and explosions booming, it is hard to realize that this is all in pursuit of a diamond that may one day grace the ring on the finger of a beautiful girl. The kimberlite is ripped out with as much sentiment as coal. Actually spotting a diamond down the mine is almost like seeing a needle in the proverbial haystack, although naturally everyone keeps an eye open, just in case. After all, the great Cullinan diamond was found many years ago protruding from the kimberlite as the mine manager made his evening rounds. Sharp-eyed miners still pick up gems from time to time. Officially, of course, they must hand in whatever they find, but the temptation to secrete the diamond and try to sell it profitably on the black market is strong. Premier discourages such deceptions, not only by tight security, but by rewards of up to $12,000. A black miner, someone remarked, happened on a diamond in the mine just recently that won him a bonus of $4,000. Not everyone is so lucky. "I've worked at Premier for fourteen years, and I've never even seen a diamond in the mine," lamented a miner sadly. The diamonds are only revealed once the kimberlite has been reduced to small pieces through the grizzlies and crushers and hauled to the surface for reduction up in the treatment plants. At Premier, 21,000 metric tons of kimberlite is processed every day to yield just 1.6 kilos of diamonds (8,000 carats), a ratio of 13 million–1.

Premier's reputation for large diamonds means that the initial treatment on the surface has to be more cautious than at most mines, where the kimberlite is usually reduced to the size of gravel before it is sorted. The Cullinan was the size of a man's fist and could be destroyed by injudicious crushing. Almost the first step on the surface, therefore, is for the rock to be screened by X-ray sorting machines. Since diamonds fluoresce, they can be identified and deflected into a bin. And at every stage of the ensuing crushing, the material is rechecked in case some fine stone has been sprung from the kimberlite. While X-rays spot many diamonds, the final round of sorting at Premier is over grease tables. The kimberlite, reduced to the size of small pebbles, cascades down a conveyer belt and is washed over moving belts covered with one tenth of an inch of grease. Diamonds, which repel water, stick to the grease, while the waste kimberlite gets wet and does not adhere. Once every forty-five minutes the tables are stopped and the diamonds scraped from the grease. They are then given an acid bath for twenty-four hours to clean them up and are ready for a preliminary sorting.

Viewing the catch is stunning. Barend Boshoff, Premier's chief sorter, comes forward with a tray covered with 13,000 carats of diamonds. "That's what we got yesterday and the day before," he says, with more than a touch of pride. In the middle of the tray is a handsome gem of 92 carats, surrounded by five other stones of over 10 carats and a pile of much smaller stuff. "We usually get about 8,000 carats a day," said Boshoff. Was there ever a day when just nothing turned up? "No, no," he laughed. "It's never as bad as that, but it might go as low as 6,000 carats." Had any really large stones been found lately? "Ah," he replied cautiously, "De Beers doesn't announce a big stone. It's up to the customer who buys it to declare it if he wishes." Did that mean another Cullinan could turn up at Premier and remain a secret? "That's right," said Boshoff, "if the customer wanted to keep it quiet." Despite such discretion, was Premier living up to its reputation for large diamonds? He pointed to a neat 25-carat diamond nestling among the recent catch in the display tray. "We'd expect to get something like that, twenty-five carats or over every week," he allowed. Eighty years after its discovery, Premier still comes up trumps with an ace in diamonds.

The Way We Were

The homemade gravel washer perched on the banks of the Vaal River looked like a Rube Goldberg fantasy. Several old oil drums had been hammered into various shapes, joined up with some leaky lengths of hose and tacked together on a wooden frame; a flywheel, with an ancient crowbar serving as a spindle, was hooked by a fraying belt to a wheezing paraffin engine. Alongside was a derrick, with a dented bucket dangling from its single spar. Every few minutes the bucket went spinning down into a crater nearby and was shortly hoisted back up, overflowing with boulders or gravel. An African in a tattered shirt emptied it out on a flat metal tray on top of the shuddering contraption. Just to one side stood an old fellow, burnt nut-brown by the sun, who presided over the operations with a casual wave of his arm to signal the raising or lowering of the bucket. He bore a powerful resemblance to the late Jimmy Durante (his voice, it soon turned out, had that same gravely tone). He wore a red safety helmet, a grubby white shirt and shorts, black socks and old black shoes patterned white with dust; a cigarette hung permanently from one corner of his mouth. He introduced himself as Gideon Charles "Hill" Austen and confided that he was sixty-nine years old.

Austen is one of a dying breed, one of the last in a long line of diamond diggers who have burrowed hereabouts along the banks and into the waters of the Vaal River for over a century. The original alluvial diggings of the 1870s were just a few miles away upriver at Klipdrift. "My grandfather came out here from England before the Boer War," Austen said, setting up his credentials. "He came up on ox wagons and started what they call

Austen's Rush. I grew up on the diggings myself; been around here since 1927 or '28. I got twelve licenses and lots of ground to prospect. It'll take me a few years yet to finish it all."

For Gideon Austen, like the others still bending their backs along the Vaal, diamond digging becomes not just a way of life, but an obsession. No one ever gives up or retires. One old fellow loved to kid journalists that he was ninety-eight; if a digger's health held out, he might well keep going that long.

I caught the mood from another veteran, who had lost his license after being charged with illicit diamond buying, before setting out from Kimberley fifty miles away. "The hope that you'll find a pocket of diamonds," he had said, "is like compulsive drinking, gambling or sex. If you get a beautiful diamond in the gravels as you turn the sieve over, it's as close to sex as you can get. There's nothing I'd like more now than to be down on the Vaal throwing a breakwater." A breakwater, one soon learns, is a technique used in the river itself to divert the flow to get at the deposits of diamonds that are often found beneath the stream bed. Diverting the river, however, is costly; most diggers, like Gideon Austen, content themselves with working a few hundred yards in from the banks on the old flood plain, where the diamonds were deposited millions of years ago as they were weathered out of the Kimberley pipes and rolled toward the sea.

Austen was working a claim about the size of a tennis court. "I've taken five thousand rand [$6,250] out of this paddock in two and a half months," he said, as we stepped to the edge of the pit. Twenty feet down, four Africans with picks and shovels were hacking through a layer of gravel and boulders, loading up the bucket each time it descended. "They'll pull all those stones out and then try to get to the bottom gravel," said Austen. "But this pick and shovel business is slow—if only I could afford a mechanical digger." He paused and called down to one of the men below to brace up some loose boulders on the side. Then he went on. "I found a few small stones when I took the top layer of clay off, but hardly enough to pay the expenses. It costs me one hundred and eighty rand a week to keep going, if there's no breakdowns, what with the boys' wages and the paraffin for the engine. Anyhow, the lower we go down, the better it gets; there's a black layer of gravel that carries the diamonds."

The bucket below was full of loose gravel, and Austen flipped his arm at the winchman to raise it. The debris rattled down on the metal tray atop the makeshift washing machine. The African astride the tray started shoveling it into a rotating mesh cylinder, tilted at an angle of about ten degrees. Water from a drum above spilled onto the gravel in the cylinder, washing the smaller pebbles (and any diamonds) through the mesh holes into a trough below, while the large stones rolled out at the far end into a barrow and were consigned to the waste pile. The rest of the wet gravel and a good deal of mud was then slopped into another drum filled with water, which Austen called his rotary washing pan. "The specific gravity of the mush in the pan is one-point-five," he said knowingly, as the drum churned around like a cement mixer, "but a diamond's specific gravity is three-point-five." This means that any diamonds, along with heavier bits of gravel, sink to the bottom, while lightweight dirt floats off the top.

After a thorough stir, an African worker opened up a little trap door at the bottom of the pan and drained the sediment into a bucket, which he then emptied into three large sieves. He carefully dipped each sieve in turn into the top of a small water tank, rotating it rhythmically by flexing his shoulder muscles, to give the gravel a final good wash. He took the sieves over to Gideon Austen, who was waiting by a small lean-to with a makeshift table covered with a piece of sacking. Austen tipped the glistening wet gravel from the first sieve onto the sack, lit another cigarette, picked up a flat, triangular metal scraper and deftly stroked it over the pebbles to smooth out the pile. Then he cut out a wedge-shaped section, spread the stones over a corner of the sacking and began picking through, stone by stone. "You sort in the shade when the gravel's wet," he said. "The big stuff —over two carats— always gravitates to the center of the pile." He lifted out two pebbles, explaining they were ironstone and red jasper which he would set aside for polishing. He raked on and on for several minutes, but not a diamond turned up. He had no luck with the next two sieves, either. "Ah, you've got to be patient," he said, poking away at the shining gravel. "I had a four-carat here in this hole a little while ago—got four thousand rand for it. Then you can keep living, man. I take the money and put it in the bank." What was the largest diamond he had ever found, I inquired? "I had a thirty-five-carat a long time ago, but it wasn't good quality, but I did get a six-carat that wasn't too bad, and you get one or two or four or five carats sometimes." Today the sole reward was a few pieces of jasper.

Austen was not perturbed. "I tap every hour," he said, as he directed the next bucket down into the pit. "We work from seven and knock off at six, usually Monday to Friday; sometimes we work on Saturdays, shifting grit and that." Most of his African helpers, ("boys," he always calls them) have been with him a long time. "The boys know me and I know them," he went on. "We get along all right; some of them work for me for ten or fifteen years. You don't want to change your boys all the time." Not least because you must trust them. If one of them spies a diamond down in the pit, his foot can cover it in a moment. Then, when no one is looking, he can pocket it or put it in his mouth. Later he will sell it to the illicit buyers who haunt the diggings. "I'll pay them just as good as anyone else if they give it to me," said Austen. "Sometimes I even give them more than it's worth, just to get the next one, too. But they often like to take them to someone else. Chap came to me yesterday and said, 'Watch that boy. I'm giving you the tip; you lost eight carats.'" Austen responded tartly that he always kept an alert eye on his crew.

When he does strike it lucky, Austen takes his diamonds up the road to the Saturday market at Barkley West. Three or four licensed buyers hold court in a sidestreet in little shops that look more like butchers' stalls. Diggers from all along the Vaal congregate there. "If you reckon your diamond is worth a lot, you take it to two or three buyers and get the best offer," said Gideon Austen, "but usually I use one buyer, and he pays me a good price. The best buyer today, according to what I heard, is De Beers, but I haven't tried them yet."

The spirit of competitive buying survives only at the alluvial diggings here on the Vaal, at Lichtenburg up in the Transvaal and at Alexander Bay on the Namaqualand coast. But as they yield only a few thousand carats a year, De Beers has not bothered too much about them for years. A De Beers buyer shows up on market day, but more to keep an eye on things than to bid aggressively. The mining house has long realized that it is more politic to leave a little gravy to the individual digger and buyer. De Beers' prime interest was to insure that diamonds stolen from their own mines were not showing up at Barkley West or Lichtenburg to be "laundered" as legitimate alluvial finds. It was no idle fear. When the Finsch mine came on stream in the early 1960s, producing diamonds with a distinctive greenish hue, green diamonds turned up simultaneously at Barkley West. There were some awkward moments as diggers from the alluvial fields nearby told tall stories of how green stones were suddenly turning up where only yellow had been found before. Gideon Austen's observation, however, that De Beers had become not just watchdogs but eager buyers matches their new determination to harvest every last gem in South Africa itself.

The old diggers, of course, just want a good price, so that they can keep at it until they drop. The hunt is never over. You suspect they would actually hate to find some great stone that would enable them to retire. And when the dull gleam of a rough diamond does turn up in the gravel, there is no ecstasy, no throwing the hat in the air. "Nowadays when I see a diamond, I don't get funny," said Gideon Austen, raking through another pile of gravel at his shady little table. "I just know at once its weight and value." But suppose he did turn up a really fine diamond one morning, would he go "funny" then? "If I find a big diamond, I'd go to England for a holiday to see where my grandpa came from," he allowed. "But I'd be back. This business keeps you fit. I'll retire when I'm dead."

3

Namibia: The Diamond Desert

Place of jackals and birds
Where bushmen hardly go
Only howling jackals heard,
Winds and sand do flow.
Greedy man's lust for wealth,
Invades this place of solitude.

The poem, penned by an unknown miner and pinned to a mess noticeboard, catches the mood of the desolate diamond coast of Namibia. For a thousand miles the southwest coast of Africa, from the Angola border south almost to Cape Town, is a wasteland of sand dunes and scrub, constantly blasted by an incessant wind gusting in from the South Atlantic ocean. For generations this "skeleton" coast was feared by sailors and avoided by all but the hardiest explorers or bushmen—avoided, that is, until the chance discovery of a diamond in the sand in 1908 by a man clearing sand from a new railway track.*

Today that diamond coast hums with activity. The most concentrated fleet of earth-moving equipment in the world burrows through the sand in pursuit of the elusive gems scattered like stardust along the shore. And out at sea a fleet of small boats probes for diamonds on the ocean floor. The hunt goes on both on South Africa's Namaqualand coast and in Namibia (formerly South-West Africa), where De Beers Consolidated Diamond Mines of South-West Africa (CDM) has enjoyed an exclusive domain for over half a century. What the German colonial rulers of South-West Africa originally dubbed the *Sperrgebeit*—the forbidden territory, once the diamonds were found—is still closed to all unauthorized visitors. This barren slice of Namibia has remained a vast private estate fenced off by De Beers from the rest of the world.

The boldness of the enterprise at CDM is immense. It involves nothing less than rolling up the desert, section by section, along a front fifty miles long and varying in width from four hundred yards to two miles. The sea has also been pushed back behind great sand walls for almost ten miles to get at the stones beneath the waves. The scale can scarcely be appreciated until you are there.

As we flew north along the coast from Cape Town in a twin-engined Beechcraft, the lush green of the Cape swiftly gave way to arid desert, pressing right to the shore. There was no sign of habitation until, an hour and a half out, the pilot began a descent towards a tiny cluster of buildings half a mile inland. He put down on a strip of bare earth that served as a runway. No one was about as the plane rolled to a halt in a cloud of dust; only a few ostrich strutting nearby gazed at us curiously. "This is Koingnaas," the pilot announced. Koingnaas is one of a series of alluvial diamond deposits along the Namaqualand coast where De Beers is expanding its operations in the 1980s. The marine terraces here and at Annex Kleinzee, Dreyers Pan and Tweepad just to the north are, between them, already producing as many diamonds as CDM in Namibia, although generally of smaller sizes. A couple of men scrambled

* See Part II, p. 46.

out of the Beechcraft and set off for the mine. We took off again. "We'll be there in forty minutes," said the pilot, leveling out at 8,000 feet. "Down there is Port Nolloth, which is about the only place on the coast where supply ships for the mines can get in."

Shortly, the Orange River came into sight, the trees on its banks making a green ribbon stretching inland. The plane landed on another strip at Alexander Bay, just on the South African side of the river. A small concrete building served as a terminal, but no one was around. Presently an old white Mercedes came bowling over the desert road. Out got a cheerful round-faced man in a blue safari suit. "I'm Derek Erickson from De Beers," he said. We set off toward the river, crossing it on a one-thousand-yard-long single-lane bridge named after Sir Ernest Oppenheimer. There were metal gates at either end; one in South Africa, the other in Namibia. CDM's domain began on the northern bank.

Although diamonds have been found around the mouths of virtually every river ushering into the Atlantic along this coast, none can equal the profusion with which they occur close to the Orange, the longest of South Africa's rivers, which sweeps through the heartland of the country for 1,300 miles. And down the Orange River, perhaps ninety million years ago, came the diamonds as they were slowly washed away by erosion from kimberlite pipes somewhere in the interior of southern Africa. A great geological guessing game is the true source of these stones. They seem to share an affinity with those found near Kimberley, but no one is yet certain.

When the diamonds reached the sea, some were deposited immediately close to the river mouth (there is a particularly rich deposit at Alexander Bay, on the South African side of the Orange estuary), but many rolled northwards, urged on by the cold Benguela current and the southwest winds. Eventually these stones came to rest in marine terraces along the beaches. The richest terraces were laid down for nearly sixty miles or so north of the Orange in Namibia and over time were buried beneath the sands. The terraces lay so deep that originally they were completely overlooked when the first diamond discoveries were made at Luderitz, further up the coast, in 1908. The diamonds there were on the surface and could be picked up by hand. Not until the late 1920s did geologists detect that the real crop was in six layers of buried marine terraces nearer the north bank of the Orange.

Since the diamond deposits around Luderitz were almost worked out, they were soon abandoned in favor of the richer fields along the Orange River, which have yielded CDM an extraordinary harvest for almost half a century. While conventional mines delving into kimberlite pipes yield a blend of gems with fragments of industrial quality, the diamonds in Namibia are essentially all gems that survived the long journey downriver and the scouring of the sea. Moreover, the sea has ground most into smooth, round pebbles, so that they can be cut and polished with a minimum of loss.

For the people at CDM the Orange River, once the conduit for diamonds, plays a vital role. "The river is our lifeline," said Derek Erickson. "We've got two farms along it that provide us with milk, meat, fruit and vegetables, and its water has been piped over the desert to create the garden town of Oranjemund." The town, an oasis of green in the sand, came into view. We drove down an avenue of wild olive trees, passing neat, white houses surrounded by hibiscus hedges. "We've got a cricket ground, a golf course, a riding club, a flying club and a yacht club," said Erickson proudly, "but it's all completely artificial. If it wasn't for diamonds none of this would exist—no town, no vegetation. The closest real town is Cape Town five hundred miles away, or Windhoek [the capital of Namibia], which is seven hundred miles northeast."

Oranjemund (meaning Orange Mouth) is truly a company town. The eight thousand inhabitants are virtually all CDM employees or their families. They live free in company houses or hostels; they shop in a company supermarket, relax at the company's cinema and send their young children to the company school. (The older children of white employees go to boarding schools in South Africa.) The only locals not on the CDM payroll are the bank and post office staff, the clergy and the police. Three thousand of the inhabitants are white, mostly mining engineers, geologists and technicians with their wives and children, together with five thousand black Namibians, of whom most are migrant workers. Only a handful of Namibians were living permanently at Oranjemund with their families

prior to independence. The majority of the migrants, on contracts of between six and twelve months, are Ovambos, a tall,
stately tribe from northern Namibia, who have provided most of
the work force at CDM for over half a century. Many Ovambos have spent their entire working lives on the diamond fields,
returning home to their families only for a few months between
each contract. In the past they have been limited to unskilled
or semiskilled tasks, but by the late 1970s, with Namibian independence in prospect, De Beers established training schools, not
only at CDM but in Ovamboland, to teach them more skilled
trades. After Namibian independence the pressure to "localize"
more jobs is likely to be intense. The days of white domination
are numbered.

The isolation of Oranjemund is such that until 1975 the town
itself was regarded as part of the security area of the mine.
Everyone drove around in company cars that could never leave.
Private cars were all parked across the Orange River in South
Africa, and everyone went through elaborate checks before
leaving. All luggage had to be submitted to the security office
hours in advance to be scrutinized for stolen diamonds, which
are all too easy to acquire in a terrain of several hundred square
miles studded with them. Furniture, radios and household ap-
pliances could not be taken out at all. There was good reason
for this. The confines of life at Oranjemund, as in prison, concentrate the mind wonderfully on how to beat the system and
smuggle out diamonds. The lesson on what could be done with
a car was learned in the early days when one engineer, who had
acquired some diamonds illicitly, carefully took several large
bolts from the chassis of his car, drilled out the inside of the
bolts, filled the cavities with diamonds, replaced the bolts,
tightened the nuts and drove through several times without
detection. After he was caught, De Beers decreed that cars
coming into Oranjemund stayed there until they were scrap.
Today, however, Oranjemund is completely outside the security
area. The checkpoint is now a couple of miles outside of town
in the desert on the fringe of the mining area itself.

Heading that way in Erickson's Mercedes, we came up to a
high, double-barbed-wire fence stretching away into the distance, through which there is a single entrance to the mining
area. Erickson left his car by a high wall covered with "Beware

of guard dog" notices. We entered a low, white building directed by signs like those to airport customs. Each of us took a plastic card and inserted it into a slot machine, whereupon a door ahead swung open into an empty passage with a door at the other end. It was a moment out of Alice in Wonderland. A closed-circuit TV camera beamed down, and presumably an unseen guard approved what he saw. The door at the far end opened automatically. "You've now been registered on the computer," said Erickson, "and when we come out it will decide whether you get a free walk or are searched."

We went into a courtyard where an array of Land Rovers, Nissan minibuses and small Toyota cars were parked. All had CDM emblazoned on the side, and most looked as if they had been sandpapered through long exposure to the desert. These vehicles, once in, never leave the mine area.

Erickson selected a minibus, and we set off up the coast. "Down here the mining area runs in from the sea for two miles, but up in the north it narrows to about four hundred yards," he explained. "We don't mine systematically because the diamonds are not evenly distributed. The larger ones are in the south. We aim at a mix in terms of grade and size, and mine about forty different patches at any one time."

Over a rise in the dunes, Erickson pulled off the road and pointed to a low bluff of gray rocks. "There is the original sea cliff running from north to south," he said. "That's the extent of the mining area. The marine terraces with the diamonds are all between that and the sea."

Half a mile ahead a great swirl of flying sand turned out to be a squadron of bulldozers and scrapers engaged in an endless minuet of stripping sand from an area about half a mile long and a quarter wide. In endless motion a scraper lined up for a run, two bulldozers tucked in behind, and they set off in a cloud of sand. When the scraper had pushed up thirty-five tons of sand, it peeled away toward growing dunes beside the new mine area, grunted to the top, ejected its load, rolled down the far side and lined up for another run. This goes on around the clock six days a week. Between thirty and sixty feet of sand has to be stripped away to reach the ancient diamondiferous gravel in the marine terraces beneath. The statistics become prodigious; close to sixty million tons of sand are moved annually by this initial stripping operation, and ultimately the proportion of waste material to diamonds recovered is two hundred million to one.

Once the sand has been peeled away to reveal the marine terraces, the back-breaking work begins. The terraces, about three feet thick, are a mix of sea-smoothed boulders and diamondiferous gravel, or conglomerate, which has to be ripped up by bulldozers and mechanical diggers, and hauled to the crushing plants. This would be relatively easy if the bedrock beneath the terraces was flat and smooth, but it was eroded by the sea millions of years ago into ravines and gullies. The diamonds, although studded all through the conglomerate, have a habit of nestling in nooks and crannies of the bedrock. Someone invented a giant vacuum cleaner to suck them out, but it has never worked as well as a good old-fashioned dustpan and brush.

That chore falls to gangs of Ovambos known as "the bedrock cleaners." We came upon a group of twenty of them, muffled up against the windblown sand in orange-colored waterproofs and caps with earmuffs, working their way slowly across a moonscape of bar rock. Most of the boulders and conglomerate of the terrace had already been hauled away, but a hydraulic excavator was tap-tapping relentlessly at odd pockets in the side of a gully twenty feet deep, like a long-necked bird pecking for insects. Along the bottom of the gully an Ovambo, with a broom in one hand and a bent metal spike in the other, swept over every particle of loose material, probing into odd corners to pry out any dirt and, hopefully, a diamond. If he finds one he gives it to the headman of his gang, who has a little tray which he turns in at the end of the shift. The lucky finder gets a reward. Once CDM paid its bedrock cleaners the same for any diamond, regardless of size, but the shrewd were then inclined to break any stone into pieces, thus claiming several rewards but ruining beautiful gems. The reward is strictly according to size now; the bigger the diamond, the bigger the reward. But the maximum is only 200 rand ($250), much less than that given in the underground mines of South Africa, where the top prize is 10,000 rand ($12,350). The best reward here is equivalent to about one month's basic pay for a bedrock cleaner.

Still, the temptation to hide a good diamond exists, and it is not difficult when working in a hidden crevice to secrete one in the mouth or the pocket. The real battle is to get it out of the mine area. Twenty-three Ovambos had been caught in a round-up shortly before my visit, in what the security staff claimed was a concerted attempt to steal diamonds to help finance the South-West Africa People's Organization (SWAPO), the foremost party fighting for true independence for Namibia from South Africa. One of the tricks employed was to take the diamonds on the bus north to the little town of Luderitz, outside the diamond area on the way home. The stones were simply carried in the pocket; if there was a spot check, the diamond was immediately dropped on the floor of the bus and written off as lost.

But picking up diamonds from nooks in the bedrock is not an everyday occurrence; they are, after all, the leftovers. Most have been hauled, still embedded in conglomerate, to the crushing plants.

The rich diamond deposits on the seashore at CDM naturally led to the conclusion that there were diamonds out to sea as well. The first man to put it to the test was an enthusiastic Texan, Sam Collins, who discovered that De Beers' lease at CDM extended only to the low-water mark. He decided that the sea beyond was open to all comers. Accordingly, in the early 1960s Collins dispatched a fleet of ships up the diamond coast to dredge up the diamondiferous gravel from the ocean bed. His foray started quite a rush. Ultimately fourteen ships were seeking diamonds offshore. The diamonds were indeed there, but the cost of sea mining was astronomical, and eventually the bubble burst. De Beers then moved in and took over Sam Collins' operations as part of a wholly owned subsidiary, Marine Diamonds Corporation, which secured exclusive concessions from the shores of Namibia to the edge of the continental shelf, thus insulating CDM from future seaborne intruders. The sea prospecting has been continued by De Beers on a limited scale. The real development, however, has been a massive thrust to push back the sea itself for nearly a quarter of a mile along a ten-mile front just north of Oranjemund.

Leaving the bedrock cleaners and their brooms, Erickson drove toward the sea, which was completely obscured by a towering man-made dune. "The bulldozers began by pushing sand into the sea," he explained, "and gradually we build up a wall sixty feet high and sixty feet thick. Once we had started, the tide and the current helped by carrying the sand north to extend the wall for us." We stopped on top of the barrier. The tracks of a jackal were clearly etched on the sand where it passed by on some foraging expedition, and far below on the beach a lone seal was scratching itself. "We're now a quarter of a mile out beyond the original beach," said Erickson, "and you can see inside the wall how we've cut out a huge box right down to the marine terrace, sixty feet below sea level. We have pumps at work around the clock to keep pace with the water seeping in." Since speed is essential before a storm can breach the wall, a giant bucket-wheel excavator has been brought in that devours sand with the enthusiasm of a monster on the "Muppet Show." It cuts great swathes through the original shore line behind the seawall, eventually revealing the diamond terraces beneath the seabed.

All the material from the excavated terraces is hauled by truck to four computer-operated treatment plants placed at strategic intervals along the coast for screening, crushing, milling and scrubbing with water. The boulders, which do not contain diamonds, are quickly eliminated by an ingenious, if deafeningly noisy, machine designed on the principle that boulders, when dropped, bounce higher than conglomerate. The boulders jump over a separator and can be dumped, while the less bouncy conglomerate passes onward to be broken up by rubber-lined crushers into pebbles no larger than gravel in a stream bed. These, in turn, are fed into the dense liquid of a heavy media separator, in which light material stays in suspension and can be skimmed off, while heavier pebbles—and diamonds—sink to the bottom. By now 90 percent of the waste material has been removed. The remainder is taken in locked dump trucks to the central recovery plant, where a final crushing takes place in sealed rooms that may be entered only by a select handful of CDM staff. Finally the gravels and the diamonds pass along conveyer belts which are scanned by X-ray separators. Diamonds fluoresce under X-ray, and the light they emit activates a compressed air jet, which literally blows them out from the gravel into a side channel. The diamonds come tumbling down a tube onto a wooden table in the sorting room, in full view of visitors segregated on the far side of a bullet-proof window.

A middle-aged lady in a white overall stands by the table as the diamonds, and some small bits of gravel that get blown along with them, arrive. Holding a pair of tweezers in her left hand, she picks out the diamonds with the dexterity of a gull pecking up shellfish on a mudflat and pops them into an orange plastic cup in her right hand. Once in a while she empties the cup into the growing pile of rough diamonds before her. This is the harvest of those bulldozers, sandscrapers and bedrock cleaners scattered along over fifty miles of coast. It amounts to around 5,000 carats of diamonds a day—enough to fill a couple of large coffee mugs. A typical day's sample is laid out beneath spot-lights in a sealed glass case beside the sorting room. There are eight large stones of between five and ten carats, perhaps a hundred ranging from one to five carats, a good pile of fifty points to one carat and a mugful of smaller stones. "The average size here is point seventy-six of a carat," said Derek Erickson. "We don't get many really big diamonds. The largest was two hundred and forty-six carats found in 1928, and we have had a couple at one hundred and sixty and one hundred and fifty-three carats. The best crop here is high-quality medium-sized gems with a good variety of color."

And that is the real secret of CDM. It is not just that it pro-duces 1.6 million carats of gem diamonds a year but that they are much more valuable because of consistent quality, size and shape (which means they can be cut and polished with much less loss). Indeed, a study commissioned by the Commonwealth Fund for Technical Cooperation reckoned that stones from CDM earned more than twice as much per carat as stones from the Namaqualand fields just to the south.

No wonder the diamond desert has been the star in De Beers' crown for so long. In the late 1960s and early 1970s, CDM ac-counted on average for up to 40 percent of De Beers' total taxed profits. Since 1974 no separate accounts have been published for CDM, but the group's annual reports have indicated a decline in its contribution. "The proportion of total profits derived from South-West Africa/Namibia, amounting in 1979 to 18 percent, is less than it used to be in the past," the De Beers' annual report stated that year. Such a share would indicate $164 million profits from CDM; still a substantial amount, although not as high as some mining analysts anticipated, given the strength of gem diamond prices in recent years. De Beers points out, however, that all-around higher working costs, especially in oil for its vast earth-moving fleet on the diamond coast, have risen rapidly, while the development of the Namaqualand and Botswana deposits inevitably reduces the share of group profits from CDM.

What no one would dispute is that although production at the diamond desert has peaked out from 2 million carats down to around 1.6 million, it is a continuing treasure trove. So the real issue, as Namibia gains its independence after over sixty years of domination by South Africa, is who will control CDM? At present it is 100 percent owned by De Beers, whose lease on the diamond desert runs until 2010. Well ahead of independence, De Beers astutely transferred CDM's head office to the Namibian capital, Windhoek. Clearly the Namibian government will eye the wealth of CDM—whose taxes constitute no less than 50 percent of their country's revenue—with special attention. Already CDM pays 64 percent of its mining profits to Namibia. Will the new regime rest content with that? Or, like their neighbors in Botswana, will they reduce De Beers' stake in CDM, perhaps opting for a 50–50 share? Outright nationalization is conceivable, especially if the left-wing-orientated SWAPO eventually gains power.

The undisputed point is that plenty of diamonds still lie hidden beneath the sands of the Namib desert and just offshore in the turbulent waters of the South Atlantic. Although production has peaked out (and De Beers is sometimes accused of having degutted the best diamonds ahead of independence), at least twenty years' work remains in the present mining area. As Harry Oppenheimer himself has stressed, "CDM will be of major importance to the emergent state of Namibia."

Whether De Beers will remain alone in the driver's seat is quite another matter. And can Oranjemund, the company town that has led such an isolated life, almost untouched by the political turmoil leading up to independence, remain so remote from the real world once there is a border post manned by Namibian customs and immigration just down the road on the banks of the Orange River? The kingdom in the Namib desert, as CDM is often called, may soon be an integral part of the republic of Namibia.

4

Botswana: The New Champions

Sharp at four o'clock on weekday afternoons a dull boom sounds across a flat expanse of veldt on the edge of the Kalahari desert, startling a few kudus and impalas browsing in the shade of the mophane trees. A pink-brown column of dust rises lazily into the air from the center of a huge, shallow, egg-shaped crater. There is silence for a few moments, and the dust soon settles; then a small blue Mazda pickup truck flying a red flag buzzes out into the middle of the pit. Two men climb out and poke around the scattered rocks for a while to confirm that all the charges have exploded. The all clear is soon sounded, and a solemn procession of dump trucks rumbles out to start collecting the pieces over the next twenty-four hours.

This ritual afternoon blasting has been going on for almost a decade out in the wilds of Botswana, on the fringe of the Kalahari desert, at what was formerly a lonely cattle post named Orapa. It began on July 1, 1971, precisely a hundred years after the first discovery of diamonds at Kimberley; just as the Kimberley mines heralded the arrival of South Africa as the world's richest gem diamond producer, so the Orapa diamond pipe signaled that a new champion had been found. Barring accidents, Botswana will be the league leader in gem diamonds by 1985. The combined production of Orapa and two other mines, Letlhakane and Jwaneng, is forecast at 11 million carats a year, of which around 3.5 million will be of gem quality. It is a remarkable transformation for this country, almost the size of France, with scarcely 700,000 inhabitants. Until the last decade, Botswana was one of the poorest of all third-world countries, half covered by the sands of the Kalahari, with some indifferent cattle rearing as the only real asset to its economy. "The wealth from Orapa," said Botswana's late President, Sir Seretse Khama, when he opened the mine, "is the key to Botswana's development."

The Botswana government has a 50 percent holding in De Beers' Botswana Mining Company (Debswana), which manages Orapa, the smaller pipe at Letlhakane thirty miles away and the new Jwaneng mine in the heart of the Kalahari, coming on stream in 1982. Originally the government took a mere 15 percent stake in the enterprise, but once De Beers revealed the true scale and wealth of Orapa and sought to renegotiate its contract to expand operations and open up Letlhakane, too, officials took the opportunity to insist upon a fifty-fifty share. Botswana now receives upwards of 70 percent of the profits of the mines, which have become the mainstay of its economy. The country's revenue from diamonds alone is expected to exceed $500 million annually by 1985, compared with $190 million from all sources just seven years earlier. And diamonds will account for almost three-quarters of all exports, giving Botswana, as one commentator put it, "one of Africa's sturdiest economies." [6]

Botswana's diamonds are equally crucial to De Beers in the eighties. They will account not only for more than half of all the group's output, but will compensate for the decline in gem yield both from the Kimberley mines and CDM in Namibia. Indeed, a smooth partnership between De Beers and Botswana is in the interests of both parties—as Harry Oppenheimer was at pains to point out in April 1980 when launching his annual report. "Revenue from diamonds is already a very important

[6] *Financial Times*, London, July 29, 1980, p. 19.

element in the national income of Botswana and will become very much more important when Jwaneng reaches full production," he observed. "It is not too much to say that the interest of the Government of Botswana in the stability and prosperity of the diamond industry is virtually as great as that of the De Beers Company itself."

Yet this fortune for Botswana and De Beers could easily have been overlooked. The original hunt for a diamond pipe had been going on for twelve years before Orapa was located in the spring of 1967. For although everyone knew that three alluvial diamonds had been found in the Motloutse River in eastern Botswana (then the Bechuanaland Protectorate) in 1955, the source of the diamonds was forever elusive. "Eventually we embarked on a systematic following up of all the drainages," recalled Jim Gibson, a quiet-spoken geologist dressed in a neatly pressed olive-green safari suit, shorts, white socks and tough brown shoes, who has been hunting diamonds in Botswana for almost twenty years and is in charge of geology at Orapa. One arm of the Motloutse was only a tiny stream, but it sat in a broad valley, an anomaly which led the geologist to believe that at one time the drainage area of the river was much more extensive. So Gibson and Dr. Gavin Lamont, then the chief De Beers geologist in Botswana, pressed westwards for a hundred thirty miles beyond the present river system right to the edge of the Kalahari desert. "Here we found garnets and other heavy minerals, which are indicators that you are in a kimberlite area. The kimberlite itself weathers quickly, and you don't find it exposed on the surface," Gibson went on, going over to a large map dotted with orange pins that covered the wall of his office. "And once you are in a kimberlite area, you know what other features to look for on aerial photographs." The aerials showed twenty-nine potential pipes in the area, including one "big daddy" a mile long. "We found it hard to believe it was all pipe," Gibson recalled, "but walking through the bush to the site we could see that it was a slightly elevated area. And when we put down some sample pits, we realized that we had one of the biggest pipes ever found." Their luck was extraordinary; the pipe is just a short stretch from the beginning of the Kalahari desert itself. "Once you've got one hundred feet of that sand over your pipe, it's much harder to find," said Gibson. Orapa was only the fourth pipe with payable diamonds found during this century in Africa, and it proved to be the biggest area in the world, except for the Williamson Pipe in Tanzania. The pipe covers more than a square mile and, at ninety million years old, is a youngster in the kimberlite stakes. The slight hump Gibson could see across the veldt was the last of the original cone that had not been weathered completely flat. "What we're mining is kimberlite debris washed back into the top of the pipe from the rim of the crater," said Gibson. "We shall have to go down nearly three hundred feet to get to the pure kimberlite pipe."

That will take quite some time. Even after nine years the miners are only skimming the top of the cone, for the area to be dug out is so vast that they have descended scarcely a hundred feet below the level of the veldt. They may get to the pure kimberlite sometime in the 1990s, and the mine is expected to last at least until the year 2050.

Thus at Orapa one can see what other famous mines, like Premier or Kimberley's Big Hole, looked like in their early days when they, too, were only shallow depressions in the ground. The only difference is that the cobweb of ropes and wires strung out to all the individual diggings at the Big Hole are missing; instead, seven dump trucks roll into the pit like clockwork night and day, bringing out the rock for crushing. A tall laconic Frenchman named Claude Lenferna, who has spent almost thirty years in Africa, is the pit superintendent. "The size here is fantastic," he said, piloting his pickup truck toward the middle of the crater down a series of gently inclining ramps, "which is why it looks as if we are only playing with it. After eight years we are just starting to expose the rim of the pipe." The excavations proceed, he explained, in giant steps eighty feet wide and thirty feet deep. But the impression is of haphazard digging because the grade of diamonds varies all the time. In the middle of the pit Lenferna pulled up and got out a map of the diggings. "The entire pit is divided into fifty-by-fifty-meter blocks, and every single one is entirely different," he said. "In the center of the pipe we've got lots of waste, so the grade is only zero point twenty-three [i.e., 0.23 carats of diamonds are found in each ton]. Next to that, there's some blue ground at zero point ninety-nine, and over there near the rim we're getting three point fifty—what a grade! On average we need a grade of one point fifty, so you are really juggling one block to another at a time. If I don't produce that average, the management clobbers me."

The actual diamonds are firmly embedded in the rock and are rarely visible to the naked eye. "I've been here eight years, and I've never seen a diamond in the pit," said Lenferna, "although some guys have the eye and pick them up—there's a reward of up to one thousand *pula* [$1,250] if they hand them in." The slim chance of spotting a diamond in the open pit means that Orapa is not much troubled with a black market in illicit finds. "Quite a change from the Williamson," remarked Lenferna. "Illicit diggers and buyers were coming over the fence like flies there all the time."

Orapa's diamonds are ultimately sprung from the rock at the huge treatment plant—the biggest in the world—which breaks down 1,250 tons of debris an hour around the clock. X-ray detectors then separate the rough diamonds, which speed along conveyer belts to the heavily guarded sorting house. Within, eighteen sorters are stationed behind a glass screen through which they poke their hands and arms into long white gloves similar to those worn by workers in nuclear research stations to isolate them from radioactivity. The intention here, of course, is to make it impossible for anyone to palm the stones they are sorting on the bench on the far side of the screen. A pile of dust, gravel and diamonds is poured out before each gloved sorter, who deftly picks out the rough with a pair of tweezers and drops it into white plastic teacups. Although one or two large diamonds of over 200 carats have turned up at Orapa, the mine is no match for Premier or CDM when it comes to size or quality. Most of the gemstones have a yellowish-brown tinge, while nearly 85 percent of the 4.5 million carats turned up at Orapa each year are tiny gray-black stones useful only to industry.

The consolation, however, comes once a day when consignments arrive at the sorting house from the two small pipes being worked at Letlhakane thirty miles to the south. Although Letlhakane boasts none of the grand scale of Orapa (the pipes are only 28.4 acres and 8.6 acres), and output measured in carats is scarcely 400,000 a year (less than one-tenth of Orapa), a remarkably high proportion are gem quality, and several good stones of up to thirty carats have been found. "Letlhakane is getting better as we go in," said Roger Price, the sorting-house manager. "It's now giving us thirteen hundred carats a day, half of them gems. Orapa is the bread and butter; Letlhakane is the cherry on top."

The real cherry crop, however, should be at the Jwaneng mine, where production will start in 1982 and reach full pitch three years later. The Jwaneng pipe is projected to turn up at least 6 million carats a year, of which 2 million should be good quality gems; it will be the largest single mine in southern Africa. The discovery and development of the mine, at a cost of $340 million, rate as an even greater technical feat than Orapa, for the mouth of the pipe is buried beneath a hundred fifty feet of Kalahari sand in the Ngwaketse district of southern Botswana. No visible evidence of diamonds was apparent on the surface at all, and De Beers geologists had to drill down through the desert and bring up pulverized samples of kimberlite for analysis. Not only does all this overburden have to be eliminated before mining can start, but an entire town has to be erected in the desert and water supplies piped in from boreholes thirty miles away.

And Orapa, Letlhakane and Jwaneng may be only the start. De Beers and other mining groups are diligently hunting through the Kalahari for more hidden pipes. "Vast areas are still not properly explored because of the deep sand cover," said geologist Jim Gibson. "It's a technical feat to find any deposits under the Kalahari."

Yet already the money generated by Orapa and Letlhakane, and the prospect of even more from Jwaneng, means that plans can be made for new schools, clinics and improved communications throughout Botswana. A slow transformation from a rural, pastoral society into an industrial one is taking place. The change is not always easy. For a start, the relatively high rate of pay available in the mines acts as a magnet that has threatened to disrupt the rest of the emerging economy. The government has been forced to put a ceiling on wages at Orapa and Letlhakane; the ordinary unskilled worker there is paid between 80 and 90 *pula* a month ($100–$112), far less than he would earn, for instance, in the diamond mines of South Africa. The government is equally insistent upon the majority of jobs going to local people. White expatriates in the chief management and technical posts comprise only 200 of the 2,100 employed at Orapa. Eventually most of the whites will also be replaced by locals, as training programs bear fruit. De Beers is already sponsoring over forty scholarships abroad to enable Botswana students to study mining, metallurgy and engineering. "In five years' time we'll be ninety-six percent localized," said Letz Pilane, the tall, gray-haired chief of public relations (a schoolteacher in Botswana before Orapa came along), "and outsiders have to be justified all the time."

Life at Orapa is certainly very different from that of the simple African village from which most workers came. The township, set on a small knoll a couple of miles from the mine, has broad streets lined with flame trees. There are swimming pools, a good golf course, a cinema, a supermarket and a seventy-two-bed hospital that caters not only to the mine, but to the surrounding villages. The football team, White Diamonds, is in the first division of the Botswana league. All the children of the mine workers go to school, a privilege in Botswana where education is not yet compulsory. Most of the employees live with their families in neat, white bungalows for which they pay only a nominal rent (ten dollars a month for the simplest). The real contrast with mines in South Africa or Namibia, which operate on the contract-labor system under which many workers come only for nine months or a year without their families, is that everyone at Orapa is encouraged to make a career; there is a special gratuity after ten years of uninterrupted work.

The sense of community is close; Orapa, like Oranjemund in Namibia, has no natural roots. The nearest real town is Frances-town, 150 miles to the east; to the west there is nothing but the Kalahari. Even the water supply has to be piped in forty miles from a specially created reservoir at Mopipi which is fed by the Okavanga swamps. The visitor is constantly reminded that a few years ago this was almost unexplored country. Sitting by the eighteenth green of the well-watered golf course in the evening, the mine dumps are just visible one way, but turn your head another and the vista is still an unspoilt plain, studded with mophane and thorn trees. "We had lions around a little while ago," said a young Botswana engineer, brushing up on his put-ting. "A male and a female with three cubs were attacking cattle on the farm. So if you stay up here late you might see a lion." He went off into the dusk, trailing his clubs on a little golf cart, very much a symbol of the new era in Botswana—a black engineer playing golf against a growing skyline of waste dumps intruding upon the vastness of the veldt.

While many of his compatriots may find it hard to abandon a pastoral life with their cattle, there is undoubtedly a feeling of pride at their new-found status in the diamond world. As I bade good-bye to Letz Pilane at Orapa's tiny airstrip, I inquired how I should address letters to him. "Just put Orapa, The Diamond Town, Botswana," he said cheerfully. "Everyone knows us."

5

The Soviet Union:
The Wild Card

The discovery of diamonds in the Soviet Union is like a scene from a Bolshoi ballet. The heroine is Larissa, the huntress. One day she is trekking through the snow-covered forest of Siberia when she spies a red fox slipping between the pines. Larissa raises her rifle, but the split second before she pulls the trigger, she notices that the fur on the fox's belly is stained blue. Instinctively she deflects her aim, and the shot goes wide. The fox bolts, but the cunning huntress tracks it to its lair. This is not, as you may have suspected, the palace of a handsome prince who has been turned into a wretched fox by a wicked witch; it is a conventional foxhole with one notable exception—it has been dug into blue kimberlite. As the observant Larissa instantly deduces, the stained fur is an omen not of blue blood, but of diamonds.

This is the tale that some Soviet propagandist has spun to dramatize the discovery on August 21, 1954, of the first real evidence that kimberlite diamond pipes existed in the vast wastes of Siberia. The huntress was actually a redoubtable lady geologist from Leningrad named L. A. Popugayeva who did indeed find a lair where the fox's digging had brought some blue ground to the surface. Her detective work was a Siberian variation on the African theme, for pipes have been located there by the energetic burrowing in the desert of armies of ants. The first pipe located through Larissa Popugayeva's work in the short Siberian summer of 1954 was aptly named Zarnitza (Dawn); it was the fifth biggest ever located, covering over fifty-three acres but was not, alas, very rich in diamonds. It heralded, however, a host of similar finds nearby all along the Vilyui River, a tributary of the Lena, one of which proved a real bonanza. According to some accounts, this pipe was also located when a geologist, Yuri Khabardin, noticed excavated blue ground near a fox's lair. Whatever the exact clue (and it is clear that more than a touch of folklore surrounds both discoveries), Khabardin sent off a coded radio message, "I am smoking the pipe of peace. The tobacco is excellent." His find was duly called *Mir* (Peace).[7]

The discovery of the Mir pipe marked the beginning of a new era in the history of diamonds. In the succeeding quarter of a century, the Soviet Union has become a formidable force in the diamond market. Indeed, by 1980 her position has become pivotal, just as in gold and platinum. The geological accident that concentrated both precious metals and diamonds in Russia and South Africa, two countries at the opposite ends of the political spectrum, gives each an exaggerated importance in the marketplace. Although the Russians have never revealed any statistics of their diamond production, it is conservatively estimated to be over 10 million carats a year (more likely between 11 and 12 million), making the Soviet Union the world's second largest producer after Zaire. But as Zaire's output is virtually all of industrial quality, while over a quarter of Russia's is reckoned to be of high-quality gems, her influence is magnified, at least until Botswana reaches full maturity in the mid-1980s. The direction of Soviet policy for the export of both rough and polished gems during the next decade will be crucial, not

[7] "Siberia. No longer a sleeping land," by John Massey Stewart, *Optima*, No. 2, 1976, pp. 85–104.

least to the continuation of the monopoly of De Beers' Central Selling Organization. "The Russian presence has been the phenomenon of the 1970s," remarked a London broker. "Today they are an essential part of our life." But the mystery that still surrounds much of Soviet mining and marketing often gives extra significance in a business that thrives on rumor. Without doubt the Soviets are, as *Forbes* magazine observed in an excellent appraisal of the scene, "the wild card in the diamond pack."

The Russians' hand has been transformed by their mines. A quarter of a century ago they were almost desperate buyers of rough industrial diamonds in all sorts of shady alleyways in the West. Indeed, in the early days of black markets for illicitly mined diamonds in West Africa and Zaire (then the Belgian Congo), the gem quality went to Antwerp, and the industrial or *boart*, moved by various back doors to Moscow. Old dealers in Beirut, whither many Lebanese operators in Africa dispatched their diamonds, recall that the diplomatic bag sent home from the Russian Embassy was often full of industrial stones.

Consequently, the priority in the immediate postwar years was for the Soviet Union to try to find a domestic source of diamonds to satisfy not only her growing needs, but those of her Eastern European satellites, too. The expansion of precision engineering and drilling made it imperative, particularly in view of the Soviet Union's desperate shortage at that time of foreign exchange. (She was selling, for instance, much more gold than she produced in the years 1953–65, reducing her reserves to a very low level.) Although there was a little production from alluvial diamond deposits discovered in the Vishera river basin close to the Ural mountains as far back as 1829, this in no way met requirements.

The prospect of diamonds in Siberia had been foreshadowed in 1941 by eminent Soviet geologist Victor Sobolev, who argued that the great Siberian shield between the Yenisey and Lena Rivers bore remarkable similarity to the raised plateau of central and southern Africa, where diamond pipes had been found. Kimberley and the province of Yakutia in Siberia had much in common, he insisted. He even predicted that the most likely spot was along the Vilyui River. Expedition after expedition failed to hit the jackpot. A few alluvial stones were found in some streams by 1948, but nothing conclusive. It was only in

1954 that Larissa Popugayeva proved Sobolev was absolutely right.[8] The search has lasted thirteen years, almost the same time, incidentally, that it took to find the Orapa mine in Botswana after the first alluvials showed the way.

The pinpointing first of the Zarnitza and then the Mir pipes along the Vilyui River, however, was no instant solution. Whereas in many parts of Africa the hurdles facing diamond miners are to create communities in desert places, in Siberia the hostile winter climate was the hazard. The Siberian province of Yakutia, between the Lena River and the Arctic Circle, is often known as "The Pole of Cold." The average January temperature is minus fifty degrees Fahrenheit and may go to minus ninety degrees. Not only do the rivers freeze, but steel becomes brittle, brake fluid freezes, oils clog and rubber crisps up like a potato chip. Schools close because it is too cold for children to stand around waiting for buses, and workers outside in the diamond fields must have at least ten minutes off in every hour to thaw out inside. They benefit also from a "northern bonus" of 40 percent over Moscow pay levels in compensation for their hardships.[9]

The terrain itself is frozen solid and not only in the winter, for the permafrost defies the summer thaw, and only a few feet of topsoil are easily workable. Recovering diamonds, therefore, either from the pipes or from the maze of alluvial deposits in the surrounding swamps and rivers, is a formidable task. Everything has to be unfrozen first, even before explosive charges can be laid. The initial technique was to use high-pressure steam hoses to burrow into the ground. These were later supplemented by jet engines positioned close to the drilling points so that the heat of their exhausts could be piped directly to specially adapted drills. The entire working area was sometimes cocooned in great sheets of plastic roofing in an effort to hold in some warm air.[10]

Each step of diamond recovery is complicated by the cold.

[8] A. A. Linari-Linholm, *Occurrence, Mining and Recovery of Diamonds* (Johannesburg, 1970), p. 6.

[9] "What It Is Like to Live in Siberia During Winter," *Smithsonian*, Vol. 4, No. 10, 1972, pp. 44–51.

[10] " 'Red' Diamonds from Siberia," *The International Diamond Annual*, London, 1970, p. 81.

After blasting, the kimberlite has to be broken up by steam shovel before it can be taken to the treatment plant for reduction. Even there the customary cold-water circuits for carrying pulverized rock over grease tables, to which diamonds adhere while the waste flows on, are useless; water turns to ice in seconds. The Russians eventually overcame this by pioneering the X-ray technique of diamond sorting, later copied by most African mines, which identifies the stones by their fluorescence and separates them from other debris on a conveyer belt by triggering a jet of air.

Since the Mir pipe turned out to be the most commercially viable along the Vilyui River, a whole community, Mirny, slowly grew up nearby as the pipe swung into full production as an open-cast mine in the early 1960s. The town of 30,000 people was created from scratch. "Everything from matches to excavating machinery was supplied over thousands of miles by way of the Trans-Siberian Railway, then hundreds of miles down the Lena River and, finally, through swamps and forests of Mirny," reported Viktor Tikhonov, the manager of the Mirny Diamond Administration. "Many supplies are flown in because the Lena River is ice-free only four months a year." [11]

The scale of problems at Mir was only magnified by the discovery of two other payable pipes, Udachnaya (Success) and Aikhal (Glory) nearly three hundred miles further to the north, virtually on the Arctic Circle. Each took a decade to bring into production, and even then output is believed to have been sporadic. The exceptionally harsh winter of 1979, for instance, caused a considerable fall in production. Other pipes dotted across the Siberian shield close to Mir, including two named "Sputnik" and "Twenty-third Congress" that would probably be profitable in easier climates, have never been properly worked at all. And it is still not clear what Yakutulmaz, the Diamond Trust that oversees Siberian production, intends to do about other rich deposits which are supposed to have been found at Anabar Tundra, well inside the Arctic Circle. The inevitable conclusion is that Soviet diamond output would be much higher if diamonds were found in more favorable regions than Siberia.

[11] Ibid., p. 82.

Even so, the consolations have been substantial. Not only have the Russians achieved self-sufficiency in their industrial diamond requirements, but the export of gemstones has become a major foreign-exchange earner. Considerable debate has taken place among geologists in the West on the relationship between gem and industrial in Soviet output. The consensus seems to be that the Mir pipe, the largest single producer over two decades, is about 20 percent gem and 80 percent industrial, while Udachnaya has a slightly higher gem ratio. The real "cream," however, comes from the alluvial deposits along the neighboring rivers, which are worked by dredges in the summer months. The gem return there is much better. This is, of course, exactly the same situation as in Africa, where the proportion of gemstones in alluvial terraces in Namibia, on the southwest coast of South Africa, and in Angola and Sierra Leone is high. The tiny fragments of *boart* tend to get lost in erosion. The significant difference in Siberia, however, is that the alluvial deposits are concentrated closer to the original pipes for the simple reason that the rivers are frozen so much of the time that the stones travel more slowly. They are also less rounded than those found, for instance, on the southwest coasts of Africa, which have been smoothed by long journeys down rivers and finally by the pounding of the sea. Allowing for the gems in alluvial deposits, up to 30 percent of Soviet production is of gem, or at least "near-gem," quality ("near-gem" meaning that it can be used either for industrial purposes or gem purposes). Taking overall Soviet output at between 11 and 12 million carats annually, the real gem content should be at least 2.5 million carats, with perhaps another 0.75 million of "near-gem." This amount is rather more than some estimates, but the Russians themselves provide no statistics. Speculation grows thicker because the Russians use all the industrial-quality goods at home and only market in the West the gem quality.

The quality of Siberian gemstones is usually rated good as is the color, which is often of a slightly greenish hue, similar to that of stones from the Finsch mine in South Africa; the average size, however, is small. Most Russian rough seen in the West is between half a carat and two carats. Large diamonds are relatively rare. The biggest from the Mir pipe, dubbed Stalingrad, was 166 carats. Characteristically, the names usually laud some special event or noble comrade. A 67-carat stone found in the spring of 1976 was called "The 25th Party Congress," a 51-carat gem honored the first woman astronaut and a 46-carat bauble was dedicated to the Mine Workers' Union; a 106-carat diamond was named Leo Tolstoy to mark the 150th anniversary of his birth.

Although mining in Siberia is the local responsibility of Yakutulmaz, this diamond trust is under the wing of the Ministry of Nonferrous Metallurgy in Moscow. The Ministry has a central division, Glavzoloto, presided over by V. P. Berezin, which looks after all gold, platinum and diamond mining. The output is also actively encouraged by both the state bank, Gosbank, and the Ministry of Foreign Trade because of its great potential as a foreign-exchange earner. The rapid rise in diamond prices in the late 1970s enabled diamond exports to net nearly $1 billion annually for the Soviet Treasury (compared to around $2 billion for gold and $300 million for platinum).

The Soviet Union first appeared as an exporter of rough gem diamonds as far back as 1959. Initially Almazyuvelireksport, the division of the Ministry of Foreign Trade which handles exports of precious metals (except gold) and jewelry, signed a contract with De Beers' Central Selling Organization in London to sell their gem-quality diamonds. That was renounced, however, in 1963 on the political grounds that the Russians could not do business directly with a company having such strong South African connections. Since then the Russians have kept a very low profile on their marketing of rough. For a while they tried to filter it out through a variety of European dealers, but that was not successful, and ultimately the Russians came back through an intermediary to the Central Selling Organization, which now sells virtually all their gem-quality rough.

At the same time, the Russians have worked hard to develop their own cutting and polishing industry, both to bypass De Beers and to maximize their own profit and provide more employment at home—in short, to become vertically integrated from Siberian mine to western jewelry manufacturer. This is where their real influence lies in the evolution of the international diamond business. As the Russians began selling more of their output to the West during the 1970s already polished, so the De Beers monopoly was short-circuited, and serious inroads were made on employment in the western cutting centers. Tel Aviv was most directly challenged, because the Russians' polished goods are mainly melees, the medium-sized diamonds on which Israeli cutters have built their reputation.

The first steps in developing a cutting industry in the Soviet Union were primitive, because all the basic skills had to be copied from abroad. The Russians toured diamond-cutting plants in the West and even recruited some experts to train craftsmen. "The Russians came around our factory at Hove years ago and looked at our process for polishing girdles [the widest point of the stone]," said Arthur Monnickendam, a leading British manufacturer. "They've been polishing girdles the same way as us ever since."

Cutting plants were gradually set up, principally in Smolensk, which has acquired the best reputation for the standard of its craftsmanship, and also in Moscow, Sverdlovsk and Kiev. But it took a while for high-quality work to emerge. "You used to be able to tell Russian polished goods easily," recalled a New York dealer; "the 'make' was crude, with the table [the flat top of a stone] off to the side and facets all over the place. And if there was a slight flaw, which a good cutter could take out, the Russians left it in." Marketing skills were also awry. "Originally they handled the sale of diamonds just like shoes or caviar or gold; they didn't realize that every diamond is different and has its price," confided an Antwerp wholesaler, who has since become one of their biggest clients. "They didn't know the real value of their goods and were taken for a ride."

A man from the ministry in Moscow also decided it might be a good idea to integrate one step further by making diamond jewelry. "Suddenly they told us, 'If you want our diamonds, you must take our jewelry,'" the Antwerp wholesaler recalled. "But it was such ugly stuff. I went to Moscow and said, 'For heaven's sake, we can't sell this junk; we're simply taking the stones out and melting down the rings.' They said they were sorry, they had a six-month program on line and could not change." However, the message eventually sank in: jewelry was scrapped, and Moscow reverted to selling loose polished stones. Slowly quality improved, until by the late 1970s the Russians could match all comers. "Their polished goods are very good today; the cut is finally perfect," said a satisfied Antwerp customer, sorting through some distinctive parcels. (The Russians wrap their diamonds in the same flimsy blue-white papers as in the West, but each sheet is slightly larger.) He did have one reservation. "The only trouble is that the finish on some of their lower-quality goods is now too good. And that makes them expensive."

The Russians can afford to do a fine job, because labor costs are less important than in highly competitive western cutting centers. Indeed, there is an old joke in the diamond trade that for every thousand cutters in a Soviet factory, there are a thousand more employees watching over them to insure they do not steal, quite apart from a further thousand making tea. Overmanning, however, is not preventing the Russians from installing automatic polishing machines in some of their factories, which will standardize high quality on their melees goods and should raise productivity.

Meanwhile, the Russians have learned to drive a hard bargain. "You get on the telex to them, ask the price and they quote a thousand dollars a carat," said a Tokyo dealer. "So you place an order, and suddenly they've put the price up to eleven hundred. Those boys are very smart." And they make sure that every last cent is earned. Once a buyer from New York was in the Almazyuvelireksport offices in Moscow, looking over parcels of polished. A tiny stone slipped from his tweezers and rolled away on the floor. The Russian salesmen brought in lamps, and everyone hunted around for two hours without success. Eventually they gave up. The American signed a contract for several million dollars and went home. A few days later he got an invoice for seven dollars for the missing diamond. In the Soviet system every single stone has to be accounted for.

The Russians have also followed the De Beers example in ruthlessly making clients take some inferior goods which they do not really want, along with the polished goods they need. For many diamond producers it is the only way to clear all the output. "You must take everything in your box, just like the Diamond Trading Company," an Antwerp buyer explained, "so you keep the good stuff and sell the rest. But you can refuse the whole box and the Russians will still invite you back again—the DTC might not."

Refusals are rare. Russian-polished goods are much sought

after. Indeed, the impression I gained both in New York and Tokyo, the gateways to the two biggest retail markets for diamonds, was that every wholesaler was eager to get on the next plane to Moscow if he could wangle an invitation. In theory, it is not even necessary to go to Moscow. An overseas arm of Almazyuvelireksport, Russelmaz, maintains offices in Antwerp, Frankfurt and Geneva as a showcase for polished goods. But the real Russelmaz role often seems to have little to do with day-to-day diamond sales. Western intelligence officials quickly noted, for instance, that when a batch of diplomats were expelled from the Soviet Embassy in London on the grounds that they were KGB agents, one or two showed up soon afterwards, working in the Russelmaz office in Antwerp. Russelmaz may indeed be a shop window for diamonds, but that can be a handy front for gathering intelligence about diamond trends, among other matters. Diamonds are also a very useful way of paying agents or of financing friendly political parties throughout the noncommunist world. There was much comment in the Bombay diamond market, for example, early in 1980 about a sudden influx of Russian polished goods just at the moment of Indira Gandhi's election triumph. Her opponents argued that her campaign had been partly financed by Russian diamonds.

Professional diamond traders know it is virtually impossible to go into a Russelmaz office and buy diamonds; everything is referred back to Moscow, and the twenty Antwerp dealers and a dozen or so in New York who buy regularly from the Russians go there to do their business. One of the rare occasions when Russelmaz is known to have sold diamonds directly to a stranger was when a young Californian, who had amassed $8.1 million by a computer fraud on the bank for which he worked, offered their Geneva office the cash against diamonds. They took him up. The only catch was that when the thief was apprehended as he returned home after "laundering" his loot into Russian polished, the bank had considerable difficulty in raising anywhere near an equal amount when it resold the stones to recoup its loss. The diamonds were eventually bought by an international wholesaler for scarcely $6 million. Admittedly, diamond prices had weakened in the meantime, but it also indicated that Russelmaz cannot resist a good profit.

That is the keynote of all the Russian activity in diamonds, just as it is nowadays in all their trading with the West in precious metals. Their gold marketing has become highly sophisticated during the last decade, with a flexible policy designed to sell only into a rising market and to buy back when prices are weak. The same, apparently, is true of diamonds. The Soviets did sell diamonds too cheaply in the early 1970s, but no more. And although some dealers in Antwerp and Tel Aviv often worry that the Russians will "dump," such a move would be entirely out of character. As a Russian salesman in Switzerland remarked, "We would never cut down the tree." And they are always mindful of the old maxim of Lenin's that when one is living among wolves, one "howls like a wolf." When dealing with the capitalist world, the Russians act like the best of capitalists.

Moreover, they have a real need for strong diamond prices. Their actual cost of production is certainly much higher than in most other countries because of the hostile climate, and that may be a crucial element in their future role in the diamond trade. In broad terms, from the mid-1950s through the late 1970s, the Russian diamond-mining industry expanded, with the great Mir pipe as the backbone of production. But by 1978 there were rumors of a slowdown. Several accounts reaching the West suggested either that the Mir pipe was not proving payable at greater depths (rather like the Williamson in Tanzania) or that the permafrost was making it almost impossible to work efficiently as the hole got deeper. Initially, the Mir was worked as an open-cast mine, very much along the same lines as the Orapa mine in Botswana. It was excavated in a series of steps or benches, progressively descending by about 40 feet a year. That would mean that by 1980 the Mir pit was nearly 800 feet deep. To get below that, it might well be necessary to start all over again, digging shafts down through the surrounding "country rock" (as at the Premier mine in South Africa) and then tunneling into the kimberlite from below. That would call for a major capital investment, even if it was practical in Arctic conditions. Precisely what is happening is not known, but the Russians have made excuses about lower level of delivery of rough since 1978, pleading the high costs of mining and production difficulties aggravated by exceptional winters.

The implication is that the main period of expansion is over, and Russian diamond production will remain on a plateau during the 1980s, perhaps in the range of 10–12 million carats. The interesting point is that De Beers is pressing ahead with massive expansion plans to step up output in both South Africa and Botswana, which will become the leading producer of gem diamonds by 1985. Such activity clearly indicates they are not too worried about similar growth from the Russians. For the whole history of the diamond business in the last century has been to try to tailor mine production to market needs. (Remember that in the 1930s South African mines were closed for years.) De Beers would certainly not be engaged in a near doubling of output if they thought the Russians were about to do the same.

The other key question for the 1980s is whether the Russians continue to expand their cutting and polishing industry, at the expense of rough sales through De Beers' Central Selling Organization. The more they manage to bypass the CSO, the more of a disruptive influence they could become. Their exports of polished goods in recent years have varied between $200 and $500 million annually, while around $600 to $700 million has been marketed as rough through London. Obviously if that ratio was reversed, the De Beers monopoly, in its present form, would be challenged. In practice, the omens indicate that the Russians do not plan to step up their own cutting rapidly. While they will definitely maintain, and perhaps improve, existing facilities, they are expected to sell most of their gem production as rough for the decade ahead. The reason is hard economics. While the Russians were on a gravy train, selling their polished goods in the boom years of 1977–78, they have found life as wholesalers of polished much tougher since. "The Russians have had one or two severe shocks recently," confided a major buyer of their goods in the summer of 1980. "They simply can't sell their polished in the present state of the market." The prospect, therefore, is that the Russians will rein in slightly on their polished plans and rely instead on continuing to market rough through the CSO in London. In difficult days the guaranteed monthly check can be most comforting.

That is not to discount the Russians' influence in the years ahead. They are formidable producers. As Nick Axelrod at the Harry Winston organization in New York observed, "I see them now as a major factor in our industry."

6

Sierra Leone:
The Heartland of IDM

From the air the terrain looks like an immense Gruyère cheese, pockmarked with holes. Trees wither where their roots have been exposed; roads suddenly become pitted for hundreds of yards; corrugated iron houses teeter on the edge of craters. This crazy moonscape may suggest that a horde of giant ants passed by or that a million bombs rained down. Actually, the devastation is the wake of an army of illicit diamond miners in search of some of the world's best gemstones. Many of them are there by day, digging and sifting, half submerged in water that swiftly fills the holes and breeds malarial mosquitoes. They pay scant attention to the mining company's security helicopter scudding overhead. And at night they are joined by thousands more, burrowing by moonlight through the topsoil to diamond-iferous gravel beneath and sorting through it for rough diamonds in the first light of dawn.

Up here in the hinterland of Sierra Leone, around the town of Koidu and in the surrounding swamp and forest along the flood plains of the Bafi and Sewa Rivers, illicit diamond mining is a way of life. A generation ago Koidu was just another African village of a dozen or so houses. Today it is a bustling shantytown of 100,000 people, built literally on diamonds. Diamonds turn up in the streets and in the garden. The muddy pond that serves as the town's water supply is thought to be filled with them. Half the houses are perilously undermined by tunnels. People go around with one eye permanently cocked to the ground, and many always seem bent in what is known as the "Koidu crouch," as they lean forward to prod the dust for a chance diamond.

They know that dealers the world over prefer their stones above all others. "Sierra Leone's diamonds are the most attractive color around," explained George Kaplan of Lazare Kaplan, the New York manufacturers, who goes there regularly to buy, "although the rough is deceptive because the surface is greenish and opaque, that is only skin-deep."

Dealers who specialize in larger goods seek them out diligently. "Sierra Leone produces a rougher rough," admitted New York dealer William Goldberg, "but the odds are in your favor that at the moment of truth, as you cut, the color gets better and better." Several of the world's handsomest diamonds have been unearthed in this tropical corner of West Africa, including the third largest ever found, a 968.9-carat monster the size of a hen's egg christened The Star of Sierra Leone, which eventually yielded seventeen polished stones.

The informal nature of proceedings means that no one is quite sure how many diamonds turn up in Sierra Leone each year. Official production is around 200,000 carats of gem quality and 270,000 carats of industrial, but the true gem output from these scattered alluvial deposits may be twice as much.

Illicit diamond mining has not always been so prevalent. When Dr. Junner, the director of the Sierra Leone Geological Service in what was then a British colony, first found diamonds at Yengema, just north of Koidu in 1930, no one locally paid much attention. The original sources of the diamonds were two small kimberlite pipes, which, 1,000 million years ago, may have stood 1,500 feet above the plain. Over time they weathered, and the diamonds were gradually dispersed into the surrounding rivers and swamps. Smaller stones were washed first down the

Bafi River, then into the Sewa, which carried some right down to the sea. The richest deposits were scattered for thousands of square miles around Yengema and near the source of another eroded diamond pipe at Tongo, fifty miles to the southwest. For almost twenty years, however, the local Africans had no notion they were living on a fortune cast at random in the wilds. And initially a British mining company, Sierra Leone Selection Trust, set about alluvial mining undisturbed. "It was not until our brothers, who had been traveling in the war, came back and told us they were worth much money that we started looking," recalled an African dealer in Koidu.

Suddenly Sierra Leone Selection Trust found the vast terrain, which was supposed to be their exclusive prospecting area, invaded by hundreds of tribesmen with buckets and spades. Among the most energetic were a tribe called the Maraccas, who are by tradition well diggers. They set about digging narrow pits down through the topsoil until, fifteen or twenty feet down, they hit the layer of gravel in which the diamonds reposed. Then they worked underground, like moles, tunneling from pit to pit, gradually extracting all the gravel. Less expert excavators simply dug vast terraced holes. Other prospectors embarked on rivers and streams in flotillas of dugout canoes from which they dived to the bottom, where, breathing through rubber tubes, they scooped up gravel in sacks which were hoisted to the surface and dumped into canoes.

Selection Trust sought vainly to contain the invasion, but it was a hopeless task. Their own security force was unarmed, lacked police powers and anyway could do little to cover effectively the four thousand square miles of bush country designated as exclusive SLST territory. Not only was no illicit digging supposed to take place in this Diamond Protected Area, but dealing was also forbidden. However, that did not stop Koidu, in the heart of the protected area, from becoming the home of the dealers. As a British mining executive explained with weary resignation, "Anything can be fixed with a little 'dash' [bribe]; this is the land of the waving palms."

The proliferation of illicit diamond digging on SLST's domain during the 1950s, together with the opening up of other alluvial fields in the surrounding countryside where all comers could prospect—provided they sold to licensed dealers—naturally attracted a host of buyers. They flocked to Sierra Leone itself and to its freewheeling neighbor Liberia, whose capital Monrovia was no more than a day's journey by dirt road over the border from Koidu. No one was more intrigued than the Lebanese, who, as great traders out of Beirut, already did business in exchange and commodities with West Africa. One of the first buyers on the scene was an Armenian exchange dealer, then living in Beirut, who has since become one of the foremost dealers in rough diamonds in Antwerp. Sitting at ease by his Antwerp swimming pool one autumn evening, he reminisced how it began. "I was sitting in the Café de la Paix in Paris one day in November 1951," he recalled, "and I overheard this very interesting conversation in Arabic at the next table about diamonds coming from Sierra Leone. So I told my brother, 'We must get some.' We gave fifteen thousand pounds to a fellow in Sierra Leone to buy them for us, but he played poker and lost the money in one night." Not deterred, the brothers persevered. They had a man in Ghana, another good source of alluvial diamonds, and he journeyed to Sierra Leone, where he found he could buy matchboxes full of stones at astonishingly low prices. The going rate was sometimes as little as one Sierra Leone pound per matchbox. As the business got more organized, the brothers decided to open a buying office across the border in Monrovia to purchase any stones that "drifted" that way and also to acquire the small diamond production of Liberia itself. They set up shop in Monrovia in 1955 and have maintained a buyer there ever since. "We were the first," said the Armenian dealer proudly, "but nine or ten others soon came along."

Among them was the De Beers Diamond Corporation. De Beers owned a share of the mining company, Selection Trust, through another wing of their empire, Charter Consolidated, so they were initially outraged at the rape of the licensed diamond concession. They were annoyed, too, that the illicitly mined diamonds were reaching the Antwerp market via Monrovia and Beirut, thus escaping the net of their Diamond Trading Company. Those were the days in the 1950s when Sir Percy Sillitoe, the former head of British intelligence, was running De Beers security, and he operated much as if he was still running the official secret service. The Armenians' dealers suddenly found they were being watched. "Sillitoe's detectives came to Beirut and tailed us," one recalled. Not that it did much good. The Armenians, like all good operators in the Middle East, had their own lines of intelligence, which swiftly tipped them off to De Beers surveillance. Eventually De Beers realized it was a mining house, not an international police force, and settled for trying to outbid rival dealers for any diamonds on offer in Sierra Leone or Monrovia. Over the years an amicable truce has evolved; each dealer keeps a watchful eye on what the other is up to. The Diamond Corporation of West Africa, a De Beers affiliate, has an office in Kenema, eighty miles up the road from Koidu, and also has a regular buyer stationed in Monrovia.

Yet De Beers has never shaken the grip of the Lebanese, who moved not only to Monrovia, but to Koidu itself. Today, legally speaking, Koidu is inside the protected area for exclusive mining by the Sierra Leone National Diamond Mining Company (NDMC), which took a 51 percent holding in Sierra Leone Selection Trust in 1969, after the country's independence. Yet not only is Koidu a living diamond mine for thousands of illicit miners, but the home of a hundred or more Lebanese dealers who buy from them. Although the Diamond Corporation of West Africa's buying office is nearby at Kenema, few think it necessary to journey that far when scores of eager buyers are just down the street. The Diamond Corporation does get stones, but often those of poorer quality. The Lebanese skillfully try to corner the finest gems. Not only will they provide prospective illicit diggers with a grubstake of a bag of rice and some shovels, but they have the best intelligence on where the diggers should go. If the National Diamond Mining Company locates a profitable new area, the Lebanese hear at once, and their diggers flood in by moonlight. Often they anticipate where the mining company will go next. Inevitably they are the ones who get rich. "We Africans usually try to sell quickly and often don't get a good price," admitted an African entrepreneur, who has been trying his hand at digging and small-time dealing for thirty years in the face of Lebanese competition. "The Lebanese have telephones, and if you don't agree to a price fast, they threaten to tell the police, so miners only get one hundred and fifty to two hundred Sierra Leone pounds, or three hundred pounds [$290] if they are very lucky. I did get eight thousand pounds [$7,500] myself for a stone last month, but that was six and three fourths carats."

The real wheeling and dealing starts among the Lebanese dealers themselves, as the stones are traded from hand to hand until they reach the three or four big dealers who have official export licenses and really control the game. Not that there is any guarantee that stones will leave through official channels. There is a 2.5 percent export duty, which is frequently avoided. "The first dealer may get double what he paid for the stone, but the main ones get much much more," said the African. He added hastily, "You won't mention my name, will you? Everything in Koidu is illicit; we have no right to do any trading, but this is where the dealers are."

Koidu is a magnet, not only for diamonds filched locally, but for stones spirited over the border from neighboring Guinea, where the alluvial mining area at Masanta is just a day's journey away. "Plenty of good-quality cape coloreds [yellowish diamonds] are coming," confided a dealer. "The crossing is easy—there's only a small stream at the border."

Although Koidu is the quickest place for anyone from Guinea or Sierra Leone to dispose of diamonds, the journey over the Liberian border to Monrovia is no hazard, except in the rainy season when the roads soon flood. "You just get in your car and drive through," said the dealer. "It takes about eight hours." The attraction of Monrovia is that diamonds are paid for in dollars, while in Koidu they are traded for Sierra Leone pounds. So anyone eager to build a dollar account outside the fence of Sierra Leone's exchange controls makes the trip over the border.

Four or five buyers are usually in residence in Monrovia, a hot, listless town on the coast. Besides the Armenian firm, which has been there since 1955, and the ubiquitous Diamond Corporation, a couple of New York dealers are regulars, and others often nose around for a few months, putting up at the Ducor Inter Continental Hotel. Harry Winston, the legendary New York dealer, stationed a buyer there for a while in 1978 just before his death, much to the chagrin of the old-timers. "Harry," sighed one, "why do you do it? It's only worth a million dollars a month." On the contrary, the young Englishman Winston sent in soon found that it was more like $8 million a month, of which, it is true, $1 million were genuine Liberian diamonds but to which one had to add the smuggled goods from Sierra Leone, Guinea and even some that "drifted" up from Ghana and Angola. Securing a foothold in a smuggler's paradise was not easy. The newcomer found he had to offer over the odds for a couple of weeks to lure the traders to his hotel. Then the bargaining was tough. Usually the parcels of rough were entrusted for sale to Senegalese couriers (who also specialize in taking them direct from Sierra Leone and other African producers direct to Antwerp). They were never in any hurry.

"They come in with a parcel which is worth sixty thousand dollars maximum to you," said Winston's man, recalling too many long, hot nights. "So you offer them forty-five thousand. They say, 'Boss, you don't appreciate it,' and walk out, leaving you looking at the diamonds. They come back three or four hours later and sit around. Eventually they suggest eighty thousand and come down to sixty-eight thousand, which means their bottom price is sixty-five thousand. Meanwhile you are up to fifty-nine thousand, so they know your top is sixty thousand. Then they fall asleep in the chair, and you wake them up to give them sixty-two thousand. So they get an extra two thousand by falling asleep. What European can compete with that?"

Europeans may not; the Lebanese can. Accordingly, they have outlasted everyone else on the West African circuit for a generation. On the other hand, they have also taught the Africans the value of diamonds. "I remember going to Africa in the late fifties," said Nick Axelrod, Harry Winston's chief buyer of rough diamonds in New York, "and you could buy a milk bottle full of diamonds, and they didn't know the value. Today if it's a single ten pointer [0.10 carat], they know the value."

Axelrod, a genial man, usually crisply turned out in an immaculate pin-striped suit and given to smoking Monte Cristo cigars in a holder, is the third generation of his family in diamonds. On his very first buying trip for his father, long before he joined Winston, he came up against Lebanese dealers in Africa and admits he suffered some bitter lessons as he learned to bargain. Patience was naturally the first virtue; then, as in poker, not the slightest hint of one's hand. "The less time I look at the merchandise the better," Axelrod said. "I look at the parcel and get a price in mind. I always try below that price, but never go higher. Now the question is, do you really need the merchandise or not? If you foolishly divulge you need it, you'll pay a higher price, but if you can persuade the dealer you are just looking, then you may be able to take a stand." Although that is no guarantee that you will win. "I remember once in Africa, trying to buy a diamond from a Lebanese," Axelrod went on. "He offered it to me at a thousand dollars a carat, and we talked round that for four hours. So finally we decided to go for dinner, and at the end he makes a toast. 'Nick,' he says, 'I've known you for five years, and I'll make you a special price and give it to you for a thousand dollars a carat.'"

The steady seepage for a generation of illicitly mined diamonds from Sierra Leone, coupled with the constant ruining of prospective mining areas by unauthorized diggers who get there first and cream off the best stones, has had serious effects on the country's economy. Diamonds should be Sierra Leone's foremost export earner, yet official production by the National Diamond Mining Company fell from 900,000 carats in 1971 to a mere 200,000 carats a decade later. Declared output from the other alluvial areas, where anyone may prospect, is also static. In an effort to attract more diamonds into regular channels, the export duty was cut from 7.5 percent to 2.5 percent in 1977, and more price competition was encouraged by inviting additional foreign buyers, thus ending the Diamond Corporation of West Africa's monopoly. NDMC's production, sold annually at three "sights," is now shared between the Diamond Corporation of West Africa (De Beers), which gets half, two New York dealers, a Swiss buyer and a local entrepreneur, Jamal Mohamed Said. Jamal Said, a Lebanese who wields exceptional influence in the business life of Sierra Leone, is also one of a handful of licensed exporters (along with the Diamond Corporation) who may buy up the output of the other alluvial deposits. The word in Sierra Leone is that most big stones find their way to Jamal Said, who disposes of them on the Antwerp market.

The decline in diamond yield may eventually be halted by improved mining techniques, both by NDMC and the mass of alluvial diggers. The rise in diamond prices since 1977 has made it worthwhile for the mining company to embark on a major development program of underground mining into the two diamond pipes at Yengema. For fifty years they have simply foraged the surrounding terrain for the diamonds that were scattered on the surface near the top of the eroded pipes. By the mid-1980s they will be delving deep into the pipes themselves. "Going underground at the source could be the saving grace for us," said a mining executive hopefully. "Illicit mining has taken fifteen years off the life of our operations here. This is the last chance."

Meanwhile, the free-lance alluvial digger is becoming more mechanized, too. The energy of one hundred thousand people burrowing for almost thirty years has cleaned out most of the readily accessible diamond gravel. Buckets and spades no longer suffice. "I'm just off to buy myself a second-hand Caterpillar bulldozer," said the African dealer in Koidu. "I'm going to work an area that NDMC has just given up. You never know what you may find. A fellow near Bo found nearly two million pounds' worth with a dredge on the river—he just pumped them up. You can still make a lot of money if you hit the jackpot."

7

Zaire to Australia

Zaire: Comic-Opera Minnow

In the league table of diamond producers, Zaire has stood out for a generation as number one. The alluvial diggings scattered through the thick rain forests of Shona province yield between twelve and fifteen million carats annually, which is seven times that of the diamond desert of Namibia, almost twice as much as South Africa and comfortably ahead even of the Soviet Union. Yet no one in the diamond trade pays much attention to the former Belgian Congo. A mining man even dismissed it contemptuously as "a minnow." "What's it worth," he wondered. "In money terms, perhaps a hundred million? That's less than two and a half percent of our intake." A trifle unjust, perhaps, to the world's largest producer, but a clear indication that the goods coming out are low grade. Zaire's weak card is that virtually all of her production is the gray industrial *boart*. With the going rate for *boart* around two to three dollars a carat, Zaire's output is no bonanza. What saves the day and makes the whole thing viable is a handful of good-looking gems which bring a handsome return. At the Miba mining area near Bak-wanga in the east of Shona province, which is the best pro-ducing region, just a scattering of gems, perhaps 3–4 percent of output, earns more than three-quarters of all the revenue.

The fortunes of Zaire have also been revived in recent years by a spirited demand for very small diamonds, near-gems, which have become the specialty of Indian diamond cutters. A gen-eration ago they were consigned to industry, but the rising prices of the late 1970s suddenly made them attractive propositions for jewelry. Indian dealers snapped up parcels of Zaire rough in the hope of finding a few "swimmers," good stones that could be cut and sold at a nice markup. The trick is to pay two or three dollars a carat for a parcel and hope to find among them three or four that will fetch a hundred or two hundred dollars each, once they are cut and polished. Such gambles fueled a real market in Zaire goods from 1976–1978. A leading Antwerp dealer, through whose hands many of the parcels went, told me that he believed De Beers Central Selling Organization was un-derestimating the quantity and value of gems filtering out of Zaire.

No one can be sure, for Zaire is also the league leader in illicit diamond mining. While official production is recorded as under nine million carats, another four to six million carats are being mined illegally and smuggled out of the country to eager buyers waiting just over the border in Burundi, or across the river Congo in Brazzaville, the capital of the Republic of Congo. In-deed, the Republic of Congo, without a single carat of local diamond production, has emerged as one of the foremost dia-mond exporters in recent years. "My guess—and it is only a guess —is that you can add up to sixty percent on the official pro-duction of Zaire to account for illicit goods," said a regular buyer.

Such chaos has increased as the economy of Zaire has spiraled downward since independence in 1960. As the infrastructure of the country has slowly collapsed, so has serious prevention of illicit mining. Moreover, with inflation at 100 percent and the International Monetary Fund insisting on massive devaluations, politicians, businessmen and the military all seize any oppor-tunity to salt away some money abroad. Smuggling out diamonds and depositing the proceeds in a discreet bank account is an ideal way.

Illicit mining has always been a hazard even in the days of Belgian rule, simply because the alluvial diamond deposits that spilled out long ago from over a score of kimberlite pipes are spread through 150,000 square miles of river and forest, which cannot be effectively policed. But it was never a serious problem before independence, simply because so much was industrial and not worth the effort (unlike Sierra Leone and Angola, where gem diamonds predominate). The first diamonds were found as far back as 1907 in alluvial gravels near Tshikapa, four hundred miles east of Kinshasa (formerly Leopoldville), and commercial production started six years later. The major discovery, however, was in 1918 at Bakwanga Hill (now known as Mbujimayi), another two hundred miles to the east, where two kimberlite pipes, Miba and Talala, proved to hold the world's biggest industrial deposits.[12] The mines were developed by the *Societé Minière de Bakwanga*, an offshoot of the Belgian Sibeka group. But De Beers were not left out in the cold; they eventually took a 20 percent share of Sibeka, and, from the early days, the De Beers Diamond Corporation lined up contracts to insure that all output was funneled through the Central Selling Organization (CSO). Besides the more formal mining in Bakwanga, diggers were also licensed to roam through nearly forty alluvial deposits located around Tshikapa and Luluabourg.

The civil war that followed Congo's independence in 1960 brought an abrupt end to such orderly arrangements. The diggings became a free-for-all. Anyone not immediately involved in the fighting—and plenty of the troops who were—collected bucket and spade and went diamond hunting. The loot turned up in Burundi and Brazzaville, where Lebanese traders, Antwerp dealers and eager buyers from the De Beers Diamond Corporation zeroed in like bees buzzing to fresh blossoms.

Throughout most of the 1960s Zaire, as it had become, was an illicit miners' paradise. Then President Mobutu, attempting to restore some order and earn badly needed foreign exchange, sought to bring the mining back under control. His government

[12] A. A. Linari-Linholm, *Occurrence, Mining and Recovery of Diamonds* (Johannesburg, 1970), p. 4.

initially nationalized *Societé Minière de Bakwanga* completely, although Sibeka later won back a 20 percent holding. He also signed a "convention" with the CSO to take all the Bakwanga diamonds for marketing. In addition, he attempted to corral diamonds from the other alluvial areas by authorizing the CSO and a Belgian dealer, Jacques Graubart, to open buying offices up-country, close to the other alluvial areas. To show he meant business, he stationed troops at the diggings, with orders to shoot diamond poachers. All outsiders without legitimate business in the region were denied landing privileges at nearby airports in an attempt to thwart buyers, who often arrived by air with suitcases bulging with cash. No one took these efforts very seriously; soldiers posted to the diamond fields often traded their rifles for shovels and spades, and set to themselves.

The more formal mining activity of *Societé Minière* concentrated at the Miba pipe has done rather better, because the area is more contained. But the general collapse of Zaire's economy in recent years has brought desperate shortages of spare parts and fuel. Replacements are hard to come by, and the machinery is, as one miner put it, "rather elderly." The Miba area should be producing around 12 million carats a year; in 1980 it managed scarcely 9.5 million. Its sole salvation has been the soaring price of small diamonds and near-gems, which have made up for other deficiencies; instead of 80 percent of Miba's revenue coming from industrials, 80 percent is now from gems. And that has provided a new lease of life. Although the alluvial areas around the pipe, where 25,000 people are employed, are largely mined out and are uneconomic, prospects in the pipe itself are good. Regular open-cast mining of kimberlite, just as at South African or Botswana mines, is expected to start in 1983, and $120 million is even being invested in a new crushing plant to handle the rock. "We've got twenty years plus still to go," said a mine director happily. And once the mining is actually in the pipe, it is easier to keep out the illicit entrepreneurs. So Zaire is not going to lose its league leadership yet.

Not that anyone expects illicit mining to stop. Out in the jungle there are still plenty of diamonds for the ordinary diggers, and no buyers in Burundi or Brazzaville are packing their bags. As one of them put it, shrugging his shoulders, "We have to make the best of Zaire. It's a rather comic-opera situation."

Angola: Shades of Bogart

If Zaire strikes some as comic opera, there has been little to laugh about across the border in neighboring Angola in recent years. The bloody civil war there, aided and abetted by the Cubans and the Russians as the Portuguese withdrew from their old colony, brought looting and murder to the rich diamond deposits of Luanda province. The local Angolans got caught in the cross fire as Cuban soldiers, European mercenaries and departing Portuguese fought to get their hands on diamonds, while the Portuguese administration collapsed. For several months the mining areas were completely abandoned and left to a rabble of diggers, who not only panned what they could but raided the vaults in search of diamond stocks left behind. Angolan diamonds, which for years had been sold along the orderly channel of De Beers Central Selling Organization, suddenly appeared anywhere from Antwerp to Rio de Janeiro, from Monrovia to Tel Aviv. One leading Israeli dealer was reported to be bidding $1.5 million for a single parcel of stolen stones. But the real action was in Lisbon, whither nearly half a million Portuguese fled, often with diamonds as their only portable asset. The tales from Lisbon would do credit to a Humphrey Bogart movie. As Diana Smith of the London *Financial Times* wrote at the time, "Thousands of carats vanished either from the mines themselves or from vaults in Luanda. Many have turned up in Lisbon, offered to amazed potential purchasers in wine bottles or even straw-covered five-liter demijohns brimming with four-, five- or ten-carat uncut or first-cut stones. Those who have the cash can buy a bottle for thirty thousand or forty thousand pounds. Some of the dealing is done with the sort of trappings associated with films of the 1940s; fleets of black, six-seater Mercedes crammed with large men in raincoats with turned-up collars, homburgs and dark glasses (at three A.M.), parked outside Lisbon's bullring." [13]

"Angola is IDB gone totally mad," sighed a De Beers executive as he returned from the back streets of Lisbon, where the CSO, like a host of other buyers, was snapping up everything on offer.

[13] *Financial Times*, London, December 4, 1977, p. 3.

And he wistfully recalled the previous fifty years, when the mining of the alluvial diamond deposits scattered along five rivers in Luanda province of north-central Angola had been firmly in the hands of *Companhia de Diamantes de Angola* (Diamang), in which Sir Ernest Oppenheimer had thoughtfully secured a good interest for De Beers back in the 1920s. His concern was genuine, for Angola's diamond fields, unlike those of neighboring Zaire, are rich in gems; indeed, taking both gem and near-gem into account, over three-quarters of Angola's diamonds are cuttable. "They are super goods," he went on, "nice color, nice size—the average is zero point six of a carat—and nice shape, so that the yield is high when they are cut and polished." The quality guaranteed that Angola's output of just over two million carats a year brought a good return. They were the second largest export earner, after coffee, netting far more than Zaire, which produced seven times the weight. The diamond trade also looked to Angola as one of the best sources of gems, representing 13 percent of all gems in 1973, the last year before chaos set in.

The caliber of Angola's diamonds had often encouraged dealers to try to break De Beers' hold on their sale. Indeed, Harry Winston from New York actually succeeded in 1955 in persuading the Portuguese to grant him a ten-year contract for all Angola's diamonds, much to the chagrin of De Beers, who briefly cut him off from their own diamond sights. Eventually a complex compromise was agreed, which involved De Beers helping the Portuguese to establish their own cutting industry in Lisbon, while Winston himself won back his invitation to the CSO sights, including, apparently, a privileged selection of high-quality gems from CDM in South-West Africa (Namibia).

The diamonds, which were first located in 1917, were all concentrated within forty or fifty miles of some twenty kimberlite pipes from which they originally eroded. The heart of the diamond-mining region covers about 300 square miles along the Luashima, Luembe, Chicapa, Cuango and Cuanza Rivers. In the days of Portuguese rule the mining company, Diamang, ran Luanda province from its headquarters at Dundo like a state within a state, complete with a private army to deter illicit miners. Diamang had 26,000 employees working forty-two alluvial deposits at a time and one payable pipe known as Camutue. Since the richest harvest was in the riverbeds, the diggers "threw breakwaters" to divert the flow and mined out the dry bed. If the river was too wide to divert completely, they simply put a breakwater down the middle for a mile or two, scoured out the gravel from the dry half and then repeated the process on the opposite shore. Even in those days, of course, the opportunities for illicit activity were rife. "The Portuguese who ran the mine always seemed to take long after-lunch siestas," recalled a mining man. Plenty of diamonds went missing from the official diggings and were spirited back to buyers in South Africa or Antwerp. IDB increased rapidly during the last years of Portuguese rule, because the local freedom fighters found that diamonds were an excellent means of exchange for buying arms. The losses were modest, however, when set against the anarchy that prevailed after 1974.

The complete abandonment then of the mining area by Diamang meant that not only were the diggings open to all comers, but that the equipment quickly became derelict in the wet, tropical climate. Angola's output, even allowing for IDB, took a complete nose dive from about 2.2 million carats in 1973 to under 0.5 million carats two years later. Obviously the new ruling MPLA group of President Agostinho Neto could not allow the disappearance of a prime source of foreign exchange. The priority was to get the mining going again. In the autumn of 1977, therefore, President Neto announced that his government was taking a majority interest in Diamang to "secure the wealth which belongs to the Angolan people and determine the most convenient way to rationalize that wealth and exploit it fully." He had one simple way to stop the illicit mining; the first few offenders were shot, and others were given twenty years in prison. Discouraging IDB, however, was not much use without securing fresh expertise to run the diamond fields. The six hundred Portuguese staff had long since gone home, and, although De Beers still had a nominal shareholding in the nationalized Diamang, they could not be invited in directly as a matter of political face because Angola was effectively at war with South Africa. A discreet compromise was for Diamang to sign on thirty out-of-work Cornish tin miners from Britain, most of whom were recruited in London by a company calling itself Mining and Technical Services (MATS). MATS is actually a Liberian-registered company which provides technical services

and manpower for mines throughout the world; it also happens
to have among its directors several mining men from De Beers.[14]

This fresh influx of professional skills, coupled with a tough
line on any illicit intruders, succeeded in restoring Diamang's
fortunes with remarkable speed. Within a couple of years production was back over one million carats and in the early 1980s
will reach its former levels of around two million carats. Meanwhile the Angolans, like many new African governments, are
full of ideas to sort, value and eventually even cut and polish
their diamonds themselves. That kind of expertise, however, is
not acquired overnight, and for the moment their diamonds are
back in the customary pipeline of the CSO. "Angola has stabi-
lized," said an insider thankfully; "it's running very well."

The Little League

The luck of the geological draw that has caused kimberlite
pipes to proliferate throughout Africa south of the Sahara means
that almost all countries here have diamonds. Besides South
Africa, Namibia, Botswana, Lesotho, Sierra Leone, Zaire and
Angola, diamonds are also to be found in Ghana, the Central
African Republic, Tanzania, Liberia, Guinea and the Ivory
Coast. The pickings, however, are relatively slim, and what
usually attracts attention is some international scandal surrounding the disposal of the stones. Would most people be aware of
the Central African Republic as a diamond producer, for instance, if it had not been for allegations in the satirical French
weekly Le Canard Enchaîné about France's President Giscard
d'Estaing receiving gifts of diamonds from the tyrannical Emperor Bokassa? President Giscard tartly replied, "One must allow
base things to die in their own poison," but the accusation certainly caused plenty of interest in this remote republic's diamonds.

Actually, the Central African Republic has been the scene of
intense diamond hunts ever since two alluvial deposits were found
at Bria four hundred miles east of the capital Bangui in 1913,
and later at Berberati in the west of the country. French, American and Canadian mining groups have searched in vain for the

[14] The Sunday Times, London, December 16, 1979, p. 60.

pipes from which they originated. But the alluvial deposits themselves have produced up to 600,000 carats a year, 40 percent of them of good gem-quality melees. Since they provided 95 percent of the CAR's mineral exports, they naturally became a political football, and under the erratic role of Bokassa, no mining company or buyer could be sure where he stood from day to day. Bokassa nationalized the mines in 1969 into a new company, Central African Diamond Exploration Company (Centrediam), whose board of directors mainly comprised his favorite ministers.

The mining areas, however, were quickly engulfed by some 40,000 illicit diggers who had for years constantly picked over the fringes of the diggings. They disposed of their diamonds to the *Comptour National du Diamant de L'État* (the state diamond bureau), which sold them to American, Belgian, French and Israeli buyers. But securing licenses was often a matter of who was last in Bangui handing out a little *baksheesh* or who could keep in the brutal Bokassa's favor. Outsiders were often dispatched abruptly on the next plane. The Israelis constantly tried to lay hands on the melees—which suited their production ideally and enabled them to bypass De Beers—but it was a frustrating business. After Bokassa visited Moscow at a time when the Russians were wooing Egypt, the Israelis were cut off without a stone. Mining schemes to exploit new prospects also proliferated. An exclusive concession, for instance, was supposed to have been granted in 1978 to a consortium of Israeli, Iranian and Swiss investors who reputedly put up $11 million. All the diamonds were to be sold to the Israeli cutting industry, and the government, which really meant Bokassa, was guaranteed 30 percent of the profits. The consortium was never heard of again. But others keep coming, especially since Emperor-for-Life Bokassa has been overthrown in a belated coup masterminded by the French. His flight into exile was the moment for many dealers to board the next plane to Bangui to see what new deals could be done. "The goods are worth about forty million dollars a year," said an Antwerp dealer. "Bangui is no paradise, but I can't ignore that."

The scramble in Ghana is a trifle more dignified, for although this West African nation is the largest diamond producer to chart an independent course from De Beers' ubiquitous Central

Selling Organization, 90 percent of its 2.2 million carats is industrial. Originally the mining there, which started in the 1920s in the Birim valley north of Accra, was run by Selection Trust, the London-based mining house that also operates the mines in Sierra Leone. However, after Ghana pioneered the way to self-rule in 1957, the new government gradually took diamonds under its own wing. From the outset, Ghana's first president, Kwame Nkrumah, refused to sell diamonds through the CSO and set up his own Diamond Marketing Corporation, which sorts and values the diamonds before putting them out to tender to licensed international buyers. Eventually, in 1973, Ghana also took a 55 percent slice of Selection Trust's holding of the Akwatia mine, which produces most of the diamonds, and christened it Ghana Consolidated Diamonds. The divorce from the CSO has won the government plenty of suitors during the last twenty years among buyers who find it difficult to get all they need from De Beers or simply do not wish to do business with a cartel. Both Israel and India, in the early days of getting established as cutting centers, dispatched regular missions to secure Ghana's diamonds. The best customer recently is reported to be China, which has found Ghana a useful source of the industrial diamonds that she requires for oil-well drilling and to modernize her industry.

Across in east Africa, however, Tanzania has always stayed faithful to the CSO for the marketing of diamonds from the great Mwadui (or Williamson) pipe. The Mwadui is not only the world's largest pipe, covering over five square miles of bush country south of Lake Victoria, but also has the most personal history of any mine. Its discovery came after a five-year search, almost a crusade, by an eccentric Canadian geologist John T. Williamson, who crisscrossed Tanganyika in a lorry with all the diligence that Richard Burton and John Hanning Speke had shown in the same terrain during their hunt for the source of the Nile. Williamson knew that a handful of rough alluvial diamonds and some barren kimberlite pipes had been found near Lake Victoria, but he became convinced that the real source of diamonds had been missed.

During a stop for lunch one day in March 1940 near a village called Mwadui, he almost literally stumbled over a diamond in the dust beneath a little hill. At first he thought the hill must be the top of the pipe and spent days dissecting it with prospecting trenches before turning his attention to the plain below, where he found a rectangular pipe more than a mile wide each way. The diamonds within proved to be fine gems, many slightly tinged with pink. The nicest ever found was fifty-four carats in the rough, which was cut into a rose-colored brilliant of 23.60 carats and given by Williamson to the present Queen Elizabeth on her wedding day in 1947.

For seventeen years Williamson treated his mine very much as his own kingdom, hardly ever leaving and feuding with buyers who came for his stones. Naturally De Beers were among the first at Mwadui to persuade him to sign up with the Diamond Corporation, so that the gems could go through the CSO. Initially Williamson agreed to a contract but then had second thoughts, and for years he simply stockpiled his diamonds, refusing to deliver them to the Diamond Corporation. Meanwhile he flirted with many other buyers, including Harry Winston from New York, who was quite convinced at one stage that he was going to get them exclusively. Williamson was also the despair of his security staff, paying little heed to thefts from the mine. Eventually young Harry Oppenheimer managed to win him over and persuaded him to deliver the goods. Then, as soon as Williamson died in 1957, Harry Oppenheimer was back at Mwadui again, sitting up all night to draft a contract to buy the mine from the heirs. Realizing that the wind of change was starting to blow as many African nations moved toward independence, Oppenheimer suggested a fifty-fifty deal with the government, which was at once accepted. After independence the mine was fully nationalized, but De Beers has always remained discreetly in the background with management advice. And although the diamonds from Mwadui are sorted and valued by the government's own officials, they all end up with the CSO in London. Tanzania thus provides one of the best examples of how De Beers still treads in many unlikely areas of Africa. Other buyers, including regular deputations from Indian diamond cutters in Bombay, have tried to persuade President Julius Nyerere to sell elsewhere, but he has resisted.

The regularity of the check from the CSO in good times and bad carries more clout in Tanzania's otherwise impoverished economy. The only disappointment is the Mwadui pipe itself.

As the miners have delved deeper into its throat, the grade of diamonds has slowly diminished. At its peak, over 500,000 carats a year were being mined, but this has fallen back to little over 200,000. The world's largest mine, sadly, is by no means the richest.

The diamond discoveries all through Africa for the last century have forced Brazil, previously the leading producer, to take a back seat. Nowadays Brazil has no bonanza, but diamonds still turn up with remarkable consistency along the rivers around Diamentina in Minas Gereis province, where they were first found around 1725, and in alluvial deposits throughout Mato Grosso and Bahia provinces. The real questions that remain are the location of the pipes from which the diamonds originally came and what will be found as the vast Amazonas region is gradually opened up during the rest of this century. Already, all kinds of intriguing mining possibilities are being discovered as the jungles are cleared; the production of gold, for instance, more than doubled in Brazil between 1978 and 1980 as thousands of independent diggers, *garimpeiros*, were lured into Amazonas by the high gold price. Just such a gold rush led to the original diamond finds in the eighteenth century. The mining houses are busy, too. Sibeka, the Belgian group in which De Beers has a 20 percent interest, is already involved with *Mineracao Tejucana*, the major Brazilian producer, whose output is around 60,000 carats a year. Anglo-American, the Oppenheimers' major finance house for gold mining, is well established as the new owner of Brazil's largest gold mine, Mineracao Morro Velho, and is prospecting throughout Brazil. In Rio de Janeiro, you get just a touch of diamond fever, as if some new breakthrough might happen any day. Indeed, I found one diamond dealer who was quite convinced that Anglo, acting for De Beers, had already found a diamond pipe but was keeping quiet until they needed the diamonds.

Rumor aside, the higher prices of gem diamonds have also spurred diamond digging by the *garimpeiros*, as well as by local mining groups in the last few years. No one is sure exactly how much is being produced, but it is certainly 350,000–400,000 carats a year, and perhaps a trifle more. Actual statistics are unreliable because most of the diamonds from the *garimpeiros* are sold quietly on the black market, often to Antwerp dealers who find that an occasional foray to Brazil pays dividends. Since official exports have to go through bureaucratic channels, and each parcel must be worth $20,000, people usually find it easier to send the goods by "submarine" to Europe. The $20,000 minimum is designed to protect the local diamond cutting and polishing industry, which employs about eight hundred craftsmen and jealously tries to guard all Brazilian production for itself. Since the local jewelry market needs, according to one dealer, at least a million carats a year, they feel it is foolish for a single diamond to go abroad. The cutters have a hard time preventing the diamonds from escaping. Outside buyers, often from New York, tend to snap up the choicest parcels from "sights" that *Mineracao Tejucana* holds in Belo Horizonte once a month, while Antwerp dealers seek out the cream of the gems. Their appetites were whetted a few years ago after one operator with a small mining operation stockpiled all the best diamonds in his safe and then took them all to Antwerp one day. He had difficulty actually selling them because he asked too high a price, but thereafter Antwerp buyers have forever been turning up in Rio and Belo Horizonte asking, "Where are all those beautiful stones?" I could well believe the tale, for a few months earlier I had lunched with an Antwerp dealer who was Belo Horizonte-bound on a diamond fishing expedition.

Such eagerness is rarely displayed for the diamonds of Venezuela, the other main source in South America. The actual output is substantial—over 800,000 carats a year—but more than 70 percent is of industrial quality, and even the gems are inclined to be small, with many black flaws. Indeed, a dealer I talked with in Caracas was remarkably scathing about the homegrown goods. "The only people who are keen on them are local cutters," he said. "If you came to Antwerp with a large parcel of Venezuelan goods you might have difficulty unloading it. The diamonds are coated, and you never know what you will end up with when you cut." Yet a question mark must hang over Venezuela, just as it does Brazil. The diamonds are found mainly in alluvial deposits along the Caroni River, a tributary of the Orinoco. The terrain is almost impassable, and the streams are exploited by *garimpeiros* with picks and shovels. The kind of step-by-step exploration that has been undertaken in Africa is not yet feasible. But the *garimpeiros*, encouraged by the gold price, are doubling their activities. Either they, or a mining company, may one day find not just gold but the fountain of those alluvial stones. Too much in South America is still uncharted.

Australia: Kimberley Two

An American journalist once sent a famous cable to his boss in New York when he did not receive an expected promotion, lamenting, "Why did you keep me on tiptoe so long if you weren't going to kiss me?"

Australia has maintained a similar teasing game in diamonds ever since 1851 when a few alluvial stones were found. At long last there are omens that consummation will take place in the 1980s. The first real whiff of success came in the spring of 1978 when Conzinc Rio Tinto of Australia (CRA) announced, in the cautious understatement that mining companies love, that a subsidiary, Ashton Mining, had located a "diamond-bearing province in the Kimberley region of Western Australia." And a CRA executive even allowed, "Prospectors are picking up diamonds off the ground." Everyone reached for their maps and pinpointed the Kimberley Plateau near the northwest coast, midway between Joseph Bonaparte Gulf and Dampier Land; like South Africa's diamond city, it had been named after the nineteenth-century British colonial secretary. It is a remote region, peopled by a handful of aborigines. At least it was until CRA came out with the news. Twenty mining companies, including De Beers and Selection Trust, hastened to hire helicopters and get out in the field. Within a few months 4,500 claims had been pegged over an area of 1,900 square miles, much to the annoyance of the Combulgurri, the aborigines in residence, who found men from De Beers' Stockdale Prospecting literally swooping out of the skies to scoop up soil samples. The Aboriginal Lands Trust, which is responsible for their welfare, momentarily got a halt called to the scramble. The aborigines then agreed to give CRA exclusive rights to their lands and prudently hired an American mineral-rights negotiator to advise them.

Once the dust had a chance to settle a little, it was clear that CRA, at least, had plenty to be pleased with. Their initial finds were a whole cluster of kimberlite pipes at Ellendale, just to the east of the township of Kimberley Downs. The first five diamond pipes sampled all held some diamonds, and the prospects of two of them improved as time went by. One of the Ellendale pipes actually contained 60 percent cuttable gems, 37 percent near-gem and only 3 percent industrial; the catch was that even the gems were tiny, with a price at the mine of under a hundred dollars a carat. Was it viable? CRA's chairman Sir Roderick Carnegie cooled everyone off a little by saying, "We have found a few stones, but . . . this is a long process, and we have to sample thousands of tons of material to arrive at a statistically significant result."

What he neglected to mention was that CRA also had another prospect up its sleeve a couple of hundred miles further east on the other side of the Kimberley Plateau. This new pipe, on the Ord River system south of the town of Kununurra, was christened Argyle. Early samples from alluvial gravels in the river near the Argyle pipe showed some astonishingly high diamond content of over sixty carats in 1.5 tons. Although that was misleading, further fieldwork showed that there were indeed plenty of small diamonds to be had. And CRA, who lacked their own in-house diamond expertise, decided early in 1980 that it was time to call in De Beers for consultations on the technical feasibility of developing mines, both at Ellendale and Argyle. Such decisions are not taken quickly; no one disputes that the diamonds are there, but can they be mined commercially? The consensus is that they can. "Argyle is the key," confided a De Beers executive. "The whole thing is very exciting. Of course, it's early days, but, you see, there will be production by the end of 1981."

PART
III

THE SALESMEN

1

The Central Selling Organization

First, Peel Your Onion

The best-known address in the diamond business is the Diamond Trading Company, Seventeen Charterhouse Street, London, E.C.1. For a generation they resided at Number Two, which was nicknamed the "glass house" because of the vast acreage of window; then in 1979 they moved across the road to more palatial quarters at Number Seventeen. The new headquarters looks more like a medieval fortress, with narrow slit windows in a marble facade. Once every five weeks three hundred or so of the world's foremost diamond dealers and manufacturers pass through the imposing entrance doors with diamond-shaped glass panels to spend close to $300 million on rough gem diamonds. Although each has to accept or reject the box of goods that is waiting for him without any real negotiation on price or content, everyone turns up for this "convocation," as one of them called it, with religious regularity. For the Diamond Trading Company (DTC), the main arm of the De Beers Central Selling Organization (CSO)—"the syndicate," to many diamond traders—rigorously controls the marketing of at least 80 percent of the world's rough diamonds.

"You can't be big in diamonds without playing ball with the syndicate," said one of Israel's foremost dealers. And despite complaints about the DTC's treatment of a client from time to time, most approach it with something close to awe. "The miracle is that with an infinite variety of diamonds—some worth fifteen thousand dollars a carat and some only three—the syndicate produces standard sets of boxes in standard amounts for buyers to take off the rack like toothpaste at the chemist's," remarked a London broker. "It's a production line worthy of Michelin tires."

Toothpaste or tires, of course, are rather cheaper. No one is invited to these ten "sights" yearly unless they can stump up at least $150,000, and the wealthiest half dozen buyers may fork out anything between $5 million and $20 million a time. The toothpaste analogy, however, helps to visualize the role not just of the Diamond Trading Company, but of the whole CSO. For it is the tube through which diamonds, both gem and industrial, from mines, not just in De Beers' own stable in South Africa, Botswana, Lesotho and Namibia, but from Angola, Russia, Sierra Leone, Tanzania and Zaire are squeezed before dispersing again to cutting and polishing centers on every continent. The tube is not always watertight, as we have seen in earlier chapters. Diamonds do leak elsewhere, but only a handful of small producers such as Brazil, the Central African Republic, Ghana, and Venezuela regularly resist the embrace of the Diamond Corporation, the De Beers buying arm for goods mined outside South Africa or Namibia.

The CSO is the sponge that absorbs diamonds in bad times and disgorges them in good. The structure of the diamond business that was originally built up by Sir Ernest Oppenheimer has survived for half a century because of the comfortable feeling of stability that it engenders in miner and manufacturer alike.* Moreover, the CSO has acquired matchless experience at tailoring the demand for diamonds by the public to suit the supply

* See Part I, 4: Building the Syndicate.

from the mines. The CSO spends upwards of $40 million an-
nually, not just to create an aura that "A diamond is forever,"
but to make sure that if the inventory is laden with a particular
size of diamonds, the customer is wooed to buy them. Such
management has established an impressive track record. The price
of rough diamonds has been moved up inexorably by the CSO's
twenty-eight price increases between September 1949 and the
beginning of 1980. A diamond sold for $1,000 in 1949 would be
priced at around $10,000 at a sight in 1980, a progression that
promises security to governments or mining houses adrift in the
volatile waves of gold, platinum, copper or tin prices. It even
gives the CSO magnetism irresistible to diamond producers such
as the Russians, who, for political reasons, would not wish to
give it the time of day.

But what exactly is the Central Selling Organization? And
where does it stand in the De Beers empire? The first fact to
absorb is that the CSO is merely a convenient umbrella name
for a whole clutch of companies concerned with the marketing
of diamonds. The three most significant under the CSO roof are
the Diamond Purchasing and Trading Company, which sorts
and values the output of South Africa and Namibia; the Diamond Trading Company, which ultimately sells all the gem and
near-gems; and De Beers Industrial Diamonds, which markets
the industrial goods. Corporate subtleties to generate profits or
lower taxes in one country rather than another abound. Indeed,
De Beers itself has no direct shareholding in the Diamond Trading Company, the great wholesaler of its diamonds, but controls
it instead through Anglo-American Investment Trust (Ana-
mint), a holding company that owns 26.4 percent of De Beers
Consolidated Mines. The endless interweaving of the De Beers
web frequently drives to despair analysts trying to estimate the
value of its share price, the size of its diamond stockpile or its
true financial reserves. "De Beers is like an onion," says a wag;
"you peel off one layer of skin, only to find another under-
neath."

In reality, this is financial and political windowdressing. The
decisions that actually shape the diamond business are all made
around the long table in the boardroom of De Beers Consolidated Mines at Kimberley. That is where the mining men and
the CSO's marketing men come together under the chairman-

ship of Harry Oppenheimer. Monty Charles, the courteous joint-managing director of the Diamond Trading Company, and Dr. Henry Dyer, who presides over the industrial diamond division, are both on the De Beers main board. Strategy to expand or cut back on diamond-mine production, to build up the diamond inventory in a recession or for the CSO to promote a particular size of diamonds will be decided there. "Can you sell the diamonds for us, Monty?" Harry Oppenheimer asked in the late 1970s when the mining side was considering a massive expansion program. Charles assured him that he could. So, for all the corporate smokescreen, the heart of the matter is that the CSO is the De Beers marketing arm, pursuing policies clearly coordinated with the mines.

No one tries to deny that it is a cartel. "We are very, very much a monopoly," said Monty Charles at the Diamond Trading Company, "but, I believe, a benevolent monopoly." The CSO certainly sees itself as the father figure leading the diamond trade, which it sometimes argues has not yet grown up, along a stable path. The view is always long-term. "Most *diamantaires* don't think beyond next month," Charles observed, "but I'm planning at least five years ahead all the time. We have to guide the industry, some of whom, if you'll excuse an old metaphor, can't see the wood for the trees."

The Diamond Trading Company is really the mainstay of the CSO, for it accounts for over 90 percent of CSO sales of close to $3 billion annually. De Beers Industrial Diamonds is equally firmly astride the industrial market, but the price for industrial goods is so low (on average $3 per carat, against up to $15,000 a carat for gems) that its earnings are a drop in the ocean. And when *diamantaires* around the world talk of "the syndicate," what they really mean is the DTC. This is the company with whom, if they are invited, they do business. And the clear boss of the syndicate is Monty Charles, whose standing in the diamond trade is unique. "What has Monty Charles told you?" was about the most frequent question I was asked as I traveled from Antwerp to Tel Aviv and from Bombay to New York. And if you inquire who were the three shining lights of the business in the last generation, the answer is usually Harry Winston, the prince of diamond salesmen, Joseph Goldfinger, the dealer who spurred Israel to become a great diamond-cutting and polishing center, and Monty Charles. "He is the backbone of the Diamond Trading Company," said a Bombay sightholder.

Talking to Charles, a quiet-spoken man in his early sixties, you begin to see why he and the Diamond Trading Company have such a reputation. Its strengths are twofold: unmatched experience in actually sorting and marketing diamonds; and unrivaled intelligence about what is going on in every corner of the diamond world. Monty Charles always keeps his office door open; he likes to see what is going on outside. "The secret of the DTC is communications," an Israeli dealer observed. "I remember buying some special goods on the sixth floor once, and then going down in the lift to the second floor to see my regular box. As I stepped out of the lift, the salesman who met me remarked on what beautiful goods I had just purchased. He already knew what I had agreed to upstairs a minute before."

The foundation, however, is diamond know-how. The DTC prides itself on the caliber of its sorters. Monty Charles recalls that when he went to work there in 1938, he spent four years sorting industrial *boart* before he was allowed to grade a real gem diamond. Progress is a trifle faster today, but the schooling is thorough.

Although some countries, like Botswana and Tanzania, prefer to undertake the initial sorting of their diamonds themselves, the real burden—eyestrain might be a better word—falls on the CSO in Kimberley and London.

3,000 Varieties

The highest building in Kimberley, Harry Oppenheimer House, is a modern twelve-story block on the edge of town, with walls of sheer concrete on three sides and dark-tinted glass that slopes inwards on the fourth. If you take the elevator up to any of the top seven floors, you step out into a long narrow room running the full width of the building. Ranged along the middle of this emporium are tables laden with neatly blue-tagged wooden boxes filled with rough diamonds. Apart from the occasional column, the wall opposite is all glass, giving a stunning view out over the head shafts of a couple of old diamond mines to the endless veldt beyond. The sky is dark blue, save for a few puffy white clouds. But the thirty-two young men and women, all immaculately turned out, who are seated at benches up against the windows all have their eyes down on little piles of diamonds spread out on white paper before them, dexterously picking through them with tweezers. "The glass slopes into the building on each floor," explained Jimmy Glover, who has been sorting there for thirty years, "so that we can place the tables close to the natural light." The light, incidentally, is from the south because we are below the equator; elsewhere, of course, diamonds are always sorted in a north light to avoid the sun's glare. Harry Oppenheimer House has been strategically placed so that direct sunlight only trickles in for a few minutes on two or three of the longest days of the year.

The diamonds from South Africa's mines and from Consolidated Diamond Mines (CDM) in Namibia all come here for initial sorting and valuation by the Diamond Purchasing and Trading Company, the South African arm of the CSO.* Every diamond is picked over by hand, although when they first arrive they are popped through a series of mechanical sieves to sort them into basic shapes, and then through another gadget like a coffee grinder that scrutinizes the stones for color and sifts out the black *boart* that is useful only for industrial purposes. Everything else, however, comes down to the sorting floor for a thorough going-over. "We do a certain size on each floor," said Jimmy Glover. "Here on the eighth they are going over the two-carat rough. They sort into seven grades of purity, and then into seven grades of color, judging them against sets of master stones. Lots of it is opinion, and we have long debates."

We went over to look at some of the rough. Glover scanned a box with a practiced eye. "These are from Kleinzee," he decided; "they are frosted, but nicely rounded. And these over here are from CDM; they have a different frosting, so they look shiny and bright. You can tell all the mines—Premier is the top end in quality and color; Finsch used to be khaki green, but the character has changed, and now they are whiter."

The degree of concentration in the room was remarkable. There was almost total silence, except when a sorter pushed back his chair and stepped softly over to collect a new batch or asked his section boss to verify his opinion of a stone. The

* De Beers Consolidated Mines has a direct 50 percent holding in this CSO company.

reason for the quiet was soon explained. Most of the sorters wore tiny earplugs linked to sockets on their workbenches. "That's four-channel radio," explained Glover, "and they can listen to what they like without disturbing anyone. Sometimes, if a soap opera is on in the afternoon, the girls sit there in total silence with tears pouring down their faces." The earplugs also make for occasional misunderstandings. A local bishop visiting Harry Oppenheimer House congratulated De Beers executives for their worthiness in providing so much employment for the deaf; no one had the heart to tell him the sorters were plugged into pop. Every sorter is crisply dressed. The men must wear either jacket and tie, or a white safari suit, with long white knee socks. All the women wear identical dresses. Most of the sorters are young; all are white. Usually they start as teenagers, often following their parents in the trade, because De Beers, for security as much as anything, likes to know the background of employees through whose hands riffle millions of dollars of diamonds a week. "It takes one to two years to get anywhere near a fair idea of sorting," said Hennie Kruger, a tall young man of twenty-eight who had worked his way up to section head in a decade. "There is a high degree of tension and concentration, and you get physically tired. The youngest staff are usually on the top floor, where we do the smallest sizes, because their eyes are better."

Once the diamonds have been sorted, they are taken down to the sixth floor for scrutiny by senior quality controllers. An agreed valuation for each shipment is then made with appraisers from the Diamond Producers Association (DPA) representing the mines, the South African government and the administration of Namibia.

With sorting and valuation complete, all the diamonds from CDM and most of those from South African mines are dispatched to the Diamond Trading Company in London. However, 10 percent of the South African diamonds are held back at Harry Oppenheimer House in Kimberley for sale directly to forty local manufacturers in South Africa, who enjoy the special advantage of getting their stones 10 percent below the price that will be charged in London.

The discount on Kimberley sights, originally instituted at the insistence of the South African government in the 1920s to encourage the local cutting industry, causes considerable resentment in the diamond trade elsewhere, especially since the South African government decided in 1978 that cutting can also be undertaken by colored workers (although not yet by blacks). Previously, cutting in South Africa was an exclusive preserve of whites. They handled only larger goods over one carat, so there was no real competition to such cutting centers as Antwerp, Tel Aviv or Bombay. After the belated approval of coloreds (against much objection from the white cutters' union), the local industry can expand to cut and polish all sizes.

The local Kimberley sights, however, are small; most diamonds from South Africa and Namibia, together with those of other African nations and Russia, go directly for sale to the Diamond Trading Company in London. "We get about fourteen shipments from different sources in every thirty-five-day cycle," explained Johnny Roux, an elegant fellow with a fine twirl of handlebar moustache, who started out as a DTC sorter back in 1948. "The diamonds just pour into London. It's often quite overwhelming, but they've all got to be sorted and checked."

The preliminary sorting, as at Kimberley, is done with metal sieves with mesh of different sizes. Then the painstaking sorting by hand begins. First, the diamonds are divided according to shapes. The perfect crystals—"stones"—go in one pile; the irregular, broken crystals in another called "cleavages"; broken pieces with parallel sides, like slips of glass, go into a third heap for "flats"; and finally triangular twinned crystals, known as "maccles," make up the fourth pile. "The maccles are the Siamese twins of diamonds," said Johnny Roux, putting us back to back. "The two gems are joined like this, and you'll see a fishbone effect with the grain going one way on the top and another on the bottom." He added, to display his credentials, "I should know. I sorted 'maccles' for twelve years."

Roux was just getting into his stride. "So we've got four shapes. Each goes to a separate department which sorts them into five grades of quality according to whether they are clean, have a few small spots near the edge or dark spots inside—the worst spots look like great lumps of coal. Each grade is then sorted again into seven colors before a north light, comparing the stones with color samples to get the perfect match. Now we've got thirty-five different categories for each shape. There's still some way to go. Next we sort out fourteen types by weight, from one carat to fourteen carats; that makes it four hundred ninety options for each shape. Multiply that by four shapes, and we have nineteen hundred sixty categories," he concluded, looking very pleased with his calculations. "And that's just a simple assortment. We're not even taking into account such things as coated stones or near-gems."

Ultimately the DTC segregates just over three thousand varieties, and has price books with an up-to-date rate for each one. Prices are all quoted in dollars. The DTC itself takes a modest 2 percent commission.

The diamonds are now ready for general layouts at which DTC executives, headed by Monty Charles, can get an overall feel for what they have to offer at the next sight. Under Charles's experienced eye, the DTC's salesmen try to match what has come in from the mines with orders from sightholders who indicate three weeks in advance their ideal requirements at the next sight. Since supply rarely matches demand, the DTC is always seeking to strike the closest balance. Not that any one sight is tailored to what has just come in; the strength of the DTC's hand is the inventory. This can be run down in a boom and increased in a recession. Since the DTC's prime concern is price stability, the trick is to judge just how much or how little the market can genuinely absorb at each sight. Moreover, since CSO contracts oblige it to buy all production, the DTC, as its sales outlet, often has to shift sizes or qualities of diamonds no one really wants. Naturally the DTC does its best to oblige its customers, but ultimately the sightholder must accept or reject the box he is offered. As a De Beers man once put it rather charmingly, "When you go into a sweetshop, you have to buy a whole box of chocolates, you can't just pick out those with the centers you prefer."

Setting Your Sights

The visit to the "sweetshop" at Charterhouse Street ten times a year is by invitation only. Securing a sight (becoming a sightholder) is the ultimate accolade in the diamond trade, and the waiting list is long. A sightholder is a true graduate, like someone awarded a "first" at Oxford or Cambridge. The examination is just about as tough.

The Diamond Trading Company is interested only in two types of customers: major dealers in rough diamonds who can supply small manufacturers not rating their own sights; and substantial manufacturers with their own cutting and polishing facilities. The DTC shies away from traders who like to get their hands on diamonds just to sell them to all comers at a profit. The three or four dealers they work with in each cutting center are carefully chosen to form a direct link on the road to the ultimate goal that De Beers envisages for every diamond—in a piece of jewelry. That target is clearly designated because of a feeling that diamonds in jewelry are a genuine long-term offtake from the market. The growing investment vogue for loose diamonds in recent years has disturbed De Beers, who fear they are a dangerous overhang that might one day be dumped back in the market's (and thus their) lap at short notice.*

The precise number of sightholders fluctuates slightly; usually there are just over three hundred, including eighty from Belgium, sixty-four from the United States, sixty-one from India and forty-five from Israel. A few of them have been around as long as the Diamond Trading Company itself. P. N. Ferstenberg in Antwerp cheerfully likes to recall that when he started out in the early 1930s the Diamond Trading Company was so hard-pressed to shift any of its inventory that it threw out the welcome mat to all comers. "Anybody could buy at the syndicate," he said, "and all the diamonds were set out on the table, and you could choose what you liked. Ah, that was another business." But most have had to win their invitations the hard way since the present system of ten sights annually was introduced in 1961. The Israeli and Indian sightholders are virtually all newcomers in the last twenty years.

The initial contact between the DTC and a prospective sightholder will often be through one of five "syndicate" brokers: Hennig, Abrahams Tooth Goldie, Bonas, Nagel and Morgan.† The brokers keep an eye on developing firms, sometimes culti-

* See Part III, 2: Investors.
† Hennig and Abrahams Tooth Goldie now work in partnership, though each retains its own clients.

vating a particular market themselves with a view eventually to introducing the main manufacturers as sightholders. Hennig played a leading role in the establishment of the cutting industry in Tel Aviv in the 1940s and now represents two-thirds of the Israeli sightholders. Similarly, Bonas paved the way in Bombay in the 1960s, getting to know Indian manufacturers before introducing them to the DTC.

The DTC itself does plenty of spadework. Their sales team visits potential customers every year. When they feel that a firm is ripe for approval, they pass the word to Monty Charles, who sets off like some examiner, with a colleague. "I usually know if it's on or off as soon as we walk in, just from the look and feel of the place," said Charles. "If it's on, we sit down and ask some questions." How long has he been in business? What is his turnover? What are his aims and growth plans? What capital is behind him? Size is not necessarily paramount. "It's not always the biggest that get in," said Charles. "We are looking at the whole picture of the diamond trade, and if we see there is not enough capacity in one specialty we look for a small firm to fill it." Youth is no barrier; an Antwerp manufacturer was accepted when he was only twenty-nine. The real aim is to find the go-ahead customer, with plans to build a new factory or open a couple of overseas sales offices if he gets his sight and help him to achieve that. "We should guide him and motivate him for the future of his business," added Monty Charles. The danger, as the DTC sees it, is that a sightholder can become lazy; a sight is such a guarantee of success that he sits back and takes it easy, going to sleep at night in the comforting knowledge that the diamonds in his safe will be worth as much, if not more, in the morning. To prevent that, the DTC will nudge him constantly to take new initiatives. Thus the DTC's seal of approval is a highly personal one, granted to an individual, rather than his company, and subject to constant scrutiny to keep his performance up to scratch. Although the diamond business is a family one, a son cannot automatically expect to retain sights as part of his inheritance. He must also prove himself worthy.

The sightholder's life is closely geared to the five-week cycle between each sight. Three weeks in advance he must advise the DTC, through his broker, of his exact requirements, although obviously they know what his basic needs are. Across the board,

New York sightholders take larger goods, Tel Aviv specializes in medium-sized goods (melees) and Bombay in small sizes. "Each manufacturer is a specialist," said Johnny Roux, running through the DTC's collation of the incoming telexes. "So we won't be sending every type of diamond to each manufacturer; we don't send him goods he can't work. If he wants five hundred thousand dollars of stones and cleavages, that's what he gets; no maccles or flats are included. And on the smaller sizes, we also separate those which can be polished direct—the makeables—and those which have to be sawn. So we take into account if you are a 'sawables' or a 'makeables' man."

Beyond that, however, there is no guarantee that the sightholder gets precisely what he wants. The DTC will make up his box with a complete spectrum of different qualities and colors, and even if the sightholder specifies only one shape, there are still 490 possible variations. The proportion he receives of each will depend very much on the state of the DTC's own inventory. "The way we do it," said Johnny Roux, "is to say, okay, he wants a million dollars of certain 'goods.' Now, what percentage is that to the total value of this particular diamond we have for sale? Let's say it is zero point two percent. So he gets that proportion of all different sizes, qualities and colors."

Major sightholders, such as the late Harry Winston, the late Joseph Goldfinger and Star Diamond, who have vied with each other for the role of number one over the last two decades, receive several boxes for delivery to different places.* Star Diamond—now rated head and shoulders above all others, both in gem and industrial diamonds—gets boxes for its London office and for affiliates in Tel Aviv, Bombay and New York, each reflecting the character of the company's business in that city. The big three's boxes have cost them $20 million a sight on occasion.

Each sightholder will be advised ahead of time the exact value of his box so that he can arrange the necessary financing with his bank. In the cutting centers, there are two or three banks specializing in loans for the diamond trade. (De Beers, incidentally, has a director on the board of the leading Antwerp and Tel Aviv banks.) The DTC insists upon payment for its rough-diamond boxes within seven days of each sight, but it will usually be three

* Winston died in 1978, Goldfinger in 1976.

or four months before the sightholder can sort, manufacture and sell his diamonds. The banks, therefore, are essential to tide him over.

Sights begin every fifth Monday and usually occupy about a week. Virtually all sightholders fly to London, and most put up at the Savoy. When they get to Charterhouse Street, the buyers go up to the second floor, accompanied by their syndicate broker, to collect their boxes. Each is ushered into a private viewing room facing north on the second floor. "The broker sees him nicely settled in," said Johnny Roux, "and he has complete privacy so he can set about looking at his diamonds. He will look at every stone, and it may take one or two days, depending on how many boxes he has. There's no rush, no hurry." Many of the sightholders work for an hour or two, then lock up the room and stroll down to the waiting room at the end of the corridor for a smoke or a chat with their fellow sightholders. Everyone knows everyone else, and a great deal of trading goes on right there.

As he works through the scores of little white paper parcels in his box, each carefully labeled with such descriptions as "collection black spotted," "blue dark spotted" or "white speculative spotted," the sightholder leaves to one side any stones on which he disputes the DTC's grading. That is really the purpose of the whole visit. The overall price and character of the assortment in his box are not debatable. But if he is unhappy about the grading of one or two stones, he calls in his broker for a second opinion, and then they may tackle the DTC's sales staff. The complaint is often about color; the DTC may have judged a stone as top color, and the client will disagree. But changing the syndicate's mind is not easy. "If there is grave doubt we will take the stone out," said Johnny Roux, "but our decision is final, and if we say no, then the customer must take it." Few sightholders recall winning such disputes, unless it is at once apparent that a genuine error has been made.

A little humor, though, can pay dividends. P. N. Ferstenberg in Antwerp, who has been buying from the syndicate longer than anyone, recalled an altercation when he complained about three stones. "The syndicate said they would not change them or take them out or reduce the invoice," he said with a twinkle in his eye, "So I told them, 'You're not like a pretty girl.'"

"What do you mean, we're not like a pretty girl?" asked the DTC salesman.

"Well, you can always ask a pretty girl to go out with you," replied Ferstenberg, "but you don't even like to be asked."

The salesman broke up, laughing. When the invoice came, it had been reduced.

Actually, the rule about accepting the entire box is not totally inflexible. In very difficult market conditions, such as the recession of 1980, the DTC will allow each sightholder to leave out three stones. They realize that the margin of profit at such times is so narrow that having to accept even a few he does not require can ruin a client. Such consideration, however, is the exception. "When the market is good, we are tough as hell," said Monty Charles.

The only occasion when the DTC is always open to genuine horse-trading is for large diamonds weighing over 14.8 carats, which are sold individually outside regular boxes. They will usually be offered to one or two chosen sightholders while they are in town. When Harry Winston was alive, he nearly always had first refusal. "I remember coming over for a sight a few years ago, and the syndicate showed me a beautiful stone—two hundred four carats in the rough—and said, 'It should belong to Mr. Winston,'" recalled Nick Axelrod, Winston's chief buyer of rough. "I looked at it and went back to the hotel and gave my opinion on the phone to Harry, and he said, 'I leave it to you.' I felt I should go ahead, and so the next day I bought it. The DTC had a bottom price, but otherwise it was negotiable." With the customary reticence of the diamond trade, Axelrod declined to say what they settled on.

Since Winston's death, no natural successor has yet emerged as the first thought when a great diamond turns up, although, of course, the organization under Ronald Winston, his son, remains one of the DTC's main clients. The best running is apparently being made by two other New York dealers, William Goldberg and Louis Glick, but the title is still open. Perhaps it will never be won. As a colleague observed, "There will never be another Harry Winston."

Once the sightholder accepts his box he still has to wait for delivery. Payment must be made first within seven days, and the goods are then dispatched, either by airmail or courier, in tough cardboard boxes bearing the DTC's seal. The prestige of having a DTC box was such that for years sightholders were often able, if they so wished, to resell the box at a profit without even breaking the seals, just by showing the accompanying invoice. During an exceptionally fervent period of diamond speculation in 1977 and 1978, DTC boxes were changing hands at up to twice the syndicate's price without even being opened (much to the annoyance of the CSO's producer clients, who were furious to find their rough commanding 100 percent premium the moment it was out of the DTC's hands). That game has been stopped in Antwerp and Tel Aviv, where all incoming boxes go through a central delivery office, which now opens them and delivers the packets of diamonds to the sightholder in large envelopes. The ending of the DTC box as a negotiable instrument is a big change in the diamond trade. The syndicate has the market back under tight rein after the most frenetic speculation in its history. For several months early in 1978 it looked as if the DTC might actually be losing its grip, arousing fears that a large secondary market in rough outside their control might be established.

The trouble, from the De Beers standpoint, arose because dealers and manufacturers, particularly in Israel, started to order at sights far more diamonds than they required. Rumors had been circulating that the overall De Beers inventory of melees— that is, medium-sized goods which are the specialty of the Israeli industry—was dangerously low. Speculation was fueled by inflation, against which diamonds were an attractive hedge. As the prices of rough in the cutting centers soared, so the fever grew. The banks, as mainstays of finance, encouraged the spiral, notably in Tel Aviv, by continuing to advance money for more purchases against the collateral of diamonds already held.

Before long the markets of Antwerp, Tel Aviv and Bombay were awash with diamonds which had been bought at inflated prices. "Knowledge meant nothing in those days," recalled a dealer. "You bought any parcel and sold it at a profit in a few days." The price of rough diamonds, in fact, which should usually be closely matched to the price for polished goods, took off on its own. De Beers, openly challenging prices as "irrational," realized that, unless they could curtail the speculation, the stable image of the diamond, with the price always moving relentlessly up, could be ruined. They feared, too, customer resistance if the soaring price of rough was passed on in full on polished goods. "It was a hairy time for us," admitted an executive. "It was really touch and go to stay in control." The DTC took three specific steps to shake out the speculators. At five sights in 1978 they slapped on a surcharge, averaging 25 percent, on all boxes to discourage sightholders from ordering more than they absolutely needed (a move which their Bombay clients rejected en masse by refusing to attend). Secondly, they warned the banks that they were extending too much credit and in particular got the low interest rate of 6 percent, which the Israeli banks had long charged, raised. Finally, they withdrew invitations to several sightholders considered guilty of fostering speculation. And ever since, all sightholders must account for their needs meticulously, a policy which caused one Antwerp sighholder to lament, "We are no longer customers but employees of the syndicate."

Without doubt, the DTC had been shaken. Even Monty Charles speaks of "those horrible years." But it was able to get back in the saddle, and the banishment of some sightholders curtailed the speculative inclination of others. Not that *diamantaires* have been cowed. They just became more discreet than usual in selling or buying goods outside DTC channels. One strategic reason advanced in Tel Aviv for the Israeli industry's reluctance to institute a proper system of bookkeeping is that it would reveal when one sightholder disposed of some of his box to another.*

No sightholder has ever wanted to be totally beholden to the DTC, not least because he cannot be sure exactly what his box will contain. "If I could go to London every five weeks and get what I need, it would be a beautiful life," said Nick Axelrod at Harry Winston, "but Winston never wanted to be limited to what the DTC allocated. If they don't give you the merchandise you need, all your projections, all your beautiful thoughts are thrown out of the window." So Winston always explored every other direct source of rough in Africa and South America. The advantage was not only in the range of

* See Part III, 2: Tel Aviv, pp. 169–185.

goods obtained but in price, too. "I'll give the syndicate credit for trying to control the price of diamonds," Axelrod added, "but, fortunately for us, they don't control it one hundred percent, so that on the open market the price can be twenty percent less than the DTC. Of course, it can also be eighty percent more, but in Brazil, Venezuela, Ghana and Sierra Leone you're dealing with individual miners, and what you get from them can often be salvation."

The DTC is fully aware that its sightholders shop around, and they will not complain if this is done in moderation and fairly openly. "I've done much more outside business in the last two years," said an Antwerp manufacturer, "because I don't get what I need at sights. I've shown De Beers my figures and said, you supply me more or I'll do more outside." But the position is always delicate. A love-hate relationship often develops between the DTC and its sightholders, who tread warily so as not to offend the syndicate. "We sometimes feel we are treated by them as naughty schoolboys," complained another Antwerp *diamantaire.* Certainly many DTC clients are reluctant to refuse their box at a sight, for fear of their standing invitation being canceled. "What I'm buying now is a total loss," admitted a sightholder; "they are giving bad goods. But you can't say, 'The market is weak, I don't need them.'" Then he added, "If you are faithful, they will look after you. At times you swear at them, but you make it up later." And in moments of genuine personal crisis, the DTC can be helpful. "Once I was ill for six months with jaundice, and they offered to leave me out of sights until I was better," another sightholder told me. "They can be very, very cooperative, and they've never tried to force me into anything."

Despite criticism from some sightholders (and more from those who are not), it is hard to find anyone in the diamond trade who wishes the monopoly to crumble. "We all resent De Beers until the going gets rough, then they take care of things," admitted a New York wholesaler in the hard times of 1980. "If they hadn't cut back now at sights, we'd all be up to our necks in trouble—importers, cutters and retailers would all go broke." The mood was shared by another New Yorker who said, "When I look in the mirror every morning as I shave, I thank God for De Beers."

From Cartel to Cooperative?

In the summer of 1979 a craggy portrait of Harry Oppenheimer, hewn out of a rough diamond, appeared on the cover of the American magazine *Forbes*, with the caption, "Is a Diamond Cartel Forever?" That question occupies the minds of many *diamantaires*, not just because of the difficulties the Diamond Trading Company had in riding herd on the speculative excursions of the previous two years, but because the rules of the game are changing. The Russians, for instance, have increasingly been selling their own high-quality polished goods direct into the market, short-circuiting the DTC. High labor costs have hit cutting centers like Antwerp very hard and threatened the closure of many specialist plants there without a nursing hand from De Beers. And the growing political isolation of South Africa makes it ever harder for other countries to justify channeling their diamonds through a syndicate of such clear South African origins. With the rise of Botswana as the foremost producer by 1985 and the independence of Namibia in prospect, the possibility of rival "third-world" sights is increasingly discussed. As a Johannesburg stockbroking firm noted in 1980, "It would be . . . foolish to discount the long-term possibility of a break with De Beers, for political reasons, and a realignment of non-South African producers to form a marketing group of their own. Angola—potentially a major gem producer—is really politically dominated by the USSR, as is the external wing of Swapo, which could some day control Namibia."

De Beers, fully aware of the dangers, has not stood idly by. While its basic response is that there is no one else around with the right expertise to set up rival sights, it has been adapting the CSO quietly to counter the new situations.

The most obvious advance has been to play a more active role in the cutting centers of Antwerp, Tel Aviv and Bombay, to help old manufacturers in difficulties and nourish new ones. "We were inclined to sit in the 'glasshouse,' as the old building in Charterhouse Street was called," said Monty Charles, "but now we get out much more into the marketplaces." In Antwerp, Tel Aviv and Lucerne a CSO subsidiary, Diamdel, is busily playing the role of local dealer in supplying rough goods to local manufacturers who do not rate sights. And a similar arrangement has started in Bombay through the establishment of the Hindustan Diamond Corporation as a joint venture with the Indian government. Simultaneously, the sorting of some rough goods has been switched since 1975 from London to Lucerne, where a few sightholders, mainly from Israel, are now invited instead of to London. "De Beers is being very careful," observed a Tel Aviv sightholder, "not to have all its eggs in one basket."

Gossip in the trade, however, has been most stirred up by the De Beers venture into polished diamonds. Not only have they helped develop two Belgian factories specializing in cleaving and sawing diamonds, but they have become substantial traders in polished goods. In Antwerp a CSO offshoot, Diatrada, has expanded so rapidly that it is now one of the foremost exporters of polished, while another polished wholesaler, Throgmorton Gems, is equally well established in Switzerland and Israel. Some *diamantaires* feel this is only the beginning of a vertical integration that will ultimately involve De Beers from mine to retail jewelry store. That projection is premature. De Beers' answer is that, on the one hand, their intervention was necessary to "save" Antwerp from annihilation by cheap competition from India, and, on the other, that it was a natural response to the Russian advance in polished goods. While Harry Oppenheimer certainly understated it when he dismissed such enterprises as "better listening posts" to help the cartel keep abreast of polished prices, De Beers clearly does not envisage a complete takeover of all aspects of polished goods. A more realistic view is that it counterbalances the Russian activities. "If the Russians sell polished, so must the syndicate," said an Antwerp dealer. Since the signs now are that the Russians will not expand their polished operations substantially during the next decade, but will prefer to market a good deal of their production still in rough form, De Beers executives also may feel they have established a firm enough presence in the polished market not to proceed much further.

The real test is whether political pressures will eventually override the economic judgment that persuades diamond producers across the political spectrum to work through the CSO. So far most governments have taken a very pragmatic view.

That even goes for the Russians. Although the marketing of their rough diamonds has been shrouded in some mystery since they broke officially with the CSO in 1963, it is an open secret that the rough is marketed on Soviet behalf by a London merchant bank through the CSO. No one talks about it much, and *diamantaires* everywhere enjoy endless speculation on what sort of contract is involved. "The CSO and the Russians play poker with each other all the time," said an Israeli dealer, "but at heart the Russians know that De Beers has more expertise in its little finger than they could learn in a lifetime."

That is the best reason for anticipating that De Beers will remain at the helm of diamond marketing for the present. Moreover, the economic hard times of the early eighties make producers more willing to lean on the financial resources of the CSO. "Our buffer stock system guarantees them regular cash payments," said Michael Granham, a DTC director. "Can you see producers getting cash elsewhere in a depressed market?" And Monty Charles summed up their best card. "When times are good people are inclined to forget us, but in a recession they really need us."

Such appreciation undoubtedly gives the CSO considerable breathing space for a few years and the chance to drum home the message that everyone benefits from its continued existence, especially in lean times. Meanwhile, they are also tactfully suggesting another way of describing their cartel. The advertisements in the financial press in the spring of 1980, accompanying the launching of the De Beers latest annual report, carefully described the Central Selling Organization as "effectively a producers' cooperative." Even the Russians could hardly object to that.

2

The Marketplaces

Antwerp: The Turntable

The illuminated sign at Antwerp's tiny airport says *Welcome to Antwerp, World Diamond Center.* And as passengers pile into taxis from the three incoming international flights daily (all from London, the home of the Diamond Trading Company), the drivers do not really have to ask where they are going; the address will surely be Pelikaanstraat or the adjoining sidestreets of Rijfstraat, Hovieniersstraat or Schupstraat close by the central station. Clustered in these back streets are the five hundred diamond dealers, manufacturers and wholesalers (including over eighty DTC sightholders) who support Antwerp's claim for the world title.

They are a cosmopolitan assortment. Jews, Armenians, Indians, Russians mingle with Flemish and French-speaking Belgians; all pride themselves on the confidential nature of their transactions and like to feel they are a law unto themselves. The Belgian government turns a benevolent blind eye to what goes on, not fencing in the *diamantaires*, as everyone calls them, with the regulations that inhibit other diamond centers. Import and export duties do not exist, exchange controls are unheard of and all trading can be done directly in dollars. No one is pressed too hard for taxes, provided they declare some profit (no one can get away with a loss). *Diamantaires* around Pelikaanstraat love to remind visitors about the tax inspector who did not realize that their ways were different and tried hard to get at the real books; after a few discreet words in Brussels, he was hastily transferred to another town. Even the official figures, which may be half the true tally, rate diamonds as Belgium's fifth most important industry. "We feed a hundred thousand mouths, one percent of the entire population," said a dealer proudly. "If the government tried to tighten up, we'd all emigrate. What happened to Amsterdam after the Dutch government tightened up? It's finished as a diamond market."

So crossing Pelikaanstraat is almost to step into some ministate within a state, like Monaco or Liechtenstein or San Marino. This is a haven where many people feel safe and at ease, not on account of the constant presence of police cars parked at strategic corners of the sidestreets, but because the climate is friendly, awkward questions are never asked and political differences are forgotten.

The tone is set by a leading Jewish manufacturer of small diamonds who comes in very late for a meeting, looking exhausted. He is full of apologies. "I was negotiating with three Arabs," he explains. "It's a big order for over a thousand carats of polished, and they keep haggling; it could go on until nine o'clock tonight. The Arabs are buying well now, and they have no hesitation in coming to Jews. Of course, they can't go to Tel Aviv, but in Antwerp Arabs and Israelis often meet. I remember during the Six Day War I put some Arab and Israeli buyers together in the same room and said, 'What do you think?' And one of the Arabs said, 'Do you believe that the blood of the children of our mothers is less red than yours?' "

This no-man's land makes smugglers feel at home, too, although Antwerp dealers politely refer to any diamonds that do not move along conventional channels as "submarine" or "outside" goods. Tall Africans, many in long flowing white robes, stride up and down Pelikaanstraat from their base at the Tourist Hotel on a ceaseless round of offices. They are just in from

Sierra Leone, Liberia, Zaire, Angola or the Central African Republic with diamonds that have escaped the Diamond Trading Company's net, either through contracts with producers (such as Ghana or the Central African Republic) who prefer not to sign on with the syndicate, or by more devious routes from illicit mining. Antwerp suits them admirably, for no less than ninety-six *diamantaires* are dealers in rough, and several have made their names as buyers of outside goods. Many of these African couriers are French-speaking Senegalese who specialize in spiriting diamonds out of Africa and smuggling back watches and gold jewelry, which they buy from several wholesalers conveniently located hard by Pelikaanstraat. The Senegalese feel at ease in Belgium, not just because there is an absence of embarrassing exchange and customs controls on the way in, but because they can speak French and telephone quickly to their principals in Africa (an essential requirement in many of their negotiations). Tel Aviv, which might otherwise be an alternative for them, is not nearly so convenient on any count.

Going the rounds of dealers in rough, the Africans always seem to be there first, sitting back leisurely while the prospective buyer goes through the stones one by one. It requires patience. At six-thirty in the evening, with Pelikaanstraat outside almost deserted, a young Indian dealer is still closeted with two Senegalese. An agreement on price eludes them by a fraction. So the Indian pushes the diamonds back, the Senegalese slowly fold them into the blue-paper parcels. "Sorry," says the Indian, "you come back next week." As the door closes on them he explains, "It often takes two or three days of bargaining. But this is the advantage of Antwerp over Bombay. There's always lots of outside goods if you are having difficulty getting them from the DTC. We've been here from Bombay since 1973, and it's much better; there are no restrictions on any kind of trading." The phone distracts him again. "What? You've got a little parcel?" he shouts over a bad line. "I can buy anything from you. I can use any business . . . no problem. Come and see me at ten o'clock tomorrow."

The Indian community expanded rapidly in Antwerp during the 1970s, finding it a convenient place not only to pick up extra rough diamonds, but to trade polished stones imported from Bombay. Sixty families have moved there permanently, and the four largest Indian firms based in Belgium have become DTC sightholders. An endless round of travelers from Bombay frequents the diamond exchanges and hotels. When one encounters an Indian in the fitness club at the Eurotel, just across the way from the diamond district, it goes without saying he is in diamonds. And the hotel menu notes cheerily, "For the special attention of our Indian guests—our hot chicken curry, Bombay style." Even the young Englishman, downing beer in the hotel bar, confides he is working as a sorter for a well-known Indian buyer of rough. He is just back from a year in Monrovia, buying stones that have been smuggled out of Sierra Leone, so he has the right eye for discerning the best outside goods that turn up in Antwerp.

The Russians are in attendance, too. Their trading outlet for polished diamonds, Russelmaz, is housed on the second and third floors of an anonymous-looking office block in Lange-Herental-sestraat, on the fringe of the diamond district. Much to the amusement of Antwerp's *diamantaires*, it is just across the road from an eight-story office block that De Beers completed in 1979. Everyone assumes they keep a wary eye on each other's comings and goings. Although Russelmaz widely proclaims itself as "exporters and direct importers of Russian polished diamonds in finest make, all sizes and qualities," it is more a shop window than a vigorous sales organization. Local dealers find it notoriously difficult to buy anything direct from Russelmaz. Most Russian diamonds, which account for 10 percent of Belgium's imports of polished, are imported by twenty-five Antwerp firms who buy from Almazyuvelireksport in Moscow. To the Russians, the benefit of this foot in the Antwerp camp is as a listening post for diamond—and other—intelligence. Alert observers did not fail to notice that one of the suspected KGB agents kicked out of the Russian Embassy in London in 1971, in a mass expulsion of 105 diplomats and "trade officials," turned up shortly afterwards in charge of Russelmaz in Antwerp.

The Russian presence is, in a sense, a compliment to Antwerp. More than anywhere else, it is the genuine marketplace where the world's rough and polished diamonds are traded. London, Tel Aviv, Bombay and New York fulfill special functions; Antwerp is the nerve center that binds them all. The annual value of its official exports at around 100 billion Belgian francs ($3.4 billion) is more than double that of Tel Aviv, and five times more than Bombay. Adding in the diamonds that leave by "submarine," the total value is closer to $5 billion or even $6 billion annually. And when other markets are down, it is often Antwerp that remains the buyer of last resort. "Antwerp has the capacity to swallow surplus polished," said Raoul Delveaux, the former director-general of the Diamond High Council which presides over the Belgium industry. "The market is in difficulty, so what happens? Tel Aviv, Bombay, even New York exports here. Altogether, we've got over one billion dollars in stock in Antwerp at the moment."

This strong suit in diamonds is long established. The diamond trade has been in Belgium for at least five centuries, ever since, so the legend goes, Lodewijk van Berckem, a citizen of Bruges, invented diamond cutting around 1476. But Belgium's early head start was eclipsed by Amsterdam, which became the chief cutting center by the mid-seventeenth century. Antwerp regained the initiative only after the South African diamond rush of 1870. The flood of stones during the "Cape era" was more than Amsterdam could cope with, and over the next generation Antwerp's business grew rapidly.

Its trading reputation was enhanced when many Jewish families, who fled from eastern Europe around the turn of the century, settled there. "My father came from Russia in 1907," recalled Maurice Schamisso, now a leading dealer in rough and polished diamonds. P. N. (Nathan) Ferstenberg, the dean of Antwerp's *diamantaires*, remembers how he came to Antwerp as a boy of fifteen from Poland and joined a diamond cutter as an apprentice. He was astonished to find how welcome the workers made him; the first day one shared his lunch with the newcomer. For a young Jewish boy, more accustomed to taunts and bullying at school in Poland, it was a revelation. "I shall never forget it," said Ferstenberg a few years ago, celebrating half a century in the Antwerp diamond business. Finding such a haven has bred fierce loyalty to Antwerp and its diamond industry.

The emigrants found a city that was becoming the foremost center for cutting and polishing diamonds. Over forty factories already existed before 1900, while the Antwerp Diamond Club

(Diamantclub van Antwerpen) was founded in 1893 as the principal trading forum. Soon the pressure was too much for the Club alone, and the Diamond Bourse (Beurs Voor Diamanthandel) was formed in 1904, followed by the Free Diamond Trade Association (Vrije Diamanthandel) in 1911. The fourth Antwerp exchange, the Diamond Ring (Antwerpsche Diamantkring) opened its doors rather later in 1929. It is a measure of Antwerp's premier position that no other diamond center has ever required more than one, or at most two, exchanges. Today four of the sixteen members of the World Federation of Diamond Bourses are located there, the others being in Amsterdam, Ida-Oberstein, Johannesburg, London, Milan, New York, Paris, Tel Aviv and Vienna.

Although many dealers, manufacturers and brokers belong to all Antwerp's exchanges and may make their way back and forth several times daily between the three trading floors (the Free Trade Association now shares facilities with the Diamond Club), each has its own character. The Bourse trades exclusively in polished diamonds and is a favorite stamping ground for foreign buyers. The Diamond Club is the home territory of local dealers and manufacturers, trading mainly polished and some rough. It prides itself on a brisk, less conservative image than the Bourse. "The Bourse," said one member of the Club a trifle disdainfully, "is only for brokers and playing cards." The Club's executives like to boast that not only is it air-conditioned, but the north light flooding through its tall windows onto the long tables where traders spread out their diamond parcels is better than in rival establishments up the street, which are hemmed in too closely by surrounding buildings. The Club also offers one of the best restaurants on Pelikaanstraat, directly off the trading floor, so that it is possible to eat a very fine *osso bucco*, washed down with good Stella Artois beer, while keeping an eye on the action.

Membership of all the exchanges is strictly controlled and is granted only to individuals, not organizations. "It's not a firm that belongs, but a person," explained Gustave Garitte, whose father started the Diamond Ring. "You may indeed belong to a firm, but when you come in here you are responsible as a private individual."

The vetting is strict. Garitte, the manager of the Ring, paused before a notice board. On it were three applications for new membership; a detailed biography of each candidate was set out alongside his photograph. Duplicates were on display in all the other clubs; every member of the diamond fraternity has an opportunity to scrutinize who is seeking admittance and can object, if he has firm grounds. On the same notice boards are pinned suspension orders for members who have erred. Any suspension applies not only to the home club but to all sixteen in the world federation. One fresh notice marked the expulsion of a member from the Diamond Club on Pelikaanstraat. "We were obliged to exclude him," said Sylvain Zucker, chairman of the Club, "for he committed the very, very serious offense of trying to steal a stone by pretending it was his, when it could be proved it was not." Suspension is tantamount to loss of livelihood, for there is little hope of readmission later. "We can't put someone out for one year," said Zucker. "We must not take half measures. A person like that doesn't belong in our midst, and that's that." The diamond business rolls on the ball bearings of trust; a verbal agreement and a handshake are binding. Anyone who violates that trust is out.

Not that everyone is happy with the policing. While Antwerp has a good reputation for dealing firmly with transgressors, some people argue that action elsewhere is often slipshod. The much vaunted strict code is sometimes violated with impunity.

Antwerp, however, is confident it takes a tough line. "The very fact of being a member of the Club here is a recommendation," says Sylvain Zucker. "You carry its prestige. We don't want anyone as a member who won't accept that responsibility."

The bustle of the exchanges does not hide the fact that many transactions take place in the privacy of offices. "Competition is so much tougher in the last few years," said a senior manufacturer, "that it's better to meet people in your office. Then no one sees what you buy or who buys from you. Even if you have to pay an extra percentage, it's better for business." The trend occasionally makes the exchanges seem like social clubs. By the late afternoon, the action is more often chess or backgammon, rather than diamonds. A tense cluster of a dozen people crowded around a table, all standing on tiptoe, does not indicate a splendid stone on view, but merely that someone is about to cry "checkmate."

The role of the exchanges may be waning, but that of the banks specializing in diamonds grows with every rise in price. Three banks on Pelikaanstraat have devoted their attention almost exclusively to diamonds for many years. The oldest is Banque Diamantaire Anversoise, started in 1934 by a consortium of Belgian banks and De Beers to help bail out the Belgian diamond industry in the worst years of the Depression. Side by side with it are Internationale Handels-en Diamantbank (IHD) and Amro Bank, a Belgian subsidiary of the Amsterdam-Rotterdam Bank. Their specialists are not only knowledgeable about diamonds, but enjoy a unique overview of the entire industry whose accounts they maintain. Their relationship with every firm is close, for a loan does not depend upon diamonds deposited as collateral (as in Israel), but simply on the management's assessment of a *diamantaire*'s standing. "We start with confidence, confidence, confidence," said a diamond banker. "I've been in the diamond business for twenty-five years, and I know everyone personally. I go to their offices, their factories, their homes. I'm lending on my judgment of the man and his firm."

The loans are substantial. "We are usually financing the diamonds bought at the last two or three sights, because it takes several weeks for the manufacturers to sort and polish the rough," the banker went on. "So we are really financing the DTC—who must be paid before they ship the stones." All eighty of Antwerp's sightholders rely on the three diamond banks to stump up most of the cash for each sight. The largest sightholder alone will require a loan of up to $4 or $5 million; between them, the banks will be called on for $80–$90 million for every sight. The inexorable rise in diamond prices will push this to over $100 million ten times a year during the early eighties. Besides financing the purchases of rough, the banks also have to underpin Antwerp's position as the premier marketplace for polished stones flowing back from other cutting centers. "I estimate that forty percent of the money in Antwerp is tied up in stock," said another Pelikaanstraat banker, "and that means that together the three banks have at least one billion dollars outstanding."

The Antwerp banks pride themselves that their informal system of credit, based on the personal instincts of their managers, enabled them to avoid the pitfalls of speculative booms, such as the one that beset Israel in 1978. Since the banks in Tel Aviv gave loans at low rates of interest against diamonds actually deposited with them, it was possible for dealers there to put in a parcel of diamonds with a declared value of $1 million, get a $1 million loan from the bank, with which they bought another parcel to deposit at the bank for another loan, in an endless scramble that pushed up prices far beyond their true level. The banks were then stuck with overvalued parcels of diamonds. "The Israeli banks fueled the crisis," said an Antwerp banker sharply. "Our system, based upon knowledge of each firm's capacity, restrained us."

The Belgian manufacturers appreciate this. "The banks here give me credit as an individual," said one of them. "The capital of my firm is only a hundred sixty thousand dollars, but if I want a million dollars I just sign. The only guarantee is me. I'm personally responsible. But the bank has the experience to know the amount of goods I can work—and that's my limit, beyond which there's no more credit."

The cluster of banks, diamond exchanges and dealers' offices around Pelikaanstraat is only one side of the Belgian diamond industry. The other is the Kempen, the rural area outside Antwerp where most of the cutting and polishing of diamonds actually takes place. The craftsmen, on whose skill much of Antwerp's reputation rests, live in little villages with typical Flemish names—Vorselaar, Grobbendonk, Berlaar and Herenthout—some twenty miles outside the city. There are few real factories. Most of the work is done by two or three people, often of the same family, in small workshops. In many ways, they are a people apart from the born traders around Pelikaanstraat. "Virtually all the workers in the Kempen are Flemish," said Raoul Delveaux of the Diamond High Council. "Whereas if you take the trade here in Antwerp itself, ninety percent are of foreign origin, and of those, over sixty percent are Jewish." Each leaves the other to get on with his own specialty. "It's very decentralized out in the Kempen," explained a leading manufacturer. "I use workshops in twenty different villages, most of them small places with five or ten people. Some of them work exclusively for certain *diamantaires*, others work for many. But they are very remote from me as the boss here in Antwerp; if I got out there once in five or six years it would be unusual."

Yet once a day the two sides come together. The owner of a small workshop in the Kempen gets up early, spends an hour or two supervising his workers and then makes his way into Antwerp to deliver finished goods or negotiate new orders. Around 11 A.M. the Antwerp traders and the Kempen manufacturers get together in the exchanges or in the offices nearby. They do business, have a drink or lunch, then each goes his own way—the manufacturer back to the countryside with consignments of rough diamonds, the trader to his office to call Paris or Geneva or New York to dispose of the newly polished goods. "It's rather a successful marriage," says Raoul Delveaux. "The Flemish worker in the Kempen is content to do a good job for his boss, and then go out and play football and drink at the weekend. He doesn't want other responsibilities. And the traders are satisfied with the quality of the workmanship which they can sell around the world."

A slightly simplistic view, perhaps, but Antwerp is a mix of traditional craftsmanship with international salesmanship. The trouble is that in an era of high labor costs, Antwerp's role as a great cutting center has been eroded. Back in the 1920s there were 29,000 workers out in the Kempen; by 1969 this was down to 19,000, and a decade later to barely 11,000. The challenge came first from Tel Aviv and more recently from Bombay. Labor costs in Belgium, combined with high social security payments, have made it hard to compete with these new cutting centers, especially in what the trade calls melees and smalls. The Kempen has had to fall back increasingly on the cleaving— or sawing—and polishing of the large and the more difficult stones, such as maccles, the Siamese twins of diamond crystals. Its plight, however, has not gone unnoticed. And none other than the Diamond Trading Company has come riding to the rescue. De Beers has been extending its operations discreetly in Antwerp and the Kempen since the mid-seventies.

They began by establishing an outlet for rough diamonds called Diamdel, which sells directly to small manufacturers in the Antwerp area who do not rate sights. Within a short time,

Diamdel was rated among the top ten traders in rough in Belgium. The move was greeted with considerable suspicion. "This is the wooden horse entering Troy," declared one member of the Diamond High Council. De Beers was not deflected. Another company, Belsort, was set up to sort rough diamonds locally, and a third outfit, Diatrada, was established to export Belgian polished goods. Out at Berlaar in the Kempen, De Beers also guided the expansion of Lens Diamond Industries, an important firm specializing in sawing and cleaving. Several independent manufacturers were also reported to be cutting and polishing stones on contract for the DTC. An official of the Diamond High Council even estimated that by 1980 at least 700 people were directly employed by De Beers companies in Belgium, and perhaps many more through subcontracting.

De Beers executives themselves are cautious in revealing the precise level of their involvement in the Belgian industry, always insisting they are in residence to preserve and stabilize the local cutting industry. But apart from nursing Antwerp through difficult days, De Beers will concede that it is establishing a foothold in polished goods in direct response to the Russians.

Antwerp and the Kempen, just a step across the Channel from London, offer ideal facilities. And the move helps to halt the decline of Belgium as a manufacturing center. The resentment of some Antwerp dealers is certainly balanced by the appreciation of craftsmen out in the Kempen, who are offered the prospect of secure employment. In recent years many have been tempted away to Israel and even on short-term contracts to Russia to help expand the cutting industry there. Now they have more reason to stay at home. Moreover, a firmer basis for the local cutting industry should insure that Antwerp sustains through the 1980s its supremacy over Tel Aviv, Bombay and New York as the world's diamond center.

Tel Aviv: Chastened Champions

The story of the diamond industry in Israel is really the story of Israel itself, although the industry prides itself on being slightly older than the state. Ask any of the *diamantaires* gathered together in the complex of skyscrapers that form the Diamond

Exchange at Ramat Gan just outside Tel Aviv where they were born and how they came to be there. The reply is always a variation on the same theme.

"I was born in Poland in 1939, taken to Siberia, escaped to Tashkent and made my way here without my parents."

"I was born in 1943 just before my parents were put into Auschwitz, where somehow they survived, and we were all reunited in Vienna and came here."

"I left Antwerp in 1935 to work on a kibbutz."

The men who forged the industry also forged the state. They fought for it in the original war for independence in the late 1940s, and again in the Suez campaigns of 1956, the Six Day War of 1967 and the Yom Kippur War of 1973. Moshe Schnitzer, the gregarious president of the Diamond Exchange, holds the rank of Colonel; so does the government's Diamond Controller, Joseph Perlmutter, and Jonah Hatsor, the representative of Hennig's, the London diamond brokers. They suffered, too. Simcha Lustig, who presides over one of the largest cutting factories, was once a tough paratrooper but now, because of war injuries, is confined to a wheelchair.

Their aggressive spirit also built the diamond business into the country's foremost export industry and made Tel Aviv the world's premier cutting center. In the record year of 1977, rather more than half of all diamond cutting and polishing took place in Israel. This achievement was marred by only one weakness. The *diamantaires* identified so closely with Israel that they created a state within a state. They came to believe that an industry which earned over $300 million a year in foreign exchange for the exchequer and fed a hundred thousand of the nation's three million mouths was its ultimate cornerstone, that without diamonds Israel could not exist. In short, they got carried away by their own success, adopting an air of self-confidence not unlike that prevailing in Israel at large before the Yom Kippur War. Then the rug was pulled out smartly. The diamond price boom of 1977–78, in which the Central Selling Organization nearly lost its grip on the market, was fed by heavy speculation in Israel, particularly by some younger dealers who thought it was more interesting (and profitable) to trade in diamonds than manufacture them. Enormous stocks of rough were built up at inflated prices just as the world was moving into recession. At the same time, De Beers, having regained its supremacy by special surcharges at several sights, was actively encouraging the expansion of rival cutting centers in India and South Africa to cut and polish melee, the medium-sized rough between 0.2 and 1.4 carats, which had long been Israel's specialty. The Russians were also busy marketing their own high-quality polished melee. Many of Israel's *diamantaires* suddenly found themselves sitting on inventories they could not shift at competitive prices. For the first time in thirty years the value of Israel's diamond exports fell in 1979, and employment declined by one-third as many small workshops closed. The *diamantaires*, for once, were put on the defensive. The years of growth had come to an abrupt halt. The moment for reappraisal and adjustment to a different future had come. The mood I encountered, therefore, at Ramat Gan was of a slightly chastened champion seeking to sustain a comeback.

The twin towers of the Diamond Exchange dominate Ramat Gan, a garden suburb twenty minutes from downtown Tel Aviv. The original Exchange skyscraper was put up in 1968 apparently because the enterprising mayor of Ramat Gan liked the idea of having the *diamantaires* in his community and could offer a good site, while the mayor of Tel Aviv was less welcoming. A second building opened in 1980 to ease hopeless overcrowding. Along with a smaller office building and cutting factories just behind, they form a complete environment, a diamond "island" on the fringe of the city, completely preoccupied with its own affairs. There are banks, a post office, restaurants, air freight and courier firms so that the *diamantaires* can start at 8 A.M. and work through until the early evening without leaving the complex. "You might say we live here," said Mordehai Noam of Orah Diamonds, one of the foremost manufacturing firms, who has put up his own office building right behind the exchange skyscrapers. An air of informality prevails because almost everyone is casually dressed in open-necked short-sleeved shirts and slacks; only the strict Hasidim in their long black coats and Japanese visitors in well-pressed business suits are more formally turned out. The bustle and overcrowding are intense, not least because ten thousand buyers from overseas trek through every year. Anyone with energy does not wait for the rare appearances of the packed lifts, unless his appointment is towards the twenty-eighth floor, but makes better time on the stairs. Even then, around the third-floor exchange it is a matter of pushing through dealers who have spilled over onto the stairways to trade diamonds or the latest gossip.

The exchange itself, a long room with high north windows, is jammed throughout the working day. Every chair at the long range of tables is constantly occupied, and a sea of diamonds is laid out on blue-white paper. As a lively trading forum the Ramat Gan exchange is without a rival; in Antwerp and New York much business goes on in the privacy of offices. At Ramat Gan the floor is still the heart of the matter. "I have a bigger choice in the club; there are so many brokers going the rounds," said a dealer, rewrapping his diamonds in their papers after concluding a deal with the customary *mazel und broche*. "If I sat in my office and waited for a broker I might miss something. If I don't come down here I feel bad— I have to get the feeling, the smell, of what is going on. How is the market reacting to some news? It's part of my life, and if I don't see the exchange every day I don't feel well."

Originally the exchange grew up in much humbler times when no one had offices. It was just a room in which the handful of traders in a nascent industry came together from sheds and barns amidst the orange groves where they were trying to master the skills of cutting and polishing. The real surprise— and pleasure—in the modern hubbub of the Ramat Gan skyscrapers is that the founders, the first generation, are still around. Late one evening after the exchange was quiet, I found Joseph Nadel, a small, gray-haired man with a cheerful, chipmunk face who specializes in trading rough diamonds, relaxing back in his office by phoning the events of the day to his New York partner. After a while he hung up (*diamantaires* thrive on long international calls) and began to reminisce about the early days. He had learned his trade, he told me, as a teenager in Antwerp in the early 1930s, before his family emigrated to what was then Palestine. "Soon after I arrived here," he said, "a man named Aaron Mortiz set up a factory for cutting and polishing and took in poor people to teach them the trade." Using his connections in Antwerp, Nadel persuaded a few Belgian dealers to send out goods for cutting, which were then shipped back to Antwerp for sale. The business was scarcely finding its feet when war came. "We sent the last shipment back to Belgium in October 1939, just as the Germans invaded the Low Countries," Nadel went on. Soon, however, many of the diamond cutters from Antwerp, who fled before the German advance, sought refuge in Palestine. The trouble was, how could they continue to work without a ready supply of stones? Most of the cutters were living in the little town of Nethanya, just up the coast from Tel Aviv. The mayor, a shrewd fellow named Oved Ben Ami, had no doubt what must be done. He went to London and sought out Sir Ernest Oppenheimer, who agreed that the Central Selling Organization would make up a regular parcel at its sights for the newly formed Diamond Manufacturers Association in Palestine. The Association then shared the rough out among its members; initially, the parcel was divided among eight cutting firms. This guaranteed supply (which was monitored carefully by the British authorities in Palestine, who feared the stones might fall into the wrong hands and get to Germany by way of Turkey) enabled the industry to flourish. By the end of the war, a much larger CSO parcel was being split among twenty-four factories employing over five thousand people.

This sound start was quickly shattered, however, when peace came. The Belgians returned to Antwerp, and regular CSO sights for them were restored. Palestine, then in the throes of the struggle for the formation of Israel, was neglected; the CSO stopped the monthly parcel. Diamond prices were also weak, and many factories closed. Those who wished to continue had little or no capital. Yet they refused to give up; they were as determined to keep the industry going as they were that Israel, born in 1948, should thrive. This era gave the Israeli diamond business its real character; it was kept alive in those difficult days by men from the floor of the cutting factories who had no capital, only the will to succeed. Almost all the older *diamantaires* at Ramat Gan began as cutters without a penny to their names. "I started with two workers," recalled Moshe Schnitzer, the president of the Diamond Exchange, "and this is the basis for the success of our industry— we're all self-made people. We had no money, so we had to sell our production. That was just the opposite to the Belgians.

They didn't sell without a good profit, but we *had* to sell, so we made it on volume and turnover."

The real hurdle was lack of ready cash. Its absence created the unique financial structure of the Israeli industry. From the outset the banks looked favorably on the young entrepreneurs. "The banks invented a fiction, which they called the 'trust receipt,' to enable them to extend money to people who had none," explained Jonah Hatsor of Hennig, the brokers. "Initially the bank advanced the money to buy diamonds. Strictly speaking, the diamonds should then be placed in the bank as collateral for the loans, but the manufacturer must have them to work on. So the bank issued a trust receipt, enabling him to take the diamonds out for specified periods for manufacture or sale." The trust receipt was the industry's salvation. "Without the bank we wouldn't exist," said Moshe Schnitzer. "My partner and I had just ten thousand dollars, and I went off to look for customers. In Finland I found I could get a hundred thousand dollars' worth of business—it was a fortune. So I came home to the manager at Bank Leumi, and he gave me a hundred thousand dollars. No normal bank would give you money like that. Yet I don't know of one occasion when the banks said no in the early days."

The Israelis had another competitive trick up their sleeve —the chain system of manufacturing. Traditionally, in Antwerp and other centers, one man worked on a diamond throughout the cutting and polishing process. Since Israel lacked enough highly skilled workers, the entrepreneurs found it was quicker and more efficient to teach half a dozen people to specialize in specific stages. It even paid off sometimes in quality, for one man could become a real master of each step. The workers were paid by the piece, so that the more they did, the more they made. The pressure was always for high volume and rapid turnover with low profit margins.

This infant Israeli industry also had one indefatigable ally in London—George Prins of Hennig, the syndicate brokers. He was the ambassador who kept a dialogue going between the Israeli manufacturers and Sir Ernest Oppenheimer's Central Selling Organization. "Sir Ernest didn't want to supply them, preferring to remain loyal to the Belgians," recalled Vivian Prins, George's son and himself a director of Hennig. "But my father persuaded him, and that unlocked the door. So we took the initiative in Israel long before our competitors, who didn't feel it would amount to anything. But as we are a Jewish family and they were Jewish people in a desperate situation, we supported them. It was an emotional factor." Such loyalty in the early struggle to survive has not gone unrewarded. As the business in Israel flourished, so Hennig was excellently placed to act as broker for the growing number of sightholders. Today the firm acts for more than thirty of Israel's forty-five CSO sightholders.

Back in the fifties, however, the CSO, despite George Prins's advocacy, kept Tel Aviv on short rations. "Our whole supply until the late 1950s was a half million pounds [$1.4 million] a month," said Joseph Nadel. "It just wasn't enough, so we had to bring goods in from Antwerp, and we also went out to look for our own supply. I went to Ghana, the Ivory Coast and Guinea to open buying offices for Israel." That tactic brought results. The CSO never welcomed rival buyers in the field, and after a while they made a new agreement with the Diamond Manufacturers Association to increase Israel's allocation at each sight to £1 million ($2.8 million).

The *diamantaires'* hand was helped by unwavering backing from successive Israeli governments, especially those of David Ben-Gurion and Golda Meir. They saw the blossoming diamond business as a crucial source both of employment and foreign exchange. "I don't say the economy would go to the dogs without diamonds," said one official, "but why take the risk?" So the government made certain that the industry got cheap credit. The central bank advanced money to the commercial banks specializing in diamond finance at a meager 4 percent interest rate, and this was made available to the manufacturers at 6 percent. For years, cheap interest was vital in giving Israel's diamond industry a competitive edge on many of their rivals in Antwerp, New York or Bombay, who were more dependent on the changing seasons of commercial rates (a fact which did not endear Israel to its competitors). And although tight exchange controls were imposed until 1977, the *diamantaires* were given a premium over the official exchange rate on dollars they brought into the country.

The authorities always keep a close, if benign, eye on what

is going on through the Diamond Controller, who holds court in the Diamond Exchange Building. "I am the authority for diamonds in Israel," said Joseph Perlmutter, a relaxed man in blue check shirt and blue slacks, who spent twenty-six years in the army before becoming the current supremo. "I issue the licenses without which you are forbidden to hold loose diamonds. I am also the customs authority. All import and export must be done through my office." He led the way down to a strong room in the basement of the Exchange building. "All diamonds pass through here, including the rough from the sights," he explained. "We check the parcels and deliver these to the banks, who deliver in turn to their customers." All outgoing diamond parcels are similarly scrutinized. While we were looking around, a young bearded dealer came in with ten small parcels he was planning to hand-carry to Europe. Perlmutter's assistant opened up one of the parcels at random and looked over the contents briefly, picking up two or three of the polished diamonds to study them more closely through a loupe. Satisfied all was in order, he put the parcels in a brown envelope, sealed it with wax and thumped down an official seal. "The exporter must show that Diamond Control stamp at the airport to certify that the goods have left the country," said Perlmutter. "We export about five million dollars in diamonds a day through this office." Until the late 1970s, most of the diamonds went by registered airmail in distinctive stiff cardboard boxes. But after a series of robberies both at Lod Airport, Tel Aviv (where almost $25 million worth of diamonds mysteriously disappeared), and overseas, this system was suspended in favor of couriers. "All the thefts have stopped since the couriers were employed," said Perlmutter happily.

Just across the strong room from Perlmutter's men, wielding their seals, were desks for the representatives of the main banking consortia that underwrite the industry. The foremost is the Bank Leumi and Union Bank consortium, run by Union Bank, which finances about 45 percent of the business; its preeminence is underlined by having a representative of the De Beers Diamond Trading Company on the board (which also provides De Beers with a unique insight on what is going on). There is also a joint operation between the Israel Discount Bank and Barclays Discount Bank, while First International

Bank and United Mizrachi Bank operate individually. Their presence in the import-export strong room underlines the special relationship the banks have with the diamond industry. In a sense a *diamantaire* never actually owns diamonds at all; they are loaned out to him, courtesy of his bank, against that all-embracing trust receipt. "You must understand that Israel is a newcomer as an economic unit, with a rather primitive level of banking," said a banker specializing in diamond finance. "So, until very recently, judgments could not be made on the basis of collateral, unlike Antwerp or London. And since the industry was very much undercapitalized, the trust receipt was created. Let's say you are a dealer and you bring in rough diamonds, which go into the bank as collateral for payment. Then how can you use those diamonds? How can you free the diamonds from the bank? There was no way without the trust vehicle." The receipt enables a dealer in rough diamonds, for instance, to take the diamonds out of the bank for 30 days while he seeks to sell them; alternatively, a manufacturer can remove his diamonds from the bank's vault for up to 120 days while he is cutting and polishing. He can even dispatch polished goods on approval to a foreign client against a trust receipt. The banks' protection is twofold; they are insured, and anyone who defaults on a trust receipt is liable to criminal charges. The diamonds also go through the banks' hands at every stage. Even when the stones leave the Diamond Controller's offices duly sealed for export, the labels on the yellow and green boxes read, for instance, "Sent by Union Bank of Israel on behalf of . . ."

The trust receipt, however, could not entirely overcome the inherent weakness of an industry growing up literally from the shop floor without capital. Consolidation in the hands of a few was inevitable. So as the industry expanded like a constantly dividing amoeba—because everyone, once they learned the ropes, wanted to be an entrepreneur—a select nucleus emerged, around which others clustered. The strong not only farmed out work to the newcomers but shouldered most of the risks as secondary bankers. The strongest of all was Joseph Goldfinger. If two men stand out as the great names of the diamond business in the last generation, one is Harry Winston in New York, the other is Joseph Goldfinger in Israel. "Goldfinger was the spirit and heart of the diamond industry here," said a director of Union Bank. "Of course, he wanted to sell diamonds himself, but he had the feeling to help other people."

Goldfinger was born in Poland in 1924. As a teenager he escaped ahead of the Nazi invasion of his homeland and managed to make his way to Moscow, en route, so he hoped, to Palestine. But to get there he had first to cross Turkey, and the Turks would not allow through any travelers for Palestine who lacked essential visas from Palestine's British rulers. The British Ambassador in Moscow denied Goldfinger a visa. "All right," said the young Polish Jew, so the story goes, "give me a letter on Embassy stationery saying you are *unable* to give me one, and sign that." The ambassador obliged. Armed with this refusal Goldfinger set out for the Turkish border, where he waved the letter on formal British Embassy notepaper. As he had gambled, the Turkish immigration officer could not read English; he saw only the Embassy seal. Goldfinger got his transit visa and duly reached Palestine.

That same spirit of initiative helped him to guide the Israeli diamond industry to maturity over the next three decades. Although his empire came to embrace manufacturing in Israel and the wholesaling of polished goods in offices around the world, the strength of his business was as a dealer in rough. He stood between the Central Selling Organization and the undercapitalized, and often inexperienced, Israeli cutters. In essence, Goldfinger, financed by the Israeli banks, secured large allocations of rough at CSO sights, which he in turn gave out on credit to the little workshops around Ramat Gan, Tel Aviv and Nethanya. Most relied upon him exclusively both for their supplies and to buy back their finished production. As the web grew, the Goldfinger companies built up such large stocks of rough and polished diamonds that they were able to act as a buffer that enabled the small manufacturers to weather recessions. The Goldfinger operation became, in fact, a miniature version of the Central Selling Organization, with Joseph Goldfinger presiding as a father figure. "He took a personal interest in everything and everyone," said a banker who worked alongside him for many years. "He was most instrumental in bringing up young people and helping them to find their feet.

But he always understood, too, the overall view of relations with the CSO, of importing, of manufacturing and of the special role of the banks. He eliminated all kinds of short circuits." The CSO itself shared that admiration. "Goldfinger became the doyen," said Monty Charles of the Diamond Trading Company, with whom he was very close. "But he wasn't just an operator for himself; he was dedicated to the whole industry and Israel. If he though something should be done, it was, even if it wasn't good for him personally. And what he said went."

By the mid-1970s Goldfinger was so omnipotent that up to half the diamonds for the Israeli market, worth as much as $20 million at each sight, went through his hands. Then one weekend in June 1976 he dropped dead of a heart attack. He was just fifty-two years old. His sudden death marked a watershed for the Israeli diamond industry. "He was a leader," said a friend wistfully, thinking of the difficult years since then. "There is no replacement."

Taking stock of the Israeli diamond business in 1976, the year of Goldfinger's death, the paramount position it had won is at once apparent. In each of the five preceding years, the country had imported over 5 million carats of rough gem diamonds, equivalent to half of world production, and the export of polished goods had topped 2 million carats each year since 1972. The declared value of the outgoing polished in 1975 was over $500 million. As a cutting center of melee, the wide middle ground of gem diamonds, Israel was without equal; the 13,000 workers employed in 650 factories and workshops cut and polished 80 percent of all melees.

Moreover, the momentum for expansion was still there. The catch, however, was that the exhilaration of becoming the world's leading cutting center was also going to some people's heads. One dealer in rough admitted candidly, "We were drunk with our own success." The intoxication brought the industry close to disaster. Initially, there was the encouragement of a genuine boom in diamond sales, especially melees, during 1977 and early 1978.

Simultaneously, the Central Selling Organization was passing out odd hints that this was rapidly depleting their inventory, especially in melees. The Israeli cutters could see some evidence of this. Israel's imports of rough gems shot up to 8.6 million carats in 1976, which amounted to 82 percent of all mine output of gems; that fact signaled that the CSO must be supplying out of stocks. Fearing a shortage, the dealers at Ramat Gan began to buy up melees, not just by trying to secure larger parcels at sights, but by scouring the open market in Antwerp. They were encouraged also by the high rate of inflation in Israel and the continuing devaluation of their currency; a good stock of diamonds seemed a shrewd hedge. The rough poured into Tel Aviv. The official statistics actually listed 11.2 million carats of imports in 1977, which was more than the entire world mine production of gems. Such an avalanche needs some explanation. A great deal of rough was being imported officially, but immediately reexported clandestinely, simply as a way of changing Israeli pounds into dollars at a favorable rate. The same diamonds were even "reimported" again without ever leaving the country. "I know of one DTC box that came through the airport twelve times," said an insider. The Israelis were also snapping up goods they would normally never consider. "They were buying up thirty- or forty-dollar goods from Zaire by the bucketful," admitted one dealer, "in the hope they might get one or two good stones—swimmers—to save the whole parcel." Despite the overblown statistics, Tel Aviv was soon awash with diamonds.

The speculation was fueled by the low interest rate of 6 percent available from the banks. And since many of the diamonds were not being manufactured (export of polished went up only 22 percent while imports of rough more than doubled), they were kept in banks which advanced 80 percent of their value— with which the speculators bought even more diamonds, put them in the banks against further advances to buy more diamonds. So it went on. The situation was made more dangerous because as the price of rough jumped by 80 percent in a single year, while the price of polished lagged far behind (rough was sometimes actually *more* expensive than the equivalent in polished), the banks accepted the inflated value in granting advances. The Israeli *diamantaires* have always been at pains to claim they were not alone in this speculative foray. That is true; other cutting centers joined the game. But Israel was the premier cutting center, and its example was imitated. Perhaps what was really missing was the guiding hand of Joseph Goldfinger. "I am sure we could have talked to him, and he would have stopped it," observed a DTC director.

As it was, it became a struggle for control of the diamond trade between Israel and the CSO. "We had a real conflict with the Diamond Trading Company in 1977," admitted Moshe Schnitzer, "because eighty percent of the world production of melees is from Israel, and melees are also the bread and butter of the Syndicate. They didn't like us to dominate the price. The issue really was, who would run the show and who would dominate the price—Israel or the Syndicate?"

The Central Selling Organization, faced with the most serious challenge to its authority in its history, fought back in the first half of 1978 with substantial surcharges all around.* On the scene in Israel, however, they were active to institute some fundamental changes, most of all in the credit available from banks. In the aftermath of the diamond speculation, the Israeli government issued new regulations forcing the banks to rein in; interest rates were raised from 6 percent to 9 percent, and the banks were forbidden to put up more than 50 percent of the value of stones left with them, compared with 80 percent previously. The banks, anyway, were beginning to find their advances to the diamond industry to be top-heavy as prices soared. They had to stump up around $70 million to finance each new sight and overall had over $850 million out to the *diamantaires* by late 1979. "I've told the Syndicate we are not without a bottom," said one banker with a hint of despair. The CSO also took its own revenge on firms it felt were guilty of fueling speculation; four firms lost the privilege of sights, cutting the total number of sightholders in Israel from forty-nine to forty-five.

The penalties for Israel were real. The era of cheap credit was over. The high prices created by the speculation cut back consumer demand. Many workshops closed, and dealers were left sitting on enormous inventories. Exports of polished goods, after thirty years of rapid growth, actually fell by 25 percent in carat terms in 1978 and a further 17 percent in 1979, when

* See pp. 139–158.

export of polished was the lowest since 1971. Even in dollar terms, exports were down over 7 percent in 1979, despite the higher prices.

A dismal market was not the only headache for the *diamantaires* at Ramat Gan. They found themselves criticized increasingly by the press and public in Israel for being reluctant to agree to keep books, for continuing to get subsidized credit and for trying to prevent a thorough and open investigation of diamond thefts at the airport for fear it might rebound on some of their own exchange members. As an editorial in the Tel Aviv newspaper *Haaretz* complained, "Most members of the public think the *diamantaires* should keep correct account books, should refrain from demanding subsidies at the expense of the taxpayer and lend a hand to uncovering criminals and wrongdoers and bring them to justice. As long as they do not do so, they should not be surprised that their public image deteriorates.[15]

The matter of account books is not unique to Israel's *diamantaires*; it is a widely expressed claim of the diamond game that they cannot keep books. The excuse is always that dealers elsewhere do not keep them, so how can they? It is a vicious circle. The initial argument was against bookkeeping in Israel pounds (which have since become shekels), because constant devaluations would have meant that dealers, doing all their trade overseas in dollars, would have made enormous paper profits every time the pound went down. The government conceded books could be in dollars. But most *diamantaires* were still unhappy when the bookkeeping program was eased in during 1980. "If you want to play keeping books, I can do it easily," said the director of one of the top five manufacturing firms at Ramat Gan, "but people who know realize it will be a sham. For tax reasons people phone you from abroad and say, 'You reduce the price by twenty percent on the invoice, and I'll give you the twenty percent on your account in another country.' If I reply, 'I can't invoice you like that, I have to do the full value,' he will say, 'Go to hell.' The customer is always right."

He shook his head sadly. "I know we have a very bad public image. People say we don't keep books, we cheat, we don't pay taxes. But we pay lots of taxes, we contribute four hundred

[15] *Haaretz*, February 19, 1979.

million dollars to the economy in added value by manufacturing diamonds and we provide employment. The government in the past has given us liberty to do as we thought fit—and we flourished."

Another leading manufacturer was equally adamant. "The diamond industry is unique," he claimed. "Keeping books will be its death. We pay taxes now; we're not an exception. It's like planting a great forest; if you give all the trees the same light and the same water, some will die because they get too much light or not enough water. You have to know how to nourish an industry like ours which is so essential to the economy."

The most pragmatic reason for avoiding paperwork, however, was put forward by a noted exporter who observed, "If you are a sightholder and you want to buy syndicate rough from another sightholder, you have to be incognito." But he conceded that books were inevitable (even if they did not tell the whole story) and concluded, "We must find a better understanding with the public."

Thus, in the eighties, Israel's *diamantaires* face reconciliation on the home front and a hard fight abroad to hang onto their position as leaders of the cutting league. And after their tussle with De Beers they are not sure how much they can rely upon the Syndicate to favor them. "Maybe they will try to divide up the market more," said Moshe Schnitzer, "especially as far as melees are concerned." But on that score the Diamond Exchange's ebullient president, who is the most renowned optimist in the world of diamonds, was not worried. "Until now no center could compete with Israel as far as knowledge of melees was concerned," Schnitzer went on. "People have tried opening up cutting centers in Hong Kong, Japan, Malaysia and even Lebanon—but they are unsuccessful. What you need is a cutting center that's also a trading center—with a real knowledge of selling; that's us."

Despite fears at Ramat Gan that De Beers may avoid having so many eggs in the Israeli basket in the future, the Syndicate is not neglecting Tel Aviv. Diamdel, De Beers' rough-diamond dealing affiliate specializing in supplying goods to small firms, has an active office there. And Lens Diamonds, the Belgian cleaving and sawing firm that is also under the De Beers wing, has opened a Tel Aviv cleaving subsidiary.

The challenge to Israel in the next decade will probably come on two fronts: from South Africa, where the government is requiring De Beers to give more diamonds at a special 10 percent discount to help the developing cutting industry among the country's colored population; and, above all from Russia. "The Russians always surprise us," said Mordehai Noam of Orah Diamonds. "They make very nice stones, and they are selling melees and small brilliants at a low price, sometimes twenty percent below the market. We'll face real competition from them."

The resilience to meet that threat is not lacking. "We have a better understanding of melees and smalls, and a good customer relationship," Noam went on. "Our customers are all close friends, almost like a family. What's more, although we have a reputation for melees, we have the knowledge for everything. We have to develop and learn to handle small stones, big stones, all makes. Melees are ABC stones; we have to offer A–Z goods, so that when the customer comes he finds everything he needs." His thoughts were shared by Moshe Schnitzer who echoed, "We have to become a bigger department store in the variety of goods we offer."

The expression "department store" foreshadows the future. "I'm afraid that over the next five years the business will concentrate on big manufacturers," said Orah's Noam. "It's very, very difficult today to keep small factories going because the rough goods are so expensive. And the Syndicate boxes are so mixed with so many items that it's too much for the small man. And that's not healthy. We need every year fresh new manufacturers, young people coming in."

The trend toward large manufacturers backed by substantial finance is also encouraged by the rapid growth of automation for diamond polishing. Israel has adopted the automatic polishers, developed by a De Beers subsidiary and known as Piermatics, more rapidly than any other cutting center. "The Americans and the Belgians found it difficult to run the machines, but we have patience, and now they are working well," said Mordehai Noam, leading the way through a maze of narrow streets behind the Diamond Exchange to his own factory. We went up a dark stairway toward a rising hum of machinery and came upon a whole floor banked with Piermatics. "I'll soon have two hundred of them," said Noam, "and one worker can look after eight or twelve of them." The machines can polish forty-eight of the fifty-eight facets of a brilliant-cut diamond. Moreover, experience has shown that they are best suited to the medium-sized stones that are Israel's specialty. The concept is not unlike a record player; the diamond is fixed in a small pot on the end of an arm projecting over the rotating cutting disk called the scaife and is then lowered onto it at a carefully calculated angle and pressure, just as the needle drops onto the turntable to play a record. The only difference is that each Piermatic has four arms, so that four stones are cut at a time. The significance of those bobbing heads is that they may help Israel, which has relatively high labor costs compared to India or South Africa or Russia, to keep its competitive edge. "Now that we are semi-automatic, we have only four workers in our 'chain' instead of six," said Noam. "The time saving is enormous." Another manufacturer, who has also installed the Piermatics, summed up, "This is a revolution."

Automation may help, but ultimately the future of Israel's diamond industry will depend on the resourcefulness of a younger generation of *diamantaires* at Ramat Gan. The first generation that built the industry against all odds, just as they built a country, is getting old. "We were idealists," said Moshe Schnitzer, "and for me it was a way of doing my part for my small country; we had great national pride in being successful. And maybe that is the hope of the future. There's still a lot of spirit in this country. We'd love to remain number one."

Bombay: Cutting the Uncuttable

Memories of the splendid diamonds that the Parisian jeweler Jean Baptista Tavernier brought back from India three centuries ago, and of the great collections acquired by such princes as the Nizam of Hyderabad, the Nawab of Dacca and the Maharajah of Jaipur (who guarded his baubles with cobras) in the days of the British Raj, seem curiously out of place in modern Bombay. For the diamonds on which India has built a new reputation in the last decade would never warrant a maharajah's glance. The first packet of rough stones that I saw in a small office near the Javeri Bazaar were just dark brown specks nestling on the blue-white paper, about the size and color of flower seeds for my garden. "If these goods were not about to be polished, they would not be worth a dollar a carat," said S. G. Javeri, whose family has been in the diamond trade in Bombay for generations. "But if I'm lucky I'll get eighty to a hundred dollars a carat when they're done. We've made gems out of semigems or industrials. It's an explosion; we can do fifty, even a hundred stones per carat." He went over to a small safe and took out a delicate pendant with three stars each set with seven tiny diamonds, some of them almost too small to enjoy with the naked eye. "We've created jewelry out of goods that could not be sold as gems before," he went on proudly. "Today not a single country can rival us in polishing small diamonds."

Such enterprise made India a dominant new force in the world of diamonds in the 1970s. She overhauled both Antwerp and Tel Aviv in the weight (but not value) of diamonds imported by her manufacturers. Sixty percent of all diamonds are now cut and polished in India, and the resulting finished goods were actually the country's top export earner in 1979, grossing nearly $900 million.

The formula for such success is simple—low labor costs. A diamond cutter in an Indian village is lucky to earn $50 a month, while his fellow in Israel would earn $750 and in Antwerp or New York $1,000. India's progress has been founded on the tapping of an enormous pool of cheap labor. The scale of the operation dwarfs her main rivals; Antwerp and Tel Aviv have employed around 15,000 cutters each in prosperous times and 10,000 in leaner years. India, on the other hand, has an estimated 350,000 at work in the busiest periods, with 250,000–275,000 regularly employed.

This multitude is scattered through two hundred towns and villages. The main concentrations are in the cities of Surat and Bhavnagar and the surrounding villages in the province of Gujerat, but you can find cutters in Bombay and the states of Kerala, Uttar Pradesh and Madhya Pradesh. The majority are peasants with little education, who can earn twice as much cutting and polishing diamonds as they would make in the fields or in most other jobs in towns. There are no factories; this is the ultimate cottage industry. Families work from their own homes in small cooperative units. No one seems quite sure how many units exist, but probably there are between thirty and forty thousand. Mechanization is almost unknown. The cutter's wheel in most rural areas, where electricity does not reach, is turned by someone, often a child, pulling a rope. Overheads are nonexistent, as are job and social security. Pay is on results. "A man working ten to twelve hours can manage one or two stones a day," said a Bombay dealer, "and he gets a dollar fifty per stone."

That is the key to India's role; a new dimension has been added to diamond cutting. "Look at these goods, it's a very different kind of rough," said Arun Mehta of B. N. Arunkumar, one of the main Bombay dealers. "It is all small pieces and full of knots; give it to someone in Antwerp or Tel Aviv, and they wouldn't know what to do. And with only ten thousand workers, how many stones can you polish, anyway? They don't have the time, and they couldn't afford it. With three hundred thousand workers, we can."

Although the cutters are legion, the dealers in Bombay, who combine the roles of importer, manufacturer and exporter much more than in other production centers, are few. The real power is in the hands of a coterie of about eight families who migrated originally from the little towns of Palanpur and Patan in Gujerat state almost a century ago. "That was the genesis of the business here," said Mahendra Mehta, the quiet, courteous former chairman of the Gem and Jewelry Export Promotion Council. "These pioneers started in the Javeri Bazaar as jewelers in emeralds and rubies, or as pearl dealers, establishing links with Basra to obtain pearls from the Gulf. Then in 1922 cultured pearls came in, destroying the confidence of the buyers here. So three or four of the families from Palanpur and Patan went into diamonds and moved to Antwerp or Amsterdam. One of them was my father, who settled in Antwerp, where I was born. These families covered the whole East, selling to Burma, Hong Kong, Malaysia and Shanghai."

The business in prewar days was in goods polished in Europe, for the Indian cutting industry was virtually dormant. An initial link with Antwerp, however, had been forged. Once the Belgian cutting center got back to work after the Second World War, the relationship was strengthened. Besides buying polished goods in Antwerp for the Indian market, three of the families in the jewelry fraternity, led by H. B. Shah, decided to purchase rough as well and establish their own workshops in India. A nucleus of families survived in Benares, with generations of experience in cutting and polishing local diamond production. A couple of these families had also moved to Surat, a town that was the traditional center of the sari industry, where they had made a living remaking old diamonds into more fashionable cuts. "There were large amounts of old diamonds in the market, and it soon became a good industry in Surat, employing five hundred to eight hundred people," Mahendra Mehta recalled. "They trained diamond cutters from other communities. When I came back here from Antwerp in 1952, there were already nearly four thousand cutters."

The hurdle was not lack of cutting talent, but lack of rough. The Indian government, plagued for years after independence with a desperate shortage of foreign exchange, constantly balked at granting official import quotas; basic raw materials and machinery rightly got priority over luxury goods. The dealers in the Javeri Bazaar were not dismayed; they simply arranged for the rough goods to be smuggled in from Antwerp, just as their fellow gold dealers were establishing excellent links with Beirut, Kuwait and Dubai for regular "black" gold supplies. As a *diamantaire* in the Bazaar remarked with a smile, "We are good business people; we know how to manipulate. Black business was soon thriving."

The smuggling in those early days was one way; just rough coming in to be cut and polished for local sales. The Suez crisis of 1956, however, opened up fresh horizons. "We suddenly thought that if Israel's production was going to be disrupted by war, why don't we sell abroad?" said Mahendra Mehta. Soon some dealers started smuggling polished back to Antwerp through Nepal, Colombo, and other devious routes.

The two-way traffic cemented the relationship with Antwerp. Several Bombay jewelers dispatched their sons to settle there, both to facilitate the purchase of rough and to sell the polished goods when they were spirited back. As the business gradually became more legitimate, virtual Indian dynasties were established in the Belgian cutting center.

The successful grafting of an Indian community onto the tightly knit Jewish haven in Antwerp was fundamental in

India's swift rise in the international diamond business. A realistic working partnership was forged, not just because both had natural trading flair, but through mutual respect for each other's strong family and religious traditions. "The maintenance of our religion and culture were qualities which brought us close," said Mahendra Mehta who was born in Antwerp. "I know Indian families—jewelers—who have settled in Europe for thirty or forty years without their values or their traditions being fragmented."

The alliance offered advantages far beyond access to the best diamond marketplace. The prime asset was finance. The inevitable delay of three to four months between a dealer buying his rough and being able to sell the finished polished goods means that bridging loans are imperative. Such financing, especially while much of the business was "black," was initially unobtainable in Bombay. But once the Indian dealers found their feet in Antwerp, the Belgian banks specializing in diamond finance came to their aid. Armed with that backing, the Indian dealers in Antwerp were eventually able to win sights at the Diamond Trading Company in London, thus gaining direct access to rough goods for onward consignment to India's blossoming cutting industry.

The real difficulty, however, was to persuade the Indian government that, by permitting the regular import of rough diamonds either via Antwerp or from London, there was much to be gained by the foreign exchange earned when the polished goods were exported. "It took us nearly fifteen years to convince the government that if we imported rough we'd make an added value of thirty percent on exports," said S. G. Javeri of London Star, one of India's foremost dealers in rough. The man who was finally convinced was a minister of commerce named Manubhai Shah. But his initial concept was to seek out original sources of rough. He assigned a buyer to go to Ghana on behalf of the Indian government to bid at the diamond auctions there. By all accounts, it was a successful foray. "He was a shrewd businessman," Javeri remembered, "and by every kind of trickery available to him, he succeeded in offering a tender of four hundred thousand pounds for two hundred thousand carats. He pressured people; he did every damn thing. The Diamond Trading Company was taken aback at someone from India coming to buy, especially in Ghana, goods which at that stage were fifty percent industrial, twenty-five percent good gem and twenty-five percent doubtful gem, and always below half a carat and on the brown side. Why did we want such stuff?"

The DTC's response was to dispatch a team to Bombay and Surat to find out what was going on. And one of the leading syndicate brokers, Bonas, also began cultivating the Bombay dealers. "Bonas did a lot of spadework here in the 1960s," said a dealer, "and it really paid off. Today more than half the sightholders here are their clients." Bonas, in fact, nurtured the Bombay market, just as Hennig, their main rival, had aided Tel Aviv. The initial outcome was that eight Bombay firms were granted sights in 1964. Their boxes were usually inexpensive; the minimum cost then was only ten thousand dollars a sight. And the boxes were filled with small, poor-quality goods, usually less than 0.2 carats, in which Antwerp and Tel Aviv had little interest. But that was the key to profitability. Since no one else wanted the stones, they came cheap. "Everyone in Antwerp and Tel Aviv wants the best five or six million carats of gem production, and then the DTC has the whip hand," said S. G. Javeri. "But here we can do another ten million or even twenty million carats that fall between gem and industrial. We buy most of our rough at between five dollars and fifteen dollars a carat and sell polished for eighty to two hundred dollars."

This margin was vital. As the Indians pioneered the cutting of poor-quality rough, they found that the wastage was inevitably high. Even on fine stones, the loss in cutting and polishing is usually more than half; that is to say, one hundred carats of rough yields, at best, forty-five to fifty carats of polished. On the inferior rough that India tackled, it was usually possible to salvage only twenty-five to thirty carats in every one hundred, producing what the trade calls small brilliants and eight-cuts.

The other ace in the Bombay dealers' sleeve was that manufacturing could expand through their cottage industry with virtually no capital expenditure on their part. It was just a matter of adding more family or village cooperatives to a widening web. "You can start with five trained people, and they will have taught a hundred in less than a year," explained one entrepreneur. "Usually the units of cutters are of ten to fifteen persons, and never more than twenty, because then you are liable under the Factory Act. Most of it is self-employed people in their own homes." The majority are also young. Keen eyesight and dexterity are essential in working on such tiny stones, and anyway, the industry is so new that few have yet grown old. "The average age of our cutters is seventeen, compared with fifty in Israel and nearly sixty-five in Antwerp," explained Kantilal Chhotalal, the Bombay agent for Bonas, the London brokers. And they remain primarily in the town of Surat or in the countryside of Gujerat. "We tried to develop cutting in Bombay," Kantilal went on, "but the costs of wages and real estate here are nearly thirty percent higher. So they stay out in the cottages, and this keeps us competitive."

The incoming rough is initially sorted in Bombay and then dispersed to the cutters through an army of middlemen. "We have around four hundred agents working for us in Bombay and Gujerat," said M. N. Wagle, the manager at B. Vijaykumar, the premier DTC sightholders in India. "They collect the rough from us and distribute it to around thirty thousand cutters who work for our group. They bring the polished back, and then we pay them the making charges." Trust in the agent is essential. "We usually start him on a small amount," Wagle explained, "and he returns in two or three days with the work. If that's satisfactory, we give him more."

Although the DTC in London first granted sights to Bombay dealers in 1964, the initial expansion, on the surface, was very slow. Six years later there were still only twelve Indian sightholders, and they took up a mere $260,000 in rough. That was deceptive. The link with Antwerp was strong, and many more diamonds came that way, both officially and unofficially. There was a 5 percent import duty on the official rough until 1978, and many dealers avoided it if they could. But the real key was the relationship of the rupee to the dollar. Throughout the late 1960s and early 1970s, the official rupee-dollar exchange rate was around 7.5 rupees to $1. The black market rate—the *hawala* rate, as the Indians call it—was often as high as eleven or twelve to one. The margin often depended on the amount of gold being smuggled into India, which had to be paid for in "black" dollars; when gold demand was strong, as it was from 1968 through 1971, the margin was wide. Diamond dealers in those days found it equally profitable to do much of their business unofficially to be sure of securing the high rate for the dollar when their production was sold overseas. The remarkable fact is that by 1973, when gold prices had shot up and smuggling of the metal into India virtually ceased, the *hawala* rate narrowed, and much more diamond trade "surfaced." Forty-four Bombay sightholders spent $37.2 million at DTC sights in 1973, well over one hundred times more than three years earlier.

The Indian banks, too, were finally coming up with the cash to tide them over. Five banks, led by the Bank of India, the Bank of Baroda and Algemene Bank Nederland, began to underwrite the Bombay boxes at each sight and grant credit to the manufacturers for the three or four months until they could sell the finished goods. The level of expertise in the banks certainly did not match that of Antwerp, and hassles over paperwork for import-export licenses meant that the DTC sometimes had to extend its strict two-week deadline for payment in cash after a sight, but the banks were eventually able to stump up as much as $20 million a sight. Indeed, when the speculative boom of 1977–78 got underway, the fifty-six Bombay sightholders were able to pitch in with $148 million at DTC sights. And whereas a decade earlier their boxes had often cost only $10,000 each, the minimum order that could be placed at a sight had risen to $150,000. The major sightholders, like B. Vijaykumar, were regularly buying well over $1 million in rough per sight. Imports rocketed; India acquired 16.8 million carats of rough in 1977 and 19.3 million carats the following year, of which around half came direct from the DTC in London to the Bombay sightholders, and the balance from Antwerp, either through the Indian sightholders there or by open-market purchases. The volume is astonishing set against world gem production, which is supposed to be only just over 10 million carats annually; it means that in each of those years India imported substantially more than the estimated world output of gems. Now Israel, as noted above, was also importing more than all gem production during the identical period. Diamonds do not grow on trees. Where was this prodigious amount coming from? In part the answer is easy. "We ate up the DTC's stockpile," said a Bombay dealer. No doubt the hoarding in the cutting centers, apparently of at least three times world output, did deplete the De Beers inventory. But the real lesson of Bombay's rapid rise in the last decade is that goods once dismissed as industrials ought now to be classified as gems. When De Beers says that world output is around 50 million carats a year, of which

10 million is graded gem and 40 million industrial, there has to be a no-man's-land in between that is difficult to label precisely. What India has done is stake out that territory; perhaps another 5 or even 10 million carats of industrial should actually be labeled as her domain. The sheer scale of imported rough in the late seventies is then easier to comprehend.

In any event, India was adding to its traditional reputation as a sponge for precious metals by soaking up liberal quantities of diamonds, too. As in Israel, imports surged well ahead of exports of polished goods, leading to inevitable accusations of hoarding by dealers. In the two years, 1977 and 1978, India imported 36 million carats of rough and exported only 7 million carats of polished; yet those imports should have yielded 12 million carats of polished diamonds, indicating stockpiling in Bombay of 5 million carats.

Clearly, Bombay dealers got carried away. Like the Israelis, they bought almost any parcel going in the hope that something cuttable might turn up and justify the whole cost. One dealer compared the boom to preparing a lettuce. "You cut it up and wash the best leaves, throwing the rest away," he said, "but if some unexpected visitors then arrive, you try to salvage the discarded leaves and mix them in the salad, too." The trouble was that too many diamonds were indigestible. The cutting industry reached its zenith in 1978; then, as exporters could not off-load their inventories, employment fell by nearly 100,000 over the next two years. The stockpiling, incidentally, did not indicate that the Indian public at large was buying up diamonds. There is some diamond investment in India, usually to hide "black" money not declared to the taxman, but these buyers prefer larger goods that are smuggled in already polished from Europe or New York.

The surcharges at sights that were the De Beers response to the speculative boom provoked a sharp response from the Bombay dealers. Displaying remarkable solidarity, they simply refused to play ball with the Central Selling Organization. All fifty-six sight-holders declined en masse to accept their surcharged boxes at the May sight in 1978. Such a revolt against the DTC by an entire block of its customers was without precedent. And it drew quiet admiration elsewhere. "When it comes to the crunch, the Indians are a closely knit group," a leading New York buyer of rough diamonds remarked shortly afterwards. "They stood up for their rights and made a collective decision. You'd never see a bunch of Antwerp diamond dealers agreeing something had to be done."

The truth is that Bombay's dealers are less overawed by the Central Selling Organization than anyone else. They see the Syndicate as a useful source of supply but are quite happy to buy up any goods available outside—even from the Russians. They want to run their own show and are forever seeing plots, real or imagined, by De Beers to outwit them. The game of cat and mouse is endless. "They have tried to control us, but they never have the upper hand," said a Bombay sightholder. "They would like to have an office here, but that has never been allowed."

Conspiracy theories aside, De Beers would certainly have liked a foothold in India for their subsidiary Diamdel, which specializes in supplying rough to small manufacturers who do not rate sights. Diamdel already operates successfully in Belgium, Israel and Switzerland; India would be the obvious advance. The Indian government, however, quite apart from the *diamantaires*, has never welcomed multinationals, especially those with strong South African connections, setting up their own shop. The authorities always prefer to try to run any game like that themselves—an operation the bureaucracy calls "canalization." Canalization in diamonds is tricky; there is already one well-known canal called the Diamond Trading Company, and any Indian government outfit in search of its own source of rough would not get far without them. Eventually a compromise was reached. The Hindustan Diamond Company was established in 1979 as a "canal" to supply rough to Indian manufacturers not rating sights; the Indian government took a 50 percent share, local investors put up 20 percent, while the remaining 30 percent was held by the Bank of Bermuda (an organization that is described as a "consultant" to the Diamond Trading Company). In essence, the Indian government and the Diamond Trading Company are in partnership. Both sides seem content. "The Hindustan Diamond Company is another trump card in India's game," observed the Antwerp magazine *Diamant*, "and for De Beers (is) a foothold in one of the world's great centers of the diamond industry."

"Our job is to supply rough to the smaller people who do not have direct access to the DTC, serving them off the shelf as they need it," explained an HDC official. "We get our rough at sights along with everyone else, but we have an edge over some of the sightholders, because we get more than they do." The implication, of course, is that the DTC carefully tailors the Hindustan Diamond Company's box to meet its advance requirements precisely, while regular sightholders, who also specify their needs beforehand, may not find them matched so exactly. The HDC certainly got plenty of diamonds: at early sights in 1980 it was receiving around $5 million worth at every sight, 25 percent of all rough allocated for Bombay's sixty-one sightholders.

The launching of HDC was also designed to reduce Bombay's dependence on supplies from Antwerp, where the resident Indian sightholders had long forwarded the requirements of small Bombay manufacturers. An attempt was actually made to phase out sights in Antwerp for the Indian dealers. The mistake was to neglect the financing. The Hindustan Diamond Company demanded cash on the nail, which was exactly what the small manufacturers lacked. Their parcels from the Indians in Antwerp, on the other hand, had always benefited from 90–120 days' credit from the Belgian banks. Suddenly that cushion was removed, and the Indian banks, already overstretched on financing to local sightholders, could not always meet the gap. In fact the HDC, at least in its early days, proved more useful to the large sightholders with better credit rating than anyone else. They could simply go to the HDC in Bombay to supplement their DTC boxes. "We are supposed to help small manufacturers," said the HDC man, "but we have to sell to anyone who has a license to trade in diamonds. We can't pick and choose."

The Antwerp-Bombay axis is not likely to be seriously undermined by this diversion. The Indians are too well embedded in the Antwerp scene, with no less than sixty-five firms in residence. And one of the finest new diamond-cutting factories to be established in the Kempen outside Antwerp was built by Mefatlal Metha, who first went to Antwerp from Bombay in 1958 to found the import-export firm Jayam. Two decades later, Jayam has become not only one of the biggest houses in Antwerp for reexporting Indian polished goods to the United States and Japan, but also a major manufacturer. Its factory in the Kempen handles large goods that are beyond the skills and equipment of Indian cutters. And Mefatlal Metha has virtually founded a Belgo-Indian dynasty, with his two eldest sons working with

him in Antwerp and his two youngest overseeing their asso-
ciate firm, Samir Diamonds, in Bombay.

The collaboration also remains essential because Bombay still
lacks its own exchange. The absence of a proper trading forum
for the 1,700 Indian exporters distinguishes Bombay from Antwerp, Tel Aviv, New York and even such cities as London,
Paris, Milan and Vienna. Of course, this does not prevent plenty
of buyers from New York—who are Bombay's best direct customers—Hong Kong, Singapore and other regional markets coming to Bombay, but they have to make the rounds of widely
scattered offices. There is nothing to match Israel's great diamond
center at Ramat Gan where everyone congregates, or the diamond
clubs along Pelikaanstraat in Antwerp where the foreigner can
speedily let everyone know he is in town. Many Bombay dealers
are confident that if they had an exchange building with banks,
a post office and other facilities under one roof, they could make
the step up from a notable production center to the marketplace
of the East. Yet they also hesitate for fear that the right climate
does not prevail. India's frustrating bureaucracy, exchange controls and high taxes make it impossible to compete with the freewheeling atmosphere of Antwerp, whose advantages are fully
utilized by Bombay traders. "I use Antwerp for all my black,"
admitted a DTC sightholder. "There's too much tax here, so I
keep my stock and capital there." Local confidence is not encouraged by a law that places the onus on anyone found with
diamonds (or gold and watches) to prove how they came by
them. "The diamond is a sensitive item in India, it's such a shelter
for black money," said a broker. "If I have a diamond stock and
I'm raided, I have to prove how I acquired it—and it's all confiscated until I can. So most people do not want to keep stock
here; as soon as manufacture is finished they send the goods to
Antwerp. They need a big stock for their clientele, but they hold
it in Belgium." Proposals for a Bombay bourse conjure up visions
of catastrophe while such a law remains. "Imagine five hundred
dealers all in one building with some black stock," said another
sightholder. "The police would surround the building, and that
would be that." He clapped his hands with an air of finality.

The bourse, anyway, is not an immediate prospect. What con-
cerns the Bombay dealers currently is how long India can retain
its unique preserve as a cheap cutting center. When a De Beers

team visited Sri Lanka to look into cutting possibilities there, the Bombay dealers were aghast. "The moment Sri Lanka or China or South Korea do what we do, we are lost," said Mahendra Mehta. But that counsel of despair may be premature. Cheap labor elsewhere may be India's Achilles heel, but its defense could prove to be the special relationship with Antwerp. That combined operation will take some beating.

New York: Gateway to Affluence

The popular image of New York's diamond market housed on the single block of West Forty-seventh Street, between Fifth Avenue and the Avenue of the Americas, is of an exciting and sometimes dangerous place. A host of emporiums christened Mr. Diamond, the Diamond Horseshoe, Futurama Diamond Center or the Diamond Center of America tempts the casual window-shopper with baubles, bangles and beads. Scurrying from doorway to doorway, amidst the daytime clutter of hot-dog stands and orange-juice vendors, are the bearded figures of the Hasidic Jews, somberly clad in black hats and black coats. They arrive in their own special buses from Brooklyn shortly before nine each morning to spend the day swapping notes about diamond prices at the curbside before hurrying off to clinch the next deal. Policemen prowl the street, and closed-circuit television keeps a watchful eye in every store, lobby and elevator. No one readily forgets that three of the street's diamond dealers have been abducted and murdered in recent years.

Yet this facade really belies what is going on in a warren of offices above. "The visitor doesn't see mainstream diamond business, although the retailers down there naturally try to create the illusion that he does," said a young dealer, sitting back safely ensconced behind the double doors of his office fifteen floors up. "And do you really imagine," he went on, "that the Hasidim, who make up less than a third of the people working in the street anyway, are actually trading diamonds in the open? They are visible only because they are the brokers, going from office to office. The mainstream are the dealers, the cutters, the polishers, the wholesalers and the manufacturing jewelers up here, whom no one ever sees."

The surprising thing to anyone more familiar with the European jewelry scene is just how much of America's diamond (and other gem) business is gathered together around West Forty-seventh Street and spilling a short way around the corner up Fifth Avenue. Within a few hundred yards one can meet several of the Diamond Trading Company's biggest sight-holders, some of the world's most talented cutters and sophisticated polishers, and many of America's best manufacturing jewelers. West Forty-seventh Street is not just a diamond trading forum, but a manufacturing center in its own right; it rivals not only Antwerp or Tel Aviv, but provincial towns like Valenza, Po in Italy and Ida-Oberstein in West Germany, traditional homes of gem craftsmen for generations.

The prime reason for New York's importance obviously is as the main threshhold to the world's largest and most affluent market for diamonds. "The beauty of it is that there are no customs men from here to Hawaii," said a New York dealer. "That gives us direct access to over two hundred million people." To satisfy them, America imports around $1.5 billion of diamonds annually, twice as much as her nearest rival Japan, and almost five times more than West Germany. New York is firmly astride that flow. Los Angeles is making a belated challenge to become a diamond distribution market but is not yet in the same league. Out of sixty-four American "sight-holders" at the Diamond Trading Company in London, more than fifty are based in New York. And the major cutting centers of Antwerp, Tel Aviv and Bombay all lean on New York as their best customer for polished goods. So do the Russians, although they have so far not opened an office there, preferring to supply New York either directly out of Moscow, through such specialist importers as S. Toepfer Inc., or via European wholesalers in Antwerp. The Russians' reluctance to set up shop on West Forty-seventh Street has much to do with the fact that their polished goods have been subject to a 10 percent import duty, against 5 percent on goods from Belgium and Israel and 3 percent on those from India; consequently some dealers find it more convenient to buy their Russian diamonds overseas and try a little astute mixing with Belgian or Israeli goods to reduce the overall duty.*

* From January 1981, duty on Belgian, Israeli and Indian goods was eliminated, but the 10 percent on Russian remains.

New York's dependence on polished goods from abroad must not overshadow its own strength as a major cutting center specializing in the bigger and more speculative stones. Aside from scores of small cutting workshops gathered around West Forty-seventh Street, several leading firms, including Harry Winston Inc. and Lazare Kaplan & Sons Inc., have established their own factories in Puerto Rico. The quality of cutting both there and in New York itself is a matter of considerable pride. "Our cutters are technically the best in the world," declared William Goldberg, the big, genial president of the Diamond Dealers' Club on West Forty-seventh Street. "You ask in Antwerp or Tel Aviv or South Africa, and they'll tell you that for fine goods there's special aptitude and skill here." And to prove his point, Goldberg proudly led the way into his own workshop, where his chief cutter, Herb Lieberman, was engrossed in the delicate task of transforming a 169-carat rough stone into three magnificent polished diamonds, a 71-carat pear-shaped and two marquises. "I was offered this stone at a sight in London two months ago, and it was my decision to say 'yes or no' on the spot," said Goldberg, putting down his cigar and taking out his loupe to study one of the emerging marquises that Lieberman handed him. He examined it for a moment. "Good, good," he mused happily, "the *gletz* is almost out." Lieberman said he was now trying to block out whether he could finish the stone for a ten carat, which might be rather flat, or a nine carat. "Take a chance on a flattish belly for a ten carat," replied Goldberg after further study. And he turned back towards his office. "I'm paying him a five-thousand-dollar bonus to cut that stone," he said as we went down the corridor. "It's a special occasion."

Special stones require superrich buyers. New York's reputation as the cutting center for fine diamonds lures them from all over the world. "The bulk of my business is with foreigners," said William Goldberg. "If we didn't have traffic with the Middle East, the Far East and Europe, we couldn't stay in business. Five or six other firms are in the same position." And a dealer in a neighboring office added, "The finest stones, like a D Flawless, are often cheaper here than in Europe just because we are a major cutting center."

This reputation, first won almost half a century ago by

Lazare Kaplan who cut the great Jonker diamond for Harry Winston during the 1930s, has been enhanced since World War II. Essentially, the New York market is a postwar phenomenon, created by the many Jews who fled Amsterdam, Antwerp and Germany to escape the Nazis, or somehow survived and came to America in the late forties to rebuild shattered lives. Before that, the market had been very much an informal curbside affair at the other end of Manhattan on the corner of Nassau and Fulton Streets, squeezed between the financial district and the fish market. The first office of the Diamond Dealers' Club, formed in 1931, was an unpretentious room in a nearby building. The Club moved to West Forty-seventh Street a decade later, but much of the trading still took place in the street itself. "We used to buy and sell on the curb," recalled William Goldberg. "The trick was to straddle it, with one foot on the sidewalk, which was concrete, and one foot on the road, which was macadam. You held the goods over the road, because if you dropped a diamond on the concrete sidewalk it might chip." Security put an end to all that. It is only the Hasidim, swapping trade gossip rather than diamonds on the sidewalk, who are a reminder of the way things were.

The focal point in the ensuing years became the Diamond Dealers' Club, a crowded, rowdy emporium on the ninth floor of Thirty West Forty-seventh Street, where some 1,800 dealers, brokers, cutters and polished wholesalers do business. Entry is strictly for members only, and there is a long waiting list. (The thwarted can join the Diamond Trade Association of America across the street, but it lacks the same *cachet*.) Primarily it is a male preserve, although one woman, Ethel Blitz, who is descended from a family of dealers, has been admitted, as have the widows of twelve former members. The main business is with polished diamonds, although some transactions in rough are always going forward.

Those who penetrate the guards and two sets of electronic doors may be excused for thinking they have entered bedlam. Shouted conversations in English, Yiddish, Hebrew, French, Flemish and German compete with a loudspeaker that constantly summons the participants in this rumpus to the telephone. The long green tables are packed with a cosmopolitan

crowd. Two Indians watch patiently as a Hasidic broker un-
wraps a small parcel and picks through the stones; beside them
an Antwerp wholesaler is arguing price with a potential client
just in from Los Angeles, and nearby the agent for a South
African cutting firm is carefully wrapping up his "parcels"
again before taking them across to an enclosure to be weighed
on electronic scales and sealed by club employees. When his
table becomes vacant, there is a scramble for places closest to
the north-facing windows. At the far end of the dealing room
is a snack bar; all food must be eaten there, as a precaution
against diamonds getting embedded accidentally (or even in-
tentionally) in a doughnut.

Each transaction is concluded, as at the other fifteen diamond
clubs around the world, with the traditional handshake and
murmured *mazel und broche*—"luck and blessing." That agreement is binding. Any member who goes back on it is likely
to find himself blackballed, not only in New York but at all
the clubs. And disagreements are sternly settled by an arbitration panel that can fine or expel. One member who mislaid a
$50,000 stone and wrongly accused a man to whom he had
shown it in the club of not returning it was ordered to make a
substantial contribution to charity.

The ceaseless round of activity suggests that all diamond
trading takes place there. In reality, more transactions are going
forward in the privacy of offices up and down the street. "Important buyers go from office to office, not to the Club," explained President William Goldberg. "In the main, the Club is
for the small man, who will sit there and look for business. But
it is more useful for the foreign buyer who doesn't have an
office of his own. It's the check-in point for him, the place to
be seen and to make contact. And then the word goes out, 'So-
and-So is in town, call him at the Club.' "

"This is a real difference between New York and Tel Aviv,"
added Joseph Schlussel, a cheerful little man who is a well-
known wholesaler of polished diamonds. Schlussel's own
Diamond Registry is a case in point. He got tired of rushing
around the Club and up and down West Forty-seventh Street
in search of stones. So he convinced a number of independent
cutters in New York, Antwerp and Tel Aviv to list their inventory with him, thus building up a centralized index of a

whole spectrum of polished stones. Initially they were on filing cards, but that soon got so complex that Schlussel transferred the inventory to a computer. "I've got between six and seven thousand stones listed now," he said, squeezing through the clutter of his tiny office to get to the terminal. "Let's say I get a request for a round-shaped diamond, weighing between one and two carats and costing between fifteen and forty thousand dollars. All I do is ask 'Harry,' my computer." He typed out instructions on the keyboard. The computer thought for a couple of minutes and then printed out a list of nineteen diamonds that filled the bill. "We are trying to match the buyer to the stone he wants as quickly as possible," said Schlussel. This centralized service has eliminated many time-consuming forays at the Diamond Dealers' Club. "A cutter in my building came in looking for certain sizes of cape stones," recalled Schlussel. "We fed the request into the computer and found him just what he wanted. The owner turned out to be another cutter on the same floor of the building. They've seen each other every day for fifteen years, but neither knew the other's specialty."

Not that the computer can entirely eliminate old-fashioned legwork. Presently an aged Hasidic broker with a long white beard that reached over his chest came into Schlussel's office. From beneath his black coat he pulled out a slim leather pouch attached by a chain to his wrist. Unzipping it, he took out a small parcel and unwrapped it to reveal an exquisite canary-yellow diamond nestling in the blue-white folds of the paper. "It's a five-carat stone worth thirty-five thousand dollars," said Schlussel. "I gave it to him to show around, but he hasn't had any luck. It's tough to be a broker, you know. He's carried that stone around all day and got nothing for it; even if he'd sold it he would have earned only three hundred and fifty dollars, because the Club rules say commission is one percent. For a broker it's all hard legwork. He is the matchmaker, he has to plead and beg—he's got to talk both sides into bending. But what happens? He does a hundred thousand dollars of business and gets a thousand dollars for himself."

Such personal matchmaking will obviously continue, especially for larger stones and what the trade calls fancy colors, like the canary-yellow stone the old broker had been circulating. Yet the trend in New York is inevitably to bypass the wheeling and dealing in the Club.

The streamlining is most evident with the major firms, especially the elite sightholders at the Diamond Trading Company in London. "You don't see DTC clients running around the street," said a leading dealer. An organization like Harry Winston, Inc., one of the biggest buyers in the DTC's history and in action as a buyer outside the Syndicate everywhere from Liberia to Venezuela, is an independent empire detached from the daily hurly-burly of the street. The Winston reputation as a purveyor of great diamonds for kings and millionaires often overshadows their large wholesale division in New York that has long been rated the foremost supplier of all types of polished diamonds to manufacturing jewelers, other wholesalers and even large retailers throughout the United States.* The structure is tightly tailored. "We eliminate a lot of steps," said Nick Axelrod, Winston's chief buyer of rough. "A stone at the Diamond Dealers' Club may go through fifteen or twenty hands before it gets to the clients. Not ours." The finest of Winston's rough is cut and polished in a small ten-bench workshop above their Fifth Avenue headquarters, while the run-of-the-mill stones go through Winston's own factories in Puerto Rico and Arizona (where a factory has been established on an Indian reservation), or to cutters on exclusive contract in Belgium, France and Israel. "I will only start with a factory if he works exclusively for us," explained Axelrod sternly. "We must have control, otherwise I lose track of what is happening to my production—it's all too easy to get someone else's diamonds returned. When you send rough to cutters, you have to know what to expect back. If you dispatch a hundred carats of rough, you know you ought to get around fifty back. But some will try playing one stone for Winston and one stone for me." After that rigorously monitored operation, the polished diamonds go immediately to a wide range of manufacturers, many of whom enjoy credit terms that are the envy of their rivals. "Winston has long been a very big factor," admitted a

* See Chapter 10 for an account of Winston's retail salon.

Los Angeles dealer admiringly. "He went out to win business, and he could offer long terms and such good availability that he got it. He's still number one in polished."

The challengers, however, abound. There is London Star Ltd., part of the multinational diamond-dealing complex built around Star Diamond in London. Beginning simply as a dealer in rough diamonds shortly after World War II, Star has blossomed. "Individually, each of the group's member firms aren't much bigger than I am," confided a rival New York dealer, "but put them together, and they're among the three largest diamond companies in the world." Indeed, the combined Star group is now rated as the biggest single customer of the Diamond Trading Company in London. Their DTC boxes are dispatched to factories in Antwerp and Tel Aviv or to their Bombay office for distribution to several thousand contract workers for cutting and polishing, before marketing through London Star in New York to American wholesalers, manufacturers and large retail chains.

Such streamlining, eliminating the tangle of small dealers and wholesalers who once thrived in the diamond clubs, is a constant goal. "It's all vertical integration these days," said Henri Ringer of the Antwerp Diamond Company, a major wholesaler of polished stones through their New York subsidiary. "Manufacturing jewelers want to get as close as possible to the source of the stones, and the source wants to get close to the consumer market. I daresay we'll have to get into cutting or manufacturing jewelry to stay in the vanguard. You're even getting American 'countryside' jewelers these days who like to say, 'I buy direct in Antwerp.' "

The way ahead has been paved, above all, by the Zale Corporation of Dallas, Texas. Zale buys its diamonds in the rough from the DTC in London, then has them cut, polished and made up into jewelry in Antwerp, Tel Aviv, New York and Puerto Rico for sale through over 1,800 of its own stores throughout the United States.

If Zale is the pattern of the future, as many believe, then New York's role as a market could suffer. An outfit that handles its own diamonds every step of the way does not necessarily have to be located in New York. Zale has always been at home in Texas. The place to watch, however, is Los Angeles.

It is already the home of the Gemological Institute of America's (GIA) extensive trade school. More significantly, the Goldfinger group of companies, a worldwide organization on a par with Harry Winston and Star Diamond, has set up its main American wholesaling of polished diamonds in Los Angeles. The precise motive behind that was to win into its fold a highly experienced diamond man named Glenn Nord, who worked there for the GIA and refused to go back east. But Nord, at ease in the California sunshine, finds he is getting plenty of company. "Los Angeles is a fast-developing market of its own," he said. "Indians and South Africans are coming here and opening offices. And a few cutters have drifted from New York—they find it's pleasant to get out of the hassle of the 'Big Apple.' If some manufacturers came out, too, Los Angeles could be an important place in diamonds in ten years. It's going to be an interesting time."

3

The Art of the Cutter:
Trimming the Fat

To the uneducated eye a rough diamond often looks like a piece of frosted broken glass. A few innocents, in fact, are regularly cheated around the diamond fields of Africa by strangers who generously offer them rough diamonds that turn out to be hewn from the bottom of a bottle. The initiated are aware that the correct test is to rub the "diamond" between finger and thumb; the real thing will feel slightly oily to the touch, the bottle bottom will not. The true skill of the diamond game is transforming that little frosted pebble into a gem that radiates fire, flashing back the colors of the spectrum. Colored stones like rubies, sapphires or emeralds are valued for the natural richness of their color; a diamond's beauty is the brilliance of the reflection from within. The art is to release that brilliance, as Michelangelo released his figures from the prison of their marble. Watching a fine diamond cutter at work on a large gem at once conjures up comparisons with a sculptor; both have to be able to visualize three-dimensional shapes in advance and then work with a degree of sensitivity and accuracy that allows little error. The tension at key moments is legendary. Joseph Asscher, the renowned Amsterdam cutter, had a doctor and two nurses in attendance when he successfully cleaved the great Cullinan diamond in 1908 and then collapsed with nervous exhaustion that put him in the hospital for three months.

"In the cutting of a diamond you reach a point of no return, the moment when you must commit yourself," said Bill Meyer, who has been practicing the art for the New York firm Lazare Kaplan International, Inc. for over thirty years. "Once you've made that commitment you cannot go back." Meyer, a big man with a bushy gray-white beard who describes himself as Kaplan's "troubleshooter," had recently finished work on a flawless pink diamond that had been christened Carlotta in memory of the late wife of the firm's founder, Lazare Kaplan. Meyer had started with a rough stone of eighty-one carats which he ultimately whittled down to a forty-three-carat, pear-shaped, brilliant-cut (meaning it has fifty-eight facets) polished gem. The Carlotta is a beauty, but Meyer shook his head wistfully. "We got a fifty-three percent yield; that's a hell of a loss of non-salvageable stuff," he said. "The Carlotta took me three months of hard physical work, and while I was doing it I often wondered if I was a sculptor or a construction manager." At least he had plenty of first-rate advice at his elbow, for the name Lazare Kaplan has been renowned in cutting circles for over half a century. The founder, who gave his name to the business, originally learned his trade in Antwerp at the turn of the century, then was marooned in New York in 1914 when World War I broke out while he was on a visit. He is in every sense the grand old man of diamond cutting. Remarkably, he is still around. Even as Meyer was talking about the Carlotta, Lazare Kaplan was taking his after-lunch nap in an adjoining room, a luxury a man of ninety-seven—who still comes in to work in the city from his New York dairy farm two or three days every week—should not be denied. At least Kaplan was supposed to be napping, but presently a wooden panel like a serving hatch from the next office was thrust aside, and he stood there, with a head loupe like the visor of a medieval knight pushed up on his brow. He was holding a partially cut diamond in one hand and an india ink pen in the other. He asked Bill Meyer to step over for a conference. The stone he had just been studying had some huge imperfections, and he had been mapping out how Meyer might be able to work them out.

Strategy is everything in cutting a diamond. As Meyer had just explained, "The less work that is done the better, because each step has its dangers. And if you're hasty, you end up with a lot of broken pieces." No one agrees more than his boss. For what really made Lazare Kaplan's name immortal in the diamond trade was his successful cutting of the 726-carat Jonker diamond, then the fourth largest ever found, back in 1936. He spent over a year just studying it and building thousands of plaster-of-paris models before he started work. Ultimately he confounded his critics, for most rival cutters who had been shown the rough stone had read all the signs wrong. Although Kaplan cut the Jonker more than forty years ago, his technique remains an object lesson in diamond cutting.

When the old man had finished debating the current problem with Meyer, he led the way down the corridor to the firm's boardroom. His eldest son, Leo Kaplan, president of the firm, joined us. Another son, George, also an expert at working diamonds, was away on a buying trip in Sierra Leone. Leo went over to a showcase in one corner of the room, removed two models of the Jonker diamond and set them on the table before his father; one was solid, the other came apart like a three-dimensional jigsaw. The Jonker itself, Lazare Kaplan recalled, had been found on alluvial diggings near Pretoria, in South Africa, and been bought for $350,000 by De Beers, who in turn sold it to Harry Winston, the New York dealer, for $700,000. It was the size of a hen's egg, with a frosted gray coating and a few skin flaws where little spots of iron oxide had been forced into tiny cracks by the action of the river. One surface of the stone was flat, and several European cutters to whom Winston initially showed it said confidently that the "grain" of the diamond ran parallel to this plane. Now, the cutter's first task is always to detect the direction of the grain. A diamond, like wood, must always be split, or cleaved, along that grain; otherwise it may shatter in a thousand fragments. In cleaving there is no middle ground, as one expert observed; it is either done perfectly, or the diamond is ruined. On the other hand, if it has to be sawn, which nowadays is often preferred, it must be cut *across* the grain. Winston was in no rush to have the Jonker worked on, and he brought it back to New York and showed it to Lazare Kaplan, who, a short while before, had cut for him another large diamond, the Pohl, which had been riddled with imperfections. Kaplan had contrived to cut the 286-carat rough stone into fifteen gems, all of which, save one, were flawless. Even the lone flawed stone sold for $50,000 (then a huge price), and Winston was suitably impressed. So he asked Kaplan to study the Jonker.

Thinking back, Lazare Kaplan took up the model of the stone; it filled his whole fist. He rubbed a gnarled thumb along the flat edge. "This gem was a freak of nature," he said slowly. "The original plan was to cleave it parallel to the flat side, but that was not the grain, and to have followed that plan would have ruined it. It took me a whole year to develop a plan of the stone. Eventually some microscopic cracks showed me where the grain was." He put his thumb into a tiny ledge on top of the model Jonker. "This small ledge opened my eyes to the mistake the European experts had made," he went on. "This showed the pattern of the grain, but there was a sixty-three-degree difference between it and the flat surface that was said to be the line of the grain." [16]

Satisfied that he knew the run of the grain, Kaplan then started calculating how to divide up the stone. To do this he also needed to be sure what it was like inside. The trick in cleaving or sawing is to try to make the divisions intersect with any internal flaws so that they can then be polished out. "The stone was frosted and you couldn't see a thing," Kaplan recalled. "So I put windows on the flat bottom to be able to look inside and plot what I could make of it." The cutter, in a sense, must project himself inside the stone and walk around to see how it may be divided, just as an architect with the overall concept of a building in mind then plots out the rooms. "You are a combination of an architect and an engineer," was how Kaplan put it. "An architect has to develop a building, and an engineer has to develop space." And then he added with a smile, "You need to be a chess player, too, to see the moves."

Projecting how to carve up the Jonker, Lazare Kaplan and his

[16] Lazare Kaplan wrote a detailed account of the cutting of the Jonker in *Natural History*, publication of the American Museum of Natural History, Vol. XXXVIII, 3 (New York, N.Y., 1936), pp. 227–236.

son Leo worked endlessly in the office and at home. "We sawed up thousands of plaster-of-paris models of the Jonker on the living room floor, to see what shapes would make the best yields and forms," Leo Kaplan chipped in, "and at mealtimes Dad would take pieces of bread and mold them into various shapes like diamonds and get us to cut them up, too."

Ultimately they agreed on a division that would turn the great Jonker into thirteen major stones. (The official story has always been that twelve gems were produced, but Kaplan confided that Winston felt it was unlucky to have thirteen offspring from one giant, so he sold a small five-carat stone from one corner separately and never let on it was from the Jonker.)

The outlines for cleaving and sawing were carefully marked on the stone in india ink, a technique that has become standard procedure in the diamond trade but was originally pioneered by Lazare Kaplan himself in Antwerp as a young man before he came to the United States. Digressing for a moment from his story of the Jonker, Kaplan explained that when he first started working on diamonds in the early 1900s, cutters had had little experience in handling irregularly shaped diamonds. They just took nice octohedrons and divided them into halves or quarters. The concept of carefully blocking out what could be done with uneven stones with flaws did not exist. "I devised the marking of stones in india ink to block out how they should be cleaved or polished," he said. "At first everyone made fun of me, and someone gave me a set of paints and an easel and suggested I become an artist." But his persistence earned him the last laugh. Go to any cutting factory around the world, and you will find the planners of rough goods sketching on stones in india ink to indicate how they must be manufactured. The lines, someone once observed, look like mule tracks on a miniature mountain.

With the Jonker duly inked up, the first and crucial step was to cleave the stone. Kaplan cut a V-shaped groove, or kerf, in the top of the diamond with a knifelike chip of another diamond, precisely in line with his assessment of the grain. Then he inserted a blunt-edged wedge and tapped the wedge lightly with a specially counterbalanced mallet. The Jonker split neatly apart as he had planned. He had divined the grain correctly.

His conception of the carve-up, however, meant that besides cleaving, which is the work of a moment (once you are ready), a great deal of sawing across the grain was also necessary. The technique of sawing a diamond is much more recent than the traditional skill of cleaving and today is often employed instead of cleaving, if the option exists, because it is less chancy. Too strong a tap of the cleaver's mallet or a wrongly placed wedge can shatter a stone. The saw eating slowly through the stone can be guided at every moment and disasters usually avoided. On a large stone, such as the Jonker, which had to be divided into many pieces, the initial task—the cleaving—was similar to cutting good strips along a filet of beef; the sawing, across the grain, was to break it down further into smaller segments for final shaping and polishing. On smaller run-of-the-mill diamonds only cleaving or sawing may be necessary; the planner judges which technique is most suited to each stone and labels it "cleavage" or "sawable." Stones that are already so well shaped, like many from the diamond desert of Namibia, that they do not need either process are called "makeables."

The diamond saw is a paper-thin disk of phospor bronze spinning at more than 4,000 revolutions per minute. Since only a diamond is hard enough to cut a diamond, the whirling edge of the blade is dressed with a paste made of diamond powder mixed with olive oil. The exact recipe varies from cutter to cutter, but usually one carat (0.2 grams) of fine diamond powder is blended with between ten and twenty drops of olive oil. The actual sawing is a slow process; it may take several hours for the blade to eat through a small diamond. The delay, however, is easily offset by the advantage of being able to cut up a large stone precisely with much less loss than if it ultimately has to be shaped by polishing.

Lazare Kaplan's division of the Jonker is a perfect example. Whereas the loss on the cutting of many diamonds is well over half, the score on the Jonker was much better. Lazare Kaplan actually saved 358 carats from the 726-carat rough. "Every stone came out exactly according to my plan," the old man recalled. "I had it all worked out on paper, and each was exactly the weight and dimension I calculated. I got seventeen percent more yield than Winston expected." And Leo Kaplan added proudly, "Dad was within a tenth of a millimeter on each stone."

With the division of the great stone successfully accomplished into twelve pieces (or thirteen, according to the count of the un-superstitious), the actual task of cutting began. The majority of diamonds are tailored, or "bruted," into rounds by trimming off the corners, but, depending on the form of the original, or of the pieces cleaved or sawn from it, there are several alternative shapes —the pear, the marquise (which is elliptical like a rugby football), the eight-sided emerald, the rectangular baguette, the square or the oval (pioneered by Lazare Kaplan in 1954), to name but a few. In the case of the Jonker, all the segments hewn from the original were fashioned into emerald cuts—a cut which accentuates the qualities of large flawless gems—except for one slim chunk that was ideal for a marquise. The largest emerald cut, which retained the name Jonker, was originally cut to 142.90 carats but was later trimmed down slightly to 125.65 carats before Winston sold it for a reputed $1 million to King Farouk of Egypt. According to Ian Balfour of Hennig, the London brokers, "In the opinion of many who have scanned the gem, it is perhaps the most perfect cut diamond in existence." [17]

The diamond to be bruted is cemented with shellac into a small metal cup, known as a dop, which is mounted on a machine similar to a lathe. Another diamond, the only substance that will cut it, is fixed in another dop screwed into the edge of a two-foot-long stick. Then, as the stone spins on the lathe, the cutter tucks the stick under his arm for support and presses the other diamond firmly to it at right angles, like a carpenter delicately turning wood on a lathe. The friction between the two diamonds chips off the rough spots and corners; gradually the prescribed outline of a round, a marquise, a pear-shape or an oval emerges. The stone is then ready for the final stages of grinding and polishing to give it the required number of facets or faces. There is no mandatory number of facets, but the most widely accepted is the "brilliant" cut of fifty-eight facets, which can be adapted to diamonds of all shapes and sizes.

The trick is to get those facets at exactly the correct angle to each other, so that the light bounces from one to another. Ideally the light should enter a diamond through the flat top—the table—

[17] *Diamant*, November 1978, p. 29. The Jonker is now owned by a Japanese collector. The other eleven diamonds were all sold privately by Winston, four of them apparently purchased by the Maharajah of Indore. The fourth largest of them, weighing 30.84 carats, fetched $300,000 when it was auctioned in New York in 1975.

and be mirrored from facet to facet until it comes back through the top in a rainbow blaze. "It's like a hall of mirrors," said Lazare Kaplan. "Each mirror should catch the light from the other mirrors, and if one is out of angle you don't get the right reflection. Each mirror must have the proper relation to the table and its neighbors to get the correct dispersion; if a mirror is not facing the light there is no brilliance." The skill is not only to position the facets accurately to maintain the correct path of light, but also to give the diamond just the right depth. If a diamond is too deep—that is to say, the distance from the table on top to the "culet" at the bottom is too far—the light disperses through the sides, and the center appears black; if the diamond is too shallow, light leaks out of the bottom, causing a watery effect.

Good judgment may be clouded by the desire not to shave too much off the diamond, for its weight is an essential factor in the ultimate price. Lazare Kaplan often compares it to a butcher who leaves too much fat on the meat. "The steak weighs more," he said, "but it's not as valuable."

The best trim for a diamond is usually reckoned to be the brilliant cut's fifty-eight facets, built up of the "table" on the top, the "culet" on the bottom (a tiny plane, often trimmed almost to a point), plus twenty-four side facets on the crown, as the top part of the stone is called, and thirty-two facets on the pavilion or lower section. The greatest girth of the stone, the girdle, is nearly three-quarters of the way up. The precise symmetry of what has come to be called the "ideal cut," which Kaplan and several other American diamond-cutting houses have adopted, was pioneered by a Belgian, Marcel Tolkowsky, who developed in 1919 an exact mathematical formula for the placing and angling of every facet to create the maximum play of light within the stone and bring out its natural brilliance. Since then, rival formulae have been conjured up by other masters of cutting, but the differences between them are so subtle that to the layman it is indeed much the same as how you prefer your steak cut. And to the cutter, like the butcher, it is whether you are trying to make a little extra on the fat.*

* The Tolkowsky formula is: diameter of girdle, 100 percent; diameter of table, 53 percent; thickness of crown, 16.2 percent; thickness of pavilion, 43.1 percent; angle of crown facets, 34° 30'; angle of pavilion facets, 40° 45'.

Regardless of the formula, each facet has to be created in an exact sequence. The facets are honed one by one on a cast-iron wheel turning at 2,500 rpm, whose surface has been deeply scored and then impregnated with the same diamond powder and olive oil paste used in sawing. The diamond is clamped onto a metal arm which is lowered onto the spinning wheel, just as the needle is placed on the turntable of a record player. The angle of play between diamond and wheel are all-important and can be subtly adjusted. The stone can only be polished with the grain. As each facet is shaped, the diamond is repositioned. The table and the culet are ground first, then the four bottom corners of the pavilion, followed by the four top corners of the crown.

Although on an important stone a single experienced cutter will probably handle manufacture from rough to final polished edition, most stones pass from hand to hand as grinding and polishing proceed. One craftsman, the "cross-cutter," puts on the first eighteen facets, another, the "brilliandeerer" tackles the remaining forty, although in Israel and India, where a "chain" system is used, these tasks may be broken down further. The job is also being shouldered increasingly on medium-sized and small stones, as noted in Tel Aviv, by the Piermatic automatic polishing machines. Yet time and again, even modest stones will be referred back to the foreman or the boss for quick scrutiny that all is proceeding according to plan.

"You may get thirty percent off a piece before you decide where to table it," said Kaplan's chief cutter, Bill Meyer, "and that's where the art comes in—the ability to work without destroying any option." Flaws in the stone also have to be whittled out where possible, and that leads to more decisions. A little weight may be sacrificed in favor of flawlessness. "One carat is the critical size," said Meyer, carefully examining a stone on the polishing wheel. "This one is just over a carat, but it's got some small imperfections near the surface, so it's worth about seventeen thousand dollars. Now if I get them out and still keep the stone over one carat, it'll get a better grade and be worth another two thousand dollars. We're working to a hundredth of a carat. You almost breathe on it to get it right."

The incessant attention to detail on even the most modest of diamonds was emphasized later when I visited P. N. Ferstenberg, who has presided over one of Antwerp's best-known cutting firms for more than half a century. A short, chubby man in his seventies, dressed in a brown shirt and natty bow tie, Ferstenberg sat at a big desk surrounded by bowls of fresh roses, sorting through parcel after parcel of rough and half-cut diamonds. He spent perhaps fifteen seconds on each, scrutinizing it through his loupe, making a small mark if necessary in india ink or just nodding with satisfaction when progress on a stone pleased him. Every twenty minutes or so his foreman popped up from the factory floor to collect a parcel or deliver a new one. Ferstenberg carried on a conversation all the time as he worked. "Some stones are twenty times in my hand," he said. "I have to see every stone, and that's the trick. Once a group of us in the Club [the Diamond Dealers' Club on Pelikaanstraat] brought together twenty rough stones and divided them into five parcels of four stones, which we agreed were each worth the same. Then each of us manufactured his parcel. Afterwards we met again and estimated the value of each parcel of polished. You know, one came out with a twenty percent profit, one with ten percent, one even, one with a five percent loss and the last with a ten percent loss." Ferstenberg modestly did not say how he rated but went on. "And that's our trade. Everyone *thinks* he's the best, but it's how you see the stone. You have to observe and change your mind as you are doing the stone; that's the secret." Ultimately, of course, much depends on the balance between weight, which often means more profit, and beauty. Most *diamantaires* like to make money.

Infinite attention and skill can never remove all the imperfections from the majority of diamonds; less than one in ten is truly "flawless," meaning it has no visible blemishes with the standard ten-power loup So most will be marred internally with dark specks of carbon, sometimes looking like a tiny cloud of bubbles, or groups of colorless crystals, while the external skin may be scratched or pitted through inexperienced, hasty cutting and polishing. The "clarity" of a stone is defined on a descending scale ranging from "flawless" through "third pique," which means that tiny imperfections are "only just visible to the naked eye," to the final dismissal as "heavily spotted," denoting dark spots within and perhaps deep scratches, too, on the exterior which are "very easily visible to the naked eye." Yet even when there is little that can be camouflaged, the cutter will always try to shape the stone in such a way that some imperfections may be concealed by the setting when the diamond is mounted in a ring. And retail jewelers selling to the innocent public often judiciously avoid mentioning the word "flaw" at all, preferring to fall back instead on such euphemisms as "nature's signature," which implies a benefit rather than a defect.

Judgment is passed not only on the clarity of the stone, but on the caliber of its overall cut—the "make," as professionals call it. How well does it fit into the precise formula of symmetry laid down by Tolkowsky or another diamond guru? Some cutting houses, such as Kaplan in America, who follow Tolkowsky's guidelines of the "ideal cut" as gospel pride themselves on their quality control. Kaplan, for instance, reckons that both its workshop in New York and the main factory in Puerto Rico (where originally many workers learned their trade by practicing on ball bearings) turn out polished goods of impeccable symmetry. "The make of our diamonds is fixed," said Leo Kaplan, the company's president. "We are so consistent with quality control that a jewelry manufacturer can order two stones of a particular classification from our list and he will know exactly what he will get; with some cutting houses he might have to pick out two himself from a selection of ten. We pride ourselves on the symmetry of our stones, and we believe we polish the best in the world."

Not all cutters or wholesale buyers agree with such dedication in confining the diamond within the rigid constraints of a mathematical formula, particularly as they feel that although Tolkowsky's calculations give a diamond more "fire" they may deprive it of "brilliance." "Tolkowsky makes a beautiful stone," said Glenn Nord of the GSI Corporation in Los Angeles and one of the most respected judges of diamonds in America, "but you can't have maximum fire and maximum brilliance. If you make the table a little higher than Tolkowsky suggests, you get more fire, but you lose brilliance. You have to sacrifice one or the other."

Such tastes, and sheer economics, mean that "make" varies widely from cutting firm to cutting firm. "Some factories do Rolls Royce jobs, others do junk," said Nick Axelrod, the chief buyer for the Winston organization. And the market for junk is surprisingly large, especially in the United States itself. While cutting houses in New York and Puerto Rico, which tend to cut larger goods, would like to feel they are in the Rolls Royce bracket, it is sometimes a different tale in other cutting centers. The head of a major Tel Aviv cutting firm put it bluntly. "I have an American customer who said to me the other day, I want three qualities from you, rubbish, garbage and *drek*—that's Yiddish for shit." Americans, many wholesale jewelers admit, often prefer flashy stones and opt for weight rather than style, which, to follow Lazare Kaplan's analogy between a diamond cutter and a butcher, frequently tallies with their eating habits, too. The French and the Japanese, on the other hand, score much better marks for their choice in quality diamonds, just as they do for cuisine.

Although the brilliant cut of fifty-eight facets is the most universal, there are infinite variations with more or fewer facets that may be best suited to particular stones. The traditional rose cut, into which many of the great diamonds coming from India in the fifteenth and sixteenth centuries were fashioned, has just twenty-five facets, and a simpler version, the Brabant rose, has only thirteen. The tiny stones that are the specialty of the Indian cutting industry today are often most easily shaped into "eight-cuts," with sixteen side facets, plus the table. At the other end of the scale, the "royal cut" calls for 154 facets, including 48 on the girdle itself, a technique which can make a small stone seem larger than it really is. Occasionally the sculpting impulse inside every cutter really gets out; hearts, crosses and stars abound. One Antwerp cutter even managed a 6.5-carat horse's head, cunningly retaining a well-placed flaw in the stone for the horse's eye.

The cut of a diamond, along with clarity and carat weight, all go toward the jingle of the four "c's" that the diamond trade promotes. The fourth "c" is color. Here the cutter has no control. The perfect diamond should not only be well cut and flawless but colorless as well, so that the spectacle comes from the light it refracts. *Diamantaires*, being individualists all, have never been able to agree how to describe color exactly. The ideal colorless diamond will be denoted "rarest white" or "river" in Scandinavia, "finest white" in Britain, "exceptional white plus" if you are talking with anyone anywhere who prefers the scale of CIBJO * or simply "D" in the United States. From such perfection, however, there is a swift drop down the color scale to muddy stones that Americans label merely from S to X, and others call yellow or dark cape.

Color, however, is not always detrimental. A diamond with a delicate blush of pink is a rarity to be treasured; "fancies," as the trade calls them, in soft hues of blue, canary, champagne, gold and even gunmetal black (like the handsome 67.50-carat Black Orloff owned by a New York collector) are often more highly valued than "white" stones. The highest price ever paid for a diamond at an auction (as opposed to a private sale) was $1,090,000 at a Sotheby's sale in Zurich in 1976 for a 22.55-carat pink diamond; the highest auction price ever paid per carat was $61,000 a carat for a 4.97 pink diamond sold by Christie's in New York in 1979. "Fancies," said a New York dealer, "sell themselves."

Even then, they must be well cut. As Lazare Kaplan's trademark sums it all up, "Beauty is in the cutting."

* *Confederation Internationale de la Bijouterie, Joaillerie, Orfevrerie, Des Diamants, Perles et Pierres.*

4

The Art of the Smuggler:
The Million-Dollar Heel

The Antwerp diamond dealer was talking about the difficulties of buying polished goods from the Russians when the
telephone rang. "I have my little packet ready; it works out
at one hundred eight thousand dollars," he said into it, without
any preliminaries. "He'll pick it up at noon? You're sure our
friend won't have left by then?" He hung up, looking a trifle
embarrassed, and reverted to the Russians. Somehow smuggling,
or "submarine goods," as it is more polite to call it in diamond
circles, is always around you but is very hard to confirm. The
closed circuit of the diamond fraternity becomes even tighter
where submarine movements are concerned. "What a wall of
silence!" an investigator trying to unravel diamond thefts once
remarked. "They scarcely admit diamonds exist."

The very nature of the "goods" makes smuggling endemic
every step of the way, from mine to cutting center to buyer.
Diamonds are just so easy to hide. I had a long conversation
once with a colonel from the diamond detective division of the

South African police in Kimberley, who specialize in trapping illicit buyers of stones stolen from the mines, while he had a ten-carat diamond, the size of a cherrystone, carefully tucked behind one of his back molars. "Hell, man," he said as he spat it out afterwards, "you didn't even know I had ten thousand dollars in my mouth. A diamond is so small, it's easy to secrete anywhere. I could conceal a fortune now in the knot of your tie." He did not need to mention Ian Fleming's phrase about carrying enough diamonds on your naked body to set you up for life. The mouth, the ears, the armpits, the navel, the rectum, the vagina or even between the toes will do for a start, unless you feel like swallowing them. Fleming, incidentally, made James Bond spirit them inside his Dunlop 65 golf balls in *Diamonds Are Forever*.

Ingenuity knows few bounds. Inside tubes of toothpaste, aerosol shaving cans, boxes of face powder and even tins of fruit salad have all been tried. One professional trick is to stud the diamonds along a strip of sticking plaster and fix that inside the false bottom of a suitcase. Another is to carry the stones in hollowed-out shoe heels, although it is unwise to pack in too many. The customs in Bombay picked up a German courier with two kilos of rough diamonds in specially made heels and soles of calf-length leather boots simply because of his uncertain gait. And U.S. customs men at Kennedy Airport picked out a fellow from Hong Kong stepping too gingerly for fear of ruining his million-dollar heels. An American, eager to get his hands on diamonds being stolen from the Mwadui mine in Tanzania, hit on the idea of establishing himself as a collector of rare birds for zoos and then simply fed them the diamonds before he left the country quite openly; he made a great reputation in East Africa as a trader in birds, and no one ever thought to question their diet. The prize, perhaps, has to go to the beautiful young lady who lost an eye in a car accident and then took to smuggling diamonds in the socket behind her false one.

The best hiding places, however, can be revealed quite innocently. When the head of a large Japanese trading house took his wife and family to Singapore on holiday, he treated his wife to a beautiful diamond ring. Just before they landed back in Tokyo, she took off the ring to hide it in her brassiere. Passing through customs, husband and wife said stoutly, "Nothing to declare." Whereupon their five-year-old piped up, "Oh, mama, you forgot to mention the ring in your bra." Customs men took them aside politely and called an appraiser to study the stone. After a while he said with a smile, "You owe us nothing. You've been sold a fake."

The amount the casual tourist gets away with (if he is not cheated in the first place) is small, of course, compared to the diamond trade's submarine network. Just for a start, the flourishing traffic in rough diamonds, either stolen in the mines themselves or mined illicitly in Zaire, Angola, Sierra Leone or Brazil, involves, at a conservative estimate, at least $100 million a year. The whole game starts again once the diamonds have been cut and polished, and radiate from the cutting centers toward their eventual destination. The diamonds themselves are by now worth much more, and the sums escalate. The wholesale value of polished goods going into Italy and Spain, for instance, is at least $250 million a year, and very little is declared; Hong Kong imports close to $700 million worth of diamonds each year, and most depart again by submarine for Japan, South Korea, Thailand, Indonesia or the Philippines. Even Iran was soaking up at least $50 million a year in smuggled goods from Antwerp or Bombay until the Ayatollah replaced the Shah. Already that is one billion dollars a year, without considering North Africa, South America, the United States or even Britain.

A glimpse of what goes on just from Antwerp to London was unveiled when Jacques Rotenberg, one of the most prominent diamond merchants in Hatton Garden, the home of Britain's diamond trade, was ordered to pay the customs £500,000 ($1.1 million) in 1976 over a little matter of £850,000 ($2 million) in polished diamonds that had been smuggled in from Belgium over a three-year period, thus avoiding £276,000 ($634,000) in various taxes. He was caught only because Scotland Yard detectives, on another investigation, learned by chance that he had been robbed of £80,000 ($184,000) in diamonds but had failed to report the theft because the stones had been smuggled originally. What made it more embarrassing was that Rotenberg had served for eleven years on the customs' own diamond evaluation committee, which provides expert appraisal of imports; he had even been awarded the O.B.E. for his voluntary advice.

The fact that Rotenberg in London, and his associates in Belgium, were highly respected diamond merchants underlines how the smuggling of goods, once they are polished, is carried on almost entirely within the diamond community. As an American customs investigator said, "It's all in the family." This is not to label all diamond dealers as rogues. Most are honest; others, especially small dealers, simply cannot resist the temptation to dispatch goods to their uncle or cousin in New York or Hong Kong or Milan without going through the formalities of paperwork. Never for a moment would they consider themselves criminals, merely participants in the old game of paying as little tax as possible. And a good deal of it is done on a remarkably casual basis. An Antwerp wholesaler in polished, for instance, going to visit a colleague in Milan will take along a nice parcel, with an invoice carefully made out to some address in South America. If he goes through customs at Milan airport unchallenged, he delivers the goods there; if, by remote chance, he is stopped, he shows the diamonds with the South American invoice, explaining he is about to ship them elsewhere.

While smuggling is often done either within the family or by close friends, regular couriers are enlisted on some routes, which professional *diamantaires* either ply less often or where they would be under close surveillance. The flow of diamonds into and out of India has long required considerable organization; the volume is substantial in both directions. The entire Indian cutting industry was originally founded on smuggled rough from Antwerp where the Diamond Trading Company granted sights to two or three dealers in the full knowledge that the goods would be wafted to Bombay; the polished goods then had to be spirited back to Antwerp. Several European syndicates, including an outfit in Geneva run by a well-known character called "Abdul," were happy to oblige with couriers from their pool who specialize in shifting gold, watches or diamonds (but usually keep clear of drugs because of the increased international police attention that attracts). Couriers are often bored taxi drivers or schoolteachers from West Germany (Frankfurt, Cologne and Dusseldorf are the best recruiting grounds), who are intrigued by the prospect of a week's trip to the Orient with all expenses paid in return for taking along a special spongebag packed with carefully doctored tooth-paste, shaving and suntan cream. The couriers are carefully briefed. They will invariably be instructed to go to their hotel and wait to be contacted (you never give a courier any contact number). They may even be drilled in tackling customs. "We caught a German girl recently, a teacher, who had been coming in twice a year regularly for a holiday," an Indian revenue intelligence man said. "She had been thoroughly briefed on what to say. In fact, she came out word for word with the same approach as another German courier we had caught a few months before. She attempted to bribe us by saying, 'It's much easier to arrange things in France or Belgium with the customs, but you fellows are impossible.' Exactly what the other chap had said."

The ideal courier, whether for diamonds, gold or even drugs, works for an airline. Diamonds seem to be the prerogative of captains, who feel, perhaps, that other things are beneath their dignity. A Sabena captain ran a nice sideline once in flying polished goods from Antwerp to New York in his shoe heels. A pilot is even more useful if he can choose his own schedule. The director of operations for a Far East airline, a married man with children, found that he needed to make a little extra cash to finance an affair with a Lufthansa air hostess who had ex-pensive tastes. So he started flying rough diamonds into Bombay when he came through from Europe and returned with polished. He carried the diamonds in his briefcase or in his top pocket, for he was so well known that no one bothered to stop him. Besides smuggling on every flight that he piloted, he often slotted himself in to go along on other flights as a training cap-tain. That was his downfall. His trips became so frequent, and he was shifting so many diamonds, that gossip reached the authorities. The airline's own security chief went to him with the warning, "Whatever you are up to, stop it now." He ig-nored the advice and shortly afterwards was trapped, handing over diamonds to an airport mechanic.

The incentive for the professional *diamantaire* to smuggle or to find a courier with a yen for travel or an expensive mis-tress to smuggle for him is less to avoid import duties nowadays as to dodge all kinds of local taxes. Customs duties on diamonds no longer exist, anyway, between Common Market countries and will be lifted in the United States from 1981,* but local value-added tax or sales taxes are often high (25 percent in Japan, for instance), to say nothing of income or profits tax. So a dealer with $100,000 of undeclared diamonds in hand stands to save a good deal. Tax avoidance often becomes such a reflex action that *diamantaires* travel from place to place with a few undeclared stones in hand without any solid reason. "We caught a young Israeli last week with a fancy pink five-point-eighty-six-carat stone worth forty thousand dollars in his rectum," said a U. S. customs investigator. "I traced the stone and found it had been cut here on Forty-seventh Street, had been sold to a Hong Kong dealer, who sold it to this fellow, who took it to Europe and then came on here. But why smuggle? There's no duty because it was cut here in the first place. The only reason can be that he didn't want it shown in his books."

Physical smuggling is not the only way to fiddle the books. Indeed, for every thousand carats that may actually be shifted unofficially, probably twice as many go openly but undervalued. The invoice says they are worth $75,000, when, in fact, the real value is $100,000. Since no two diamonds are alike, and the price of any diamond is open to debate, the room for maneuver when making up an invoice is immense, especially if a variety of diamonds of different sizes and colors are all mingled in the same parcel (although such mingling should alert a customs' appraiser that something is up). "Ninety-nine percent of all shipments are well sorted, so if you find a parcel with one stone at five hundred dollars a carat and the next at fifty dollars a carat, you know it's to throw you off," said Robert Kramer, until recently the chief diamond appraiser for United States Customs in New York.

Kramer and his fellow appraisers work out of a little office above the diamond market on Forty-seventh Street. All official incoming diamond parcels are channeled through them, so they live diamonds as much as any professional and know all the tricks. "You play games," said Kramer. "Importers test the appraiser all the time, especially if he's a new one, to see what they can get away with. A wholesaler often claims he got a good

---

* Except for Russian diamonds.

buy; someone in Tel Aviv was clearing inventory, so he got the goods cheap, but we still appraise them at the market value. If he yells and screams and persists, then maybe we give a little to iron it out. It depends if we've had trouble with the same importer before. We know that certain dealers in Antwerp and Tel Aviv will give an importer here any invoice he wants."

The technique is simple. The New York buyer goes over and agrees to buy $100,000 of polished goods. He pays a $20,000 cash deposit and then asks for an invoice of $80,000, which he will subsequently remit by check. So check matches invoice, and he shows them to customs to "prove" the value of the consignment. Naturally he neglects to mention the $20,000 cash also paid, so he has that amount of diamonds on his books free of all tax liabilities.

Underinvoicing can also be a handy way of skirting exchange controls. A Bombay dealer, for instance, anxious to avoid the tangle of Indian exchange regulations, will ship a consignment of polished goods to Antwerp against an invoice for $50,000. In fact, he has already agreed with the buyer in Antwerp on a price of $65,000, but the balancing $15,000 is tucked into his bank account overseas. The skill in all this is to judge just how little one can get away with on the invoice; an absurdly low figure obviously attracts attention.

Underinvoicing, of course, is only one side of smuggling by paperwork; overinvoicing may be equally advantageous from time to time. As a Tel Aviv dealer explained, "If you look at our exports to New York, they are almost all underinvoiced; I reckon you could add almost thirty percent to the official figures to get the true value. But to Hong Kong, everything is overinvoiced by the same amount to allow kickbacks to Chinese dealers." That is to say, the goods will actually be worth $100,000 but will be invoiced at $130,000. A subtle variation on this theme is that diamonds coming into the United States for some investment companies, as opposed to jewelry manufacturers, are overinvoiced, too. This tactic is designed to enable the investment house to persuade its client that they are charging only a low markup over the "wholesale" price paid in Antwerp; in reality the house paid much less than the invoice shows. Such fraud, incidentally, is not limited to imports. A customs' appraiser told me that he was once visiting a wholesaler when a retailer telephoned to buy a $3,000 diamond. The wholesaler said he could mail it that day, whereupon the retailer added, "Make me out a memo for five thousand dollars, will you? I'm giving it to a friend 'at cost,' so I need the bill to show him."

Doctored invoices can also obscure the true origin of the goods. For many years Russian polished diamonds coming into the United States were liable to a higher duty than goods from Europe or Israel. So dealers often attempted to pass off Russian goods as polished from Tel Aviv or Antwerp. A New York firm, to save 5 percent duty, once declared that two boxes with $350,000 of polished Russian goods came from a prestigious London manufacturer. Their homework, however, was sloppy. They left the diamonds nestling in the original Russian parcel papers. These look similar to the blue-white papers used everywhere in the trade, but the New York appraiser knew that Russian papers are one centimeter wider and two centimeters longer when folded than the traditional ones. From past experience he also recognized the handwriting of the Russian sorters on the parcels. "It was an ironclad case of fraud," recalled Robert Kramer. "Usually they have the sense at least to change the parcel papers."

Hoodwinking the appraisers is not easy even then. "We had a classic one a few years ago," said Kramer. "A half-million-dollar shipment in two boxes from Israel, all in Israeli parcel papers with Hebrew writing on them. I looked at them and said to the importers, 'They're Russian.' But, 'No, no,' they claimed, 'you know Russian goods don't come into Israel.' However, the 'make' convinced me." Kramer explained that in the early days of Russian polished sales it had been easy to detect the goods because they were poorly cut and polished. Nowadays, with more experience, the Russian quality is excellent, but the stones still have certain identifying characteristics. "You have fully polished girdles, especially on melees, which other cutters won't do because you lose too much weight," said Kramer. "The Russians will also leave pinpoint flaws in the stone because they are working automatically by the book, whereas a good cutter, using his initiative, would take them out." Investigation proved Kramer's identification to be correct. The Israeli shipper had bought the Russian goods in West Germany, shipped them to Tel Aviv (labeled as West German), repackaged them and dispatched them to New York as Israeli goods—all to avoid an extra $25,000 duty.

Smuggling is not limited to the diamond trade trying to save on its tax bills. Diamonds are forever being employed to transfer undeclared income from one country to another, to launder stolen money, to pay for consignments of drugs or to finance secret agents in fostering political agitation. A young dealer in investment diamonds from Los Angeles gave me an elaborate explanation of how he had helped a wealthy doctor shift $100,000 discreetly from California to a Swiss bank for a commission of $10,000, which actually meant the doctor would have $90,000 safely "laundered." "I got the one hundred thousand dollars from him," said the diamond dealer, "and went to New York where I bought seven diamonds. One was two and three-quarter carats, the others were smaller stones, but all had GIA certificates. I put the certificates in my suitcase along with other documents, and the stones in an envelope taped inside the inside breast pocket of my jacket. Then I took a plane to Luxembourg and went by train through France to Switzerland. I was also carrying with me some rare gold coins which I showed at customs, so they were too interested to think of asking about diamonds. When I got to Zurich, I sold the diamonds to a Swiss importer for ninety-six thousand dollars. That was four thousand dollars less than I had paid in New York, but I'd still made myself six thousand dollars tax free. I put ninety thousand dollars in a Swiss bank for my friend."

The loss of $4,000 on the stones between New York and Zurich, however, underlines the vagueness of the international diamond price, which would be a greater hazard for an amateur at the same game. The Los Angeles dealer, as a professional, could be sure of securing only a narrow spread between buy and sell. The novice paying out $100,000 might well be able to sell for only $50,000.

The classic case of an innocent abroad was the young man in the computer department of a Los Angeles bank, who managed over a period of many months to defraud the bank of nearly $9 million by instructing the computer to pay money into various special accounts he set up. Eventually he took off with a great bundle of cash and hastened to Geneva with what he thought was the smart idea of laundering his loot into Rus-

sian diamonds. He approached the Geneva sales office of Russelmaz, the exporters of Soviet polished goods, and after some
discussion paid $8.1 million for a nice parcel of diamonds. Then
he headed home, right into the welcoming arms of the FBI,
who confiscated the diamonds and gave them to his former
employers. They hawked the parcel of Russian goods around
for quite some time before settling for a disappointing $5.9
million, a loss of 30 percent.

Such a cautionary tale will not diminish the diamond's appeal
for those with the right connections in the trade. The stability
of its price and its international acceptability offer immense advantages to criminals, either to hide their loot or to make payments abroad without the inconvenience of resorting to bank
accounts, which can be investigated or blocked. They know,
too, that a diamond is remarkably anonymous, unlike numbered
banknotes, travelers' checks, or even stolen paintings.*

So loose polished diamonds are increasingly being used, for
instance, to finance cocaine smuggled into the United States
from Colombia. A single courier can take the entire payment
inside him on the plane from New York or Miami to Bogotá
with little fear of detection. The diamonds themselves are often
stolen in the first place. The U. S. Drug Enforcement Agency
has established a clear link between several robberies of loose
diamonds and the cocaine trade. On one occasion, $100,000 in
small diamonds between one-quarter and two carats, wrapped in
the usual parcels, were stolen from a salesman in Hawaii. In
less than twenty-four hours the stones were in New York, being
shown to a go-between for the cocaine traffickers; terms were
agreed, and the diamonds went to Bogotá that night hidden in an
aerosol shaving can. "Unfortunately, diamonds are one of the
easiest things to trade for hard drugs," said a New York wholesaler, who lost a consignment of polished goods that also ended
up in South America.

Diamonds also buy political intelligence. As Russia's diamond-
cutting and polishing industry grew up in the 1970s, the KGB
realized that polished stones were a discreet way of paying their

---

* A Chicago firm, Gemprint Ltd., is successfully marketing a machine
that "fingerprints" a diamond by means of pictures on positive/negative
film that record its reflective patterns under a low-level laser beam, but
Gemprint's central diamond-print file is still very limited.

agents abroad. Not only did this avoid the inconvenience of changing rubles into dollars in the first place, but it also eliminated all the dangers of feeding funds into bank accounts that might be detected by counterintelligence. The "mole" in *The Honourable Schoolboy*, devotees of John Le Carré will recall, was initially tracked through funds pumped into a special account at Banque L'Indochine in Vientiane, Laos. Polished diamonds, on the other hand, can easily be smuggled to agents who sell them for local currency, avoiding all exchange complications. Occasionally the KGB overdoes it. Between 5,000 and 10,000 carats of Russian polished diamonds, worth nearly $3 million, suddenly turned up in the Bombay market just before the elections in 1980 that returned Indira Gandhi to power. Indians, who thrive on political intrigue, had no doubt about what was going on. Since the import of all polished diamonds, let alone Russian, is prohibited in India, the stones must have been smuggled. Moreover, diamond prices in Bombay were very weak, and the diamonds could have commanded a better price in Europe or America. Whoever brought them in, therefore, was not concerned with profit, but with buying political clout. "This diamond connection . . . has provided Russia with a well-established pipeline for raising rupees within India to finance their chosen candidates at elections," decided the news magazine *Onlooker* under a headline, "Poll Ripoff—Why Russian Diamonds Are Suddenly Here." [18] The exposure of the KGB's little ruse, however, caused only a ripple. Nothing was proved; the story was dismissed by politicians as malicious opposition rumor and soon forgotten. No one was caught.

This is the eternal attraction of diamond smuggling. The risks are small; the profits, either financial or political, can be great. As an Antwerp dealer summed up, "Diamond smugglers are like *anguillas*—eels—you'll never catch them."

[18] *Onlooker*, Bombay, January 1, 1980, p. 11.

PART
IV

THE BUYERS

1

Lovers

Triggering the Mystic Signal

A new advertisement caught the eye of Americans flipping through the September issue of *Ladies' Home Journal* in 1939 as the first rumbles of World War II sounded far away in Europe. Beneath a sentimental painting of a mother and young daughter captioned, FROM YOUR HAND, A GREATER TREASURE, the copy intoned: "Love of beauty is one of the greatest gifts a mother can send with her children into the future. One who finds pleasure in the delicate lines of a fine portrait—glory in the sleepless fires of a jewel—is apt to find all of life the richer." Eventually came the punch line, "Traditionally, your husband is the donor of your most precious ornaments—your diamonds. But you may give him this advice in their selection . . . color, weight, quality and cut influence the price of diamonds . . . current prices of quality diamonds—one-half carat, $100 to $200/one carat $325 to $600." In these stilted phrases De Beers fired the first shots in their long-running campaign to build an image for the diamond. After a while the prose was polished up a little to alliterate color, cut, clarity and carat weight (the four "c's," as they became known), and the message was finally crystalized, in 1948, into the slogan, "A Diamond Is Forever."

The original advertising campaign was the outcome of a meeting between Sir Ernest Oppenheimer's young son Harry and a New York advertising agency, N. W. Ayer. The aim was to whittle down the huge stocks of diamonds that had built up at the Diamond Trading Company in London during the disastrous days of the Depression. The Oppenheimers hoped they might be able to foster the idea that diamonds were not just "big rocks for the affluent." The agency's brief was "to extol the prestige and emotional connotations surrounding the giving or wearing of an engagement diamond." Ever since the days of Cecil Rhodes (who had once worked out that four million couples got engaged each year), the diamond magnates had known that their best potential market was the engagement ring, especially in America, which for fifty years had taken up more than half of all diamonds produced. During the Depression, however, many American couples had inevitably forsaken the purchase of a ring; scarcely half of all new brides received one. Sitting down together in New York, Harry Oppenheimer and the men at N. W. Ayer decided to woo them.

Forty years later, the seduction is complete. Pushing the diamond as a symbol of love, N. W. Ayer, who remain De Beers' American agency to this day, have persuaded more than three-quarters of all American first-time brides to wear a diamond engagement ring. Even among "repeat brides" (a very important element in a country where nearly one in two marriages ends in divorce), almost half have diamond rings. "I think we've saturated the market," said Dale Wyatt, who masterminds research at N. W. Ayer. "The people left over are either unconvincable, ignorant or too poor."

The original pursuit of the American bride was only the start. De Beers promotion has long since been extended to embrace all diamond jewelry, for both men and women. And the slogan "A Diamond Is Forever" has become familiar in glossy magazines around the world. Yet America remains the cornerstone of the diamond market; of $14 billion spent at retail level on diamonds in 1980, $4.5 billion was spent in the United States.

Japan was a substantial runner-up with $3 billion, but West Germany was a poor third with $1 billion, while France and Italy trailed as equal fourths with $450 million each. The dependence on America remains an inherent weakness in the diamond business. "The American economy has only to cough and the diamond industry can be in trouble," explained Vivian Prins of Hennig, the London diamond brokers. "If a recession in America cut diamond purchases there by twenty percent, that means almost a ten percent reduction in the total number of diamonds being moved around. And in a finely balanced market, that is disaster. The market is almost Dickensian in balance. As Mr. Micawber said, 'Annual income twenty pounds, annual expenditure nineteen nineteen six, result happiness. Annual income twenty pounds, annual expenditure twenty pounds ought and six, result misery.' "

In search of happiness, De Beers spends over $40 million annually on diamond promotion, of which over $15 million is channeled through N. W. Ayer to the American campaign. Of the remainder, $6 million goes to J. Walter Thompson in Tokyo to woo the Japanese, and the remaining $19 million is devoted to carrying the message to the unconverted everywhere from Frankfurt to Rio de Janeiro. The West Germans have a long way to go; a mere 32 percent of brides receive a diamond ring (DER), since the German custom is a gold ring at engagement that is exchanged for a new one at the marriage ceremony. The Spaniards are even farther behind with DERs acquired by only 13 percent of brides, while in Brazil scarcely 6 percent can afford one. But De Beers takes heart from the way the Japanese have been won over. When they first began advertising in Japan in 1967 that *Daiyamondo wa eien no kagayaki* (A diamond is brilliance eternal), a mere 6 percent of brides favored DERs; a decade later the advertisements had helped to win over more than 60 percent. And so the theme is driven home everywhere. *Ein Diamant ist Unverganglich*, the Germans are told; *Un diamente es para siempre*, the Spanish are reminded. The theme song is never changed; to the French it is *Un Diamant est Eternel*, to the Norwegians *En Diamant varer evig* and to the Dutch *Een Diamant is voor altijd*.

Europeans, however, are less susceptible to such propaganda and are more pragmatic in their approach to the diamond; they buy with an eye for investment as much as beauty. The sentimental selling of the diamond has always been most successful in the United States. "In Europe diamonds are often for a rainy day," said Mort Sarett, the ebullient fellow who runs the Jewelry Industry Council in New York, "but America is a romantic country at heart, and the diamond here has always been identified with romance."

The romantic image has certainly been carefully propagated by N. W. Ayer, on behalf of De Beers. The relationship between De Beers and their New York advertising agency is, incidentally, unique. American antitrust legislation makes it impossible for the mining house, as an effective monopoly in diamonds, to maintain any presence in the United States. So from the commanding heights of its offices in the forty-first floor of 1345 Avenue of the Americas, the agency takes care of all advertising and market research in America. To keep out of arms' reach of the U.S. government trust-busters, De Beers' executives cannot even visit the Ayer offices in New York, and all formal meetings have to be held in London. When anyone from De Beers does venture on American soil, it must be on holiday, and even an innocent vacation tour of Ayer's offices is not encouraged. Lunch at "21" can be regarded as safe ground. But no one takes risks, and De Beers has long resigned itself to keeping the Atlantic between themselves and the principal destination of their diamonds.

Despite De Beers' enforced absence, N. W. Ayer has made sure that a whole generation of Americans has grown up to magazines filled with advertisements showing dewy-eyed couples skipping barefoot along the shore, or strolling arm in arm through sun-lit woods, while romantic copy extols the virtues of love and diamonds. Over the years the prose has naturally become a little less gushy. The would-be bride of the 1980s can hardly be won as her mother was in the spring campaign of 1947, when the ads showed delicate pink and yellow butterflies flitting by a dark-haired girl, and the copy warbled:

> *From all the garden's host, one butterfly on dancing wings hovers before her, spending its brief hour with joy to symbolize her love. Just so, the diamond on her finger will some day gleam more brilliant than any other, reflecting her*

love's own image. Her engagement ring stone should be chosen, then, for its proud place.

The modern version is more likely to show a husky college boy and his demure girl sharing an ice-cream soda beneath the headline, "Our diamond means we now have the best of both worlds. Yours and mine." And the caption purrs, "I still remember the day you made this nearsighted musician see how exciting a game of football could be. And the time you sat through a concert without falling asleep. Being in love means we want to know what each other's all about. And our diamond says we want to explore those two special worlds for a long, long time."

The two ads, incidentally, are a subtle reminder of a diamond's soaring value. The 1947 one noted that a half-carat diamond retailed at $230 to $500; the half-carat diamond the college footballer gave his musician girl friend in the 1979 advertisement was listed as "available for about $1,950."

The diamond marketeers have responded also to the changing moral climate. The siren song to lure a woman in her thirties embarking on her second marriage into the jewelry store cannot be the same as that for a co-ed. As a De Beers man bluntly put it, "We couldn't say, 'When you get married again, luv, buy a ring.'" Instead the theme was "How do I feel on getting a diamond engagement ring at thirty-two?" And since the bride might well have children of her previous marriage, they were included, too. One advertisement showed children peeking out of the windows at the lovers sitting on the porch, over the inscription, "Last night when I said, 'Will you marry me?' they said yes."

De Beers is happy with the second-time brides. Although only about half actually receive a new engagement ring (but almost invariably get rid of the old one), they are usually more affluent and thus can afford a better diamond; the mean price for repeat-bride rings is over $650, a hundred dollars more than for the first time around. And the women seem more satisfied with them. "They often say, 'This new ring is much better,'" said N. W. Ayer's Dale Wyatt, "by which they may be making an invidious comparison with their first husband."

For many brides the ring itself seems to symbolize the moment of engagement more than anything else. When an N. W. Ayer team went trekking through shopping malls in the eastern and midwestern United States to tap the opinions of the newly engaged, they found in answer to the question, "What constitutes, or defines, engagement?" that the majority opted for "Having a DER." Proposal and acceptance, announcing plans to parents or informing friends all rated lower. The significance of the ring was underlined by a young man at Quaker Bridge in Bucks County, Pennsylvania, who confided that he and his girl had known each other for a couple of years and she had moved in with him. They had talked about marriage, discussed it with family and friends and had even set a date. But they were hung up because he was waiting for a check for $400, which he had earmarked for an engagement ring. "We can't get engaged till I get that check," he lamented. The marketing men went home happy that day that the message had really gotten through.

The researchers, ever eager to learn just what makes people decide to buy a diamond, have decided it all revolves around "the mystic signal." This is some kind of code between lovers by which the girl, who is protesting she does not want money wasted on a ring, is really desperately trying to indicate that she does. (The signal also operates, apparently, when wives hint to husbands they would love a new diamond bracelet or earrings for their birthday or Christmas.) Usually the semaphore is understood, but signals sometimes get mixed. A few brides break down in tears and confess to the diamond inquisitors that their secret yearnings are never detected. Still, the signal normally gets through, and the lovers head for the jewelry store.

There the debate takes a different turn. As a marketing man, just back from the rough-and-tumble of research in Kansas City, put it, "It's like a Masters and Johnson sex study—the men want size, the women want quality." The women, it turns out, usually have their way. "The man," intoned the formal account of the field adventures for the advertising agency, "takes a back seat in the selection process."

But he can take comfort. The marketing men are on his side when it comes to the question of size. The biggest worry facing them, since diamond prices started to rise sharply in the late 1970s, has been a phenomenon known as "carat erosion." This is not a geological fault in the mine but means that as prices go up, the size of diamonds in engagement rings goes down. This is because most couples going shopping for a ring (or other diamond jewelry, for that matter) often have a top price, say $600, in mind, rather than any notion that they want a one-quarter-carat diamond with very slight inclusions. Six hundred dollars now buys a smaller diamond. The evidence of erosion is clear, not just in the United States but worldwide. The average caratage of the diamond in engagement rings in America in 1972 was .47 of a carat; by 1979 it was down to .26. In West Germany it was down from .25 of a carat in 1972 to .15 seven years later, while in Britain the diamonds were rapidly getting almost too small to see as erosion dropped the median weight from .15 of a carat in 1972 down to .10.

In response to this decline, De Beers has had to consider a change of tune for the first time in a generation. Education is replacing emotion. As Dale Wyatt at N. W. Ayer put it, "Since 1939 we've said a diamond is a symbol of love, but faced with this erosion problem, we now have to go for more informative campaigns explaining why one diamond costs more than another."

And much of that effort is directed at men. After all, the poor fellow may be so preoccupied with work that he misses all those "mystic signals" that his girl friend, wife or mistress is transmitting about her deep desires for a diamond. De Beers tries to help reception. "He's had nudges from his wife, we give him an extra nudge," said Keith Ives, the De Beers market research chief. That nudge is carefully tuned to hit American men at a moment of least resistance. As they sit down in front of the television, can of beer in hand, to watch the season's best football games in the six weeks before Christmas, the screen is suddenly diamond studded in almost every commercial break. N. W. Ayer spends over $1.5 million, 10 percent of their entire annual budget, on ads at the pre-Christmas football games. The strategy is simple. "The men need prompting," says Ayer's Dale Wyatt. "The wife has been after her husband in a million subtle ways all year, and the football ads are the final trigger—do it now." The men go out in droves after the game to oblige; half of all diamond jewelry sales (excluding engagement rings) take place in December.

And while their defenses are down, men are occasionally persuaded to buy the odd bauble for themselves. As De Beers has sought to widen the market for diamonds over the last decade, men have naturally been encouraged to purchase their own diamond rings, tie clips, fraternity pins and cuff links. The response, however, is slow. The drawback, apparently, is the image created by a flamboyant fellow named Diamond Jim Brady. At least that is how Mort Sarett, at the Jewelry Industry Council, sees it. "Brady," recalled Sarett, "was a colorful salesman-cum-swindler around the racetracks in the Gay Nineties who had a collection of two thousand diamonds. Unfortunately, he made them a sign of vulgarity, so an elegant man didn't wear diamonds because it made him seem some kind of gangster like Diamond Jim." Brady's legacy lasts. Scarcely one American male in fifty buys himself (or is given) a piece of diamond jewelry each year, and only one in five possesses a single stone.

Luckily for De Beers, diamonds are still a girl's best friend. Wedding, eternity and cocktail rings, earrings, bracelets, pendants, necklaces and even diamond-studded watches sell by the million. And whereas in the late 1960s engagement rings comprised almost half of all diamond jewelry sales in America, a decade later they accounted for under one-fifth.

This growth has been achieved by De Beers deciding to promote every possible red-letter day in the calendar, from wedding anniversaries and Mother's Day to Father's Day and graduation, while tailoring its marketing campaigns to suit its inventory. If the boxes in the vaults of the Diamond Trading Company at Charterhouse Street in London become overstocked with diamonds of a certain shape or size, then an advertising campaign is conceived to try to shift them. Ideally, demand is shaped to conform with supply. When slow sales during 1973, at the height of the original oil crisis, led to the buildup of large stocks of small stones, the marketing men came up with the notion of a campaign for eternity rings. A couple of years later a surplus of large stones led to a spate of advertisements on such themes as "The Taming of a Rough Diamond," that showed a three-carat emerald-cut diamond hewn from a seven-point-two-carat rough. "It is a rare breed," intoned the copy, "because it is large, and large diamonds are becoming scarcer every day." This was followed by a similar drive to move medium-quality one-carat stones under the label of "The diamond solitaire . . . a rare gift . . . set simply and elegantly . . . to sparkle on its own . . . the one shown here is worth about $5,950."

Designers are also constantly encouraged to explore fresh and exotic avenues through the annual Diamonds International Awards which De Beers has sponsored since 1954. Originally the contest was won by the traditional New York store, Tiffany's, where Truman Capote's Holly Golightly once feasted her eyes at breakfasttime on the window displays. But over the years the rather heavy, ornate American designs have been challenged by a new breed of brisk, young designers from Britain, France, West Germany and, above all, from Italy and Japan, producing slim and elegant designs. Although the Japanese came rather late to diamonds, such designers as Yasuko Okumura, Sakiko Iida and Jun Okina almost swept the board by the mid-1970s. At the twenty-sixth Diamonds International Awards in 1980, which attracted 1,413 entries from thirty-one nations, Japan's Tadashi Honma won the $25,000 grand prize, with an eighteen-carat white-gold ring set with sixty-seven tapered-cut baguette diamonds, weighing six point twelve carats. In all, the Japanese took four of the ten prizes. The competition has now become a landmark in the jewelry year; even the Soviet Union, eager to enhance the growing reputation of its polished diamond industry, sent seven entries. While more conservative retailers often shrink initially from some of the bolder forms of modern jewelry that have fascinated young designers, De Beers welcomes originality. "We must keep the image of the diamond up-to-date," insisted De Beers' Keith Ives.

Over the last generation no one has helped them embellish that image more than Harry Winston in New York. As a salesman of the diamond he was without peer. And although he died in 1978, the reputation that he created for his Fifth Avenue salon in New York has lingered on.

La Crème de la Crème

That eccentric Edinburgh schoolmistress Miss Jean Brodie regarded her "gels" as *la crème de la crème*. In diamonds, *la crème de la crème* is indisputably to be found at the establishment of Harry Winston, Inc., 718 Fifth Avenue, New York. A sign over the imposing portals outside declares, "Rare Jewels of the World." The emphasis is on the rare. In a small lobby within, a polite, upright young lady in black dress, black stockings and black shoes distinguishes the casual buyer with a few hundred dollars in his pocket from the serious client intent on spending the $10,000 minimum that gains entrance. (While that inquisition is going forward, a hidden camera has photographed the would-be client just for good security measure.)

The approved, or the famous and truly wealthy, are then ushered through a beige screen door into the Salon. It is a high, spacious room, with an ornate chandelier suspended from the ceiling and a black carpet crisscrossed with a diamond pattern of white lines. On the walls are seven discreet showcases displaying a handful of necklaces and earrings, but otherwise little jewelry is in sight. The Salon is sparsely furnished with five black-topped antique desks. Behind each sits a middle-aged man in dark suit, white shirt and sober tie, while beside each a dark-haired young lady, attired completely in black, hovers in attendance, ready to bear from some secret safe whatever jewel the customer may desire. The emphasis on black is intentional; nothing is permitted to distract from the splendid fire of the stones.

At the center desk, the command post, sits Richard Winston, a courtly figure in his early fifties, with a heavy gold bracelet around one wrist and ornate RW cufflinks. His uncle, Harry Winston, who founded the business and ran it until his death in 1978 groomed him for a generation to take over the Salon. (Winston's own son, Ronald, has controled the extensive wholesale diamond-dealing and manufacturing side of the family's jewel empire since his father died.) In the Salon the spirit of Harry Winston lingers on. "You still feel he's sitting here," said Richard Winston. "He had a unique flair, taste and style. He taught me, too, to care for and live with every sale."

Buying a diamond, or other glorious stones, in the Winston Salon is no spot decision. "It's a big event for most people to come in," explained Richard Winston. "Our doorway is internationally imposing." Once inside, the clients take their time. "I've just finished a deal that took seven months," he went on. "Husband and wife or man and girl friend often cannot agree. I had a couple the other day who walked in cold. He was all ready to buy a diamond. He liked a big one, a D VVSI [the finest color, with only the tiniest of flaws], but she wanted a D Flawless. Then it turned out he wanted a pear shape, and she wanted an emerald cut. So I didn't make the sale then, but they'll be back. I feel it; they have taken the bait."

The casual customer, once he has been to Winston's, will return. "Seventy-five percent of my best friends came in unknown through that doorway," said Richard Winston. "You get to know them well; I go to their birthdays and their weddings. It's a very personal thing, selling them jewels." Once that bond of friendship is formed, the entire relationship changes. "A customer will call me from St. Louis," he continued, "and say, 'Richard, it's my wife's birthday next week, you put a little something you feel she'll like in the mail.' Well, I know she had a bracelet last year, and earrings before that, so I say, 'How about a necklace? I can suggest something at fifty-five thousand dollars or eighty-five thousand dollars or one hundred and fifty thousand dollars.' And he'll say, 'Send the two at eighty-five thousand dollars and one hundred and fifty thousand dollars.' I know I'll only get one back. You get to know people, their tastes and their spending power."

Richard Winston, like his uncle Harry before him, gets carried away by his enthusiasm. "I can get really excited about a fine diamond," he confided. "I often feel it's like a perfect martini—cool and sexy."

That spirit of excitement long drew those selling or in search of fine diamonds to Harry Winston. In a career spanning over half a century he handled more than sixty of the world's major diamonds. Anyone who found a large rough diamond sought an offer from Harry Winston; the 726-carat Jonker diamond from the Premier mine in South Africa, the 968.80-carat Star of Sierra Leone (the largest stone ever found in West Africa), the 601-carat Lesotho diamond from the Letseng-la-Terai diggings in the mountains of Lesotho, the 155-carat Liberator from the diamond fields of southern Venezuela and the 726-carat Presidente Vargas from the San Antonio River in Minas Gerais province of Brazil all came to his door. So, too, did such historic stones as the 43.38-carat Nassak and the 79.41-carat Nepal that were found centuries ago, probably at Golconda in India, and adorned the collections of Indian maharajahs for generations before passing into his hands. His customers over a lifetime included everyone from King Farouk of Egypt, King Ibn Saud of Saudi Arabia and the Shah of Iran to Texas oil millionaires and Greek shipping tycoons. Stavros Niarchos paid Winston $2 million for a blue-white pear-shaped diamond of 128 carats that had been cut from a 426-carat rough diamond found at the Premier mine and for which Winston originally paid $280,000. King Ibn Saud bought the beautiful heart-shaped 62.50-carat Winston diamond that had been cut from a 154-carat rough diamond found at the Jagersfontein mine in South Africa in 1952. (The purchase and cutting of this diamond were described by Lillian Ross in a famous *New Yorker* profile of Harry Winston.) The King, however, ultimately returned the stone to Winston in part payment for $2 million of other jewelry, explaining that he really needed four big diamonds exactly alike, one for each of his wives.

These deals made Harry Winston a legend. "He was an unbelievable salesman and promoter," recalled Vivian Prins of Hennig's, the London diamond brokers, who acted as intermediaries in many of Winston's purchases. "Watching him sell was the best theater you could want. It was beautiful, like a great actor at work."

The sale is not the end of the affair. A diamond, after all, is forever. Kings are deposed, millionaires die or fall on hard times and their diamonds come back again. And the surge in diamond prices during the late 1970s also prompted several Winston clients to profit from the windfall. As Richard Winston, on whom Harry Winston's mantle has fallen, observed, "I paid a client six hundred thousand dollars the other day for a diamond he bought from me for two hundred and ninety-four thousand dollars just three years ago." To that end, Richard Winston keeps careful track of every diamond he sells. He reached over and unlocked a drawer in his desk and revealed within a stack of small black account books. "In those books are the details of every client and every stone I've sold since the 1950s," he said. "Someone can phone me to discuss a new purchase, and as we are chatting about the weather or his vacation, I can get out my black book and see exactly what he has bought from us. My life's in there."

And although the days of wealthy Indian maharajahs and bejeweled rulers may be dying, Richard Winston finds that inflation and high taxes have not ruined the market. "Younger people are coming in now," he explained, "not just buying jewels for their wives, but putting their money into diamonds for investment. Of course, we're a jewel house, but we've got this enviable selection of quality stones, so they come to us. Money hasn't disappeared in this country. Sometimes I feel there's no limit."

No Flaws in the Bride

The sightseeing tour of any Japanese jeweler visiting California nowadays includes three musts: Universal Studios, Disneyland and the Gemological Institute of America's training school at Santa Monica. Their enthusiasm to pick up a little know-how on their travels underscores Japan's rapid growth as a prime market for diamonds during the last decade. The fortunes of the diamond business, which have for so long relied mainly on American dollars, now benefit almost as much from the yen, as the Japanese spend more than $3 billion a year on diamonds. Twenty years ago the diamond was almost unknown in Japan; today over 25 percent of the world's diamond jewelry is sold there. Moreover, the taste and discrimination of the Japanese have been welcomed in cutting centers accustomed to the huge American demand for "garbage." The phrase "Japanese goods" has become synonymous with top quality. The Japanese dealers diligently seek fine diamonds without a *kizu*—a flaw—because the Japanese husband-to-be is quite ready to shell out $1,000 or more for his fiancée's diamond engagement ring (double the American average).

The blooming of the diamond market in Japan naturally owes much to the Japanese "economic miracle" which has created the underlying purchasing power, with the twice-yearly bonus of a month's extra salary in June and December providing the ready cash for such luxuries as diamonds. But it has also been carefully nurtured by De Beers. In some ways the task has been an easy one, for De Beers was starting with nothing. "Japan is a country without a jewelry tradition because jewels are not worn with the kimono," said Tom de Graw, a quiet American who has made his home in Tokyo where he masterminds the De Beers campaign. What little jewelry was used was adorned with the native pearl before De Beers came along. A few wealthy Japanese families had bought diamonds before the Second World War, but during hostilities they were required to surrender them to the Bank of Japan, for sale to help the war effort. After the war all diamond imports were forbidden until 1960, but it was not until several years later, when De Beers came upon the scene with their first advertisements, that the real expansion started. "We were faced with a vacuum," recalled de Graw. "There was no ownership of diamonds in Japan; back in 1967 only five percent of Japanese brides wore diamond engagement rings." Fourteen years later, De Beers basks in the knowledge that over 60 percent of brides have one. "The diamond ring," added de Graw, "is now an essential part of the engagement in most socioeconomic groups."

Quality is all-important, because it reflects the purity of the bride herself. The nightmare of Japanese parents is that either their daughter or her ring might be *kizu mono*—scratched goods. The bride must be a virgin; her diamond must be flawless.

The need for such perfection has made Japan a favored client of many of the best cutting firms. "Almost all our overseas sales are to Japan," said Leo Kaplan of Lazare Kaplan International in New York, "and they want the finest cuts a manufacturer can make." What also delights the dealers is that Japan has virtually no cutting industry of its own. A joint venture between the trading company Sumitomo, which is the largest single importer of polished diamonds, and De Beers to create a cutting factory called Oriental Diamonds has never really flourished. There was no cutting tradition in Japan, and high labor costs have made it difficult for Oriental Diamonds, the only DTC sightholder in Japan, to compete with finished goods from Tel Aviv, Antwerp, Bombay and New York. The Russians have also been eager to secure a firm foothold in such a lucrative market and in 1979 succeeded in selling almost $30 million in polished goods to the Japanese. Many dealers have found it worthwhile to open offices in Tokyo or to enter into sales contracts with Sumitomo, C. Itoh and Nichimen, the three leading trading companies for diamond imports. "Japan is a very, very powerful market," said Hermann Schamisso, an Antwerp wholesaler, "and the scope for expansion is still very important."

What really encourages dealers is that, despite successful sales for almost a decade, they have still scarcely tapped the market. The diamond engagement ring may be in vogue for today's brides, but few of their mothers possess a gem. According to De Beers, only 23 percent of married women in Japan own any diamond jewelry at all. As for the men, they have hardly begun to buy. "Japanese men feel it is feminine to wear a ring," said Masaharu Lizuka, who works on the De Beers campaigns. "I myself have a real resistance to wearing any jewelry. Perhaps we can invent a purse or wallet for men set with tiny diamonds."

De Beers puts most effort into wooing women. The Japanese male, unlike the American, is not besieged with jingles for gems as he watches sports on television. "The prime target here is the wife because she controls the budget," said Tom de Graw. "The man gives his basic salary and his bonus to his wife, and she then gives him a spending allowance. So there's none of the surprise, 'Hello honey, happy birthday, here's a diamond ring,' that we encourage in America. The Japanese may go to the store together, but she buys."

The commercials, happily, cannot change all traditions. There is still one occasion when every Japanese woman will refuse to wear her diamond ring—the formal tea ceremony. Simplicity is then the essence; a diamond is forever forbidden. As a Japanese lady explained, "It might scratch the teabowl."

Uncharted Waters

The first reaction of any American or European to the gold *souks* of the Middle East is usually amazement at the sheer lavishness of the gold jewelry cascading down the windows of perhaps thirty to forty shops in a single street. To step into the narrow alleyway of a gold *souk* anywhere from Kuwait to Casablanca or Istanbul to Jidda is to be transported into an Ali Baba's cave. The impact is so stunning that visitors, who elsewhere might go into a jeweler's only to buy something for a special occasion, often feel compelled to buy. How can one walk through such a treasure trove without purchasing a golden souvenir?

But where are the diamonds? Not a single ornament in that waterfall of gold in the windows is set with gems. For generations gold has been not only the basic means of saving but also formed such an integral part of the marriage ceremony—the bride's status being judged by her endowment in gold—that diamonds have yet to make their mark among the Middle Eastern population. The really wealthy families of the oil sheikhs have bought fine diamonds, of course, but usually on excursions to Europe. The wind of change, however, is starting to blow. The gold shops are slowly weaning their customers onto diamonds. Late one evening in the Kuwait *souk*, I watched Youssef

Tarazi, a gregarious fellow whose shop is invariably as busy as a railway terminus, slip on a ring set with a one-carat yellow diamond and flaunt it back and forth before a group of veiled women looking at gold trinkets. His display had the desired effect; they pushed the gold bracelets aside and asked about the diamond. They talked for half an hour, with much banter and laughter about the price, and then left. "They'll be back," said Youssef Tarazi knowingly. "I have many rich customers now. I go to Moscow to buy from the Russians, and I'm selling fifteen million dollars in diamonds a year." A slight exaggeration, perhaps, but an indication that the Middle East's oil wealth is rapidly widening the market.

The dealers in Antwerp notice it, too. Their offices are filled day and night with Arab buyers, who may not know much about diamonds but are never short of cash. "One fellow came in with nine thousand dollars and asked for melees," said a wholesaler, "so I spread out some goods, and he picked out yellow colors. He didn't use a loupe, and when I offered him one, he held it *under* the diamond. But he was back the next week with twenty-seven thousand dollars, and now he comes regularly for three hundred thousand dollars a shot." Not all are innocents. "Two other Arabs came in recently," he went on. "They were scruffily dressed—one looked like a beggar—but they had a letter of recommendation from an Egyptian I know, so I saw them. Now, they really knew diamonds, but I said, 'My dear friend, I'd like to see some money.' The one dressed like a beggar took out a certified bank check for forty thousand dollars and said he had another three hundred thousand dollars in bank checks at the hotel." When the deal was concluded, the wholesaler was asked to ship the goods to Saudi Arabia. "I'll have to include one thousand eighty-four dollars of insurance on the invoice," he explained. The Arabs replied that that was not necessary. No one would steal the diamonds; in Saudi Arabia anyone who steals has his hand cut off.

The blossoming demand in the Middle East is but one sign that the market for diamonds, which has been so dependent for a century on the United States and, latterly, Japan, is broadening. Yet the habits of lovers in those regions remain uncharted. De Beers marketing men concentrate all their efforts on just twenty countries in which they actively promote diamonds and where they calculate 80 percent of all diamonds are purchased. The rest of the world is largely *terra incognita* on their map. Undoubtedly tracking the diamonds through the Middle East, Southeast Asia or South America is not easy; too many goods travel by "submarine." So some diamonds which supposedly are sold in the United States actually end up in Venezuela, Colombia or Argentina, while others that ought to be adorning the fingers of Japanese brides are really sparkling at Korean weddings. "As far as I can see, every bride in South Korea now has a diamond ring," said a marketing man just back from Seoul. Totting up how many diamonds are bought is another matter. Even in Europe it is hard enough, trying to ferret out what goes on. "In Spain and Italy it's useless trying to work out statistics—we might be out one hundred million dollars because the market is all black," lamented an investigator. "So where does one start on Southeast Asia? We can see lots of diamonds going into Hong Kong—they are the fourth largest importers of polished goods—but apparently none coming out."

The trail actually leads to Thailand, the Philippines, Malaysia and Indonesia, but is most discreetly blazed. "Hong Kong is the clearinghouse," explained a Bangkok dealer over lunch on the terrace of the Oriental Hotel. "We've all been buying heavily since 1976. Some of us have quadrupled our orders—in fact, we bought so many goods that Hong Kong dealers stopped allowing us three months' credit and insisted on spot cash." The goods all take a "submarine" route because of a 20 percent import duty in Thailand. But the dealer has little difficulty justifying them on his books. "I go to a pawnbroker," he confided, "and say, 'Sell me a bill of sale for some diamonds, and I'll give you a quarter percent.' So then I have them on my books. Or I break two hundred and fifty rings of old stock, and if the tax people come around, I say I just broke up some old jewelry." Who was buying all his diamonds? Usually, he said, his customers were successful businessmen purchasing either for wives or mistresses, or simply to salt away their undeclared profits into a highly mobile asset. They had seen the difficulties facing many Vietnamese entrepreneurs who were unable to carry out all their gold from Saigon and were determined not to be caught the same way. "But I'm very careful," he concluded, "to keep clear of army or police officers. They have plenty of corrupt money, but what can you do if they don't pay up?"

The story is the same in the Philippines and Indonesia (which is rapidly becoming the best client of a burgeoning diamond market in nearby Singapore). Flourishing black markets are underpinned by the proceeds of corruption and nourished, too, by the fear that one day diamonds may be the best ally in a hasty exit to safer climes. The resourcefulness in obtaining the goods is astounding. A well-known trick often employed by ladies in Manila, to avoid the local import duties, is to take a trip to Hong Kong. On the way out they declare a necklace or bracelet of diamonds at the airport, neglecting to mention that the stones are fakes. Then they buy the real goods in Hong Kong, have them set in the jewelry and return, flourishing the certificate stating they took them out originally.

The popularity of the diamond may well be enhanced accidentally by the spectacular rise in the price of gold since early 1980. Gold shops in the Middle East and Southeast Asia not only found it was becoming increasingly hard to finance the large stocks of ornaments with which their windows have traditionally been laden, but also that the volatility of the gold price threatened to wipe them out if they judged the market wrong. Diamonds were a safer bet because of relative stability. "Gold is so jumpy that people who have it don't sleep," observed a Middle East dealer. "But if you have a diamond you can sleep." And the leading jeweler in Penang, Malaysia, shrewdly pointed out, "Diamonds are cheap in relation to gold. It used to be two ounces of gold for one carat of diamonds of small sizes; now it's one ounce to one carat. So some dealers are selling their gold and buying up diamonds." He offered a word of caution. The old habit of buying gold jewelry as the basic form of saving and adornment dies hard. "Most people know gold better," he said. "The diamond is still for the educated."

2

Investors

"The Hardest Hard Money"

*Good evening, Mr. . . . How are you? . . .
GOOD. This is Mr. . . . of American Diamond Brokers calling. Now that you've read
through your Diamond Portfolio, it's all I
promised, isn't it? (Wait for answer) You
may be wondering why all the publicity and
attention on diamonds, and the reasons are
obvious! In the last ten years, the price of diamonds has increased in excess of 300 percent.
In the last year alone, over 50 percent. That's
better than I.B.M., U. S. Steel, Xerox, gold
and coffee futures. The price of diamonds has
never taken any downside movement in over
twenty-five years. Can you imagine how
much the dollar has lost in twenty-five years?
Look, Mr. . . . the Japanese, West German,
European, all sophisticated investors, are turn-*

ing from DOLLARS TO DIAMONDS. Un-
like paper investments, you will have in your
possession a tangible asset, unlike paper
money. You will receive physical possession
of your diamonds . . . the diamonds are sent
to you contained within a tamper-proof see-
through container. That's a real nice feeling
of security, isn't it? Mr. . . .

Such smooth, insidious patter from "the drive script" of a telephone salesman touting diamonds has become familiar to thousands of American investors in recent years. As the decline of the dollar and rising inflation precipitated a search for tangible securities, the diamond, to the unwary, often shone out as the ideal answer. Diamonds became not just a symbol of love but of financial salvation. This new role swiftly spawned a spate of diamond investment companies from coast to coast, all touting the virtues of the stone. "One of the World's Most Brilliant Blue-Chip Investments," proclaimed advertisements in the *Wall Street Journal* for Mayor's, a Florida outfit that offered "With a minimum hundred-thousand-dollar portfolio purchase you get CERTIFIED DIAMONDS SOLD AT TEN PERCENT ABOVE OUR COST from the diamond cutter and fully notarized by affidavits." And from La Jolla Diamond Inc., in California, came a brochure lauding "Diamonds . . . the Hardest Hard Money . . . Just as ancient man once used diamonds in amulets to ward off evil spirits, the modern investor can use diamonds in a portfolio to resist financial ills and offset the decline in value of the U. S. dollar, all of which threatens to erode accumulated wealth." In short, as another California firm headlined their advertisements, "Today, diamonds are an investor's best friend."

The investment houses all stressed the track record for diamond prices. They had risen steadily since the early 1930s, thanks to the careful control of De Beers' Diamond Trading Company. Would-be investors were reassured with cheerful charts showing how prices had risen by 850 percent since 1948 alone. Also, the big surge in diamond prices in 1978 gave them an exceptional performance on the *New York Times* Investment/Inflation Scoreboard for that year. The Scoreboard showed that while an investment in General Motors stock had gone up precisely 0.6 percent, a one-year Treasury bill had yielded interest of 7.05 percent, gold has risen 26.5 percent and the price of a house in Scarsdale, New York, by 32 percent, diamonds were up no less than 66.5 percent. Moreover, the Economist Intelligence Unit, in a special study of precious materials as "Inflation Shelters," was predicting further price rises going into the early 1980s. The diamond, the potential investor came to feel, was an asset he could trust in an age of uncertainty.

The vogue is by no means exclusively American. Diamonds have achieved worldwide appeal as an essential hedge against inflation, currency upheavals and political instability. And their portability has attracted much "black money"—that is to say, money not declared to the tax man—and "funk" money—nest eggs built up in politically insecure countries by people who fear that one day they may have to do a moonlight flit over the border. Worldwide investment in diamonds is over $1 billion a year. A young Belgian banker, who specializes in diamond investment, remarked early in 1980, "I estimate the American market for investment at five hundred million dollars a year, the Far East—including Japan—at three hundred million, Europe at about two hundred million, with France accounting for nearly half that, and the Middle East at one hundred million."

An executive of the Diamond High Council in Antwerp, confirming the trend, reckoned that 20 percent of all diamonds over half a carat was now destined for investors. The demand for some types of diamonds was so intense that they became almost unobtainable. The top-quality one-carat D Flawless acquired the cachet of a rare stamp; between 1978 and 1980 its price rocketed from around $10,000 to over $70,000.* Anyone fortunate enough to have one sat tight. "I'm holding several D Flawless," a Belgian exchange dealer confided over lunch at the Diamond Dealers' Club in Antwerp. "They are a terrific investment. You can't find any around now."

The price, however, was clearly distorted because so few D

* In May 1980 the one-carat round brilliant D Flawless was quoted as high as $77,000. The next category down, either an E color or a VVSI quality, was quoted at around $51,000. By comparison, a flawless J color was only $9,600.

Flawless are available. One estimate suggests that out of about
11 million carats of gem-quality diamonds mined each year, only
125,000 carats (say 1 percent) fall into the range of over half
a carat preferred by investors, and of these scarcely 750 are D
Flawless of about 1 carat.[19] A switch into diamonds by investors,
therefore, pushes the price of a relatively small number of the
finest stones completely out of proportion to run-of-the-mill
small gems.

The original rush into investment diamonds came from Italy
in 1973, when the impending collapse of the lira initiated a
scramble by Italians to turn their paper assets into diamonds
(and gold). They hurried across the Swiss border to Chiasso,
Lugano and Locarno, loaded down with suitcases stuffed with
lira notes, straight into the welcoming arms of salesmen from
a host of instant diamond investment companies. The investment
firms peddled what one dealer later admitted "was any old
rubbish from cutters," and their naive clients knew no better.
A great many Italians found to their bitter cost that they had
paid four or five times too much for their diamonds but had
no recourse. The investment houses were long closed up, and
the diamonds had been bought with funds taken illegally from
Italy.

The Italians were not the only ones taken for a ride during
the initial European diamond rush of the mid-seventies. A leading Dutch bank put several of its investment portfolio holders
into diamonds, only to discover too late that they had been sold
stones of poor "make" by cutters, who found the investment fad
handy for palming off some stones they might not have been
able to sell easily to more sophisticated wholesalers for the jewelry trade.

But lessons were not learned easily. The death of General
Franco in Spain provoked a flurry of diamond buying by
wealthy people who suddenly felt insecure about the future of
their country. In France the possibility that the left wing
would win the 1978 elections gave additional impetus to a
growing vogue for diamond investment. The variation on the
investment theme in France is that it has been channeled largely
through the banks; leading commercial banks, including Crédit

[19] *Preciousstones Newsletter*, April 1980, pp. 6–11.

Lyonnais, Banque Nationale de Paris and Banque de L'Indochine et de Suez, all became involved, as did the private Banque
Rothschild in Paris. One or two were reported to be handling
up to $20 million a year in diamond purchases for clients as the
total French demand rose to at least $100 million annually.

By contrast in West Germany, where diamond investment
also became more widespread, the main commercial banks, after
one or two preliminary forays, shied away. They felt that
dabbling in diamonds was too hazardous. So investment in Germany has become the territory of private investment companies,
as it has in Britain. The British, not usually ones for seeking their
refuge in tangible assets other than property, have been cautious, and purchases do not compare with those of the French,
the Germans or even, apparently, the Scandinavians. But one
London diamond investment outfit confided that its clients included everyone from titled families and captains of industry
to a wealthy vet and a successful pig breeder.

Farther afield, rich Mexicans sought refuge in diamonds when
the peso weakened in the years immediately before the latest
oil discoveries, and several wealthy Venezuelan families started
adding diamonds to their extensive investments in Florida
(where they prefer to hold many of their assets, just in case of
revolution at home). In India the ever-tightening regulations
on private gold holding and fear of overnight demonetization
of large-denomination notes drove much "black" money into
diamonds. And Bangkok diamond dealers found that demand
rose in tandem with increasing political tension in Southeast
Asia. As diamond investment caught on in Australia, American
Express even arranged for its clients to buy them by credit
card.

The keenest interest, however, came from the Middle East,
as the wealth created by the soaring oil prices enabled the richest
families in the Gulf and Saudi Arabia to buy not only fine new
diamonds, but to set records in the auction rooms as splendid
stones of the past came back under the hammer. The Saudi
Arabian royal family is notably intrigued by diamonds and has
taken the wise precaution of purchasing through a banker, who
is also a fully qualified gemologist with his own laboratory for
studying stones at home. While most of the diamond investment
business involves commissions handed out liberally on all sides,

the Saudi's buyer always refuses kickbacks from the cutters from whom he buys, much to their surprise. "Too many people in diamond investment are crooks," he said. "I have to be super-clean."

Most diamond investment is discreet, but the trend was clearly signaled early on by the record prices notched up by the great auction houses Sotheby's and Christie's at sales of fine jewels in New York, Zurich, Geneva and Monte Carlo. Sotheby's sold a 24.44-carat lilac-pink diamond for $1.09 million to a Saudi Arabian jeweler at $44,564 per carat. Christie's knocked down a 4.97-carat pink diamond for $305,000, achieving a record $61,000 a carat; Christie's also secured $581,395 for a 15.26-carat white diamond, at $38,000 a carat. The potential profits were underlined when Elizabeth Taylor sold for $2.5 million in 1979 the 69.42-carat Cartier diamond, which Richard Burton had originally bought for her at Sotheby's in 1969 for $1.05 million. Behind that $1.4 million profit, however, there is a cautionary tale; Ms. Taylor hoped to get $4 million for her diamond, but when it came up for regrading in New York, it was found to be of color slightly inferior to that originally certified before Burton acquired it. The price suffered accordingly. Over-grading is a continuing hazard of diamond investment at every level of wealth.

The Boiler-Room Boys

Exotic deals by movie stars or ultrarich Saudi princes apart, no market rivals the United States for regular purchases of diamonds by a wide spectrum of investors nor matches the brashness with which they are sold. Diamond investment in America has been taken to absurd (and often corrupt) extremes.

Although a handful of the diamond investment firms started since 1975 in the United States have made some attempt to educate their clients, many have been run by unscrupulous operators. Peddling diamonds became the latest racket for the "boiler-room boys," as Americans call them, the successor to selling Florida's swamps for retirement homes or Arizona desert as desirable ranchland. Gullible investors were persuaded to part with their savings for diamonds that were supposedly being

sold at wholesale price but were often more expensive than anything available from the neighborhood jewelry store and were
not always of the quality promised. A few of these "Lie-by-day,
fly-by-night" operators, as they were christened by Joel Windman, the tough New York lawyer who presides over the Jewelers' Vigilance Committee, simply cashed the checks and ran.
By the time the puzzled customer wondered where his diamonds
were and phoned to find out, the line was disconnected. A
doctor from Gadsden, Alabama, for instance, was wooed over
the phone by a saleslady who got him so enthusiastic about
diamond prospects that he mailed a $13,000 check to a Miami
address; he never saw a single solitaire. Eventually he complained to the Florida attorney general's department which dispatched an investigator, but the diamond saleslady was long
gone. "I'm a damn sucker," conceded the doctor sadly, "but
they're such great talkers." [20]

Weaving a spell with meaningless chatter that pandered to
the potential client's worries about his savings was the heart of
the matter. A salesman's knowledge of diamonds was irrelevant
compared to his gift of gab, as recruiting advertisements in
newspapers indicated. "TELEPHONE PROS, experienced
only," a New York Times advertisement declared. "Don't beat
about the bush for leads! We have the best job in town. Sell
investment quality diamonds. Direct from the cutter!!!" The
lack of experience was such that one New York cutter even sold
an investment firm $80,000 worth of diamond simulants made
from cubic zirconia; no one was any the wiser until the ultimate
client went to have his new stones independently appraised.

The most notorious investment firm in Scottsdale, Arizona,
which brashly called itself De Beers Diamond Investment Ltd.
(and neglected to make clear it had nothing to do with De
Beers Consolidated Mines, Ltd., of South Africa), even dispatched a team to London to hire salesmen with British accents.
But their activities soon attracted the attention of detectives
from New Scotland Yard, who felt they were more interested
in confidence tricksters than diamond experts. The recruiters
left in a hurry, neglecting to pay their hotel bill, but not before

[20] Miami Herald, March 4, 1979.

they had signed on fifteen salesmen of assorted English, South African and Australian origins who returned with them to Arizona.

The job prospects sounded tempting. Salesmen were paid 5 percent commissions on diamonds and 10 percent on colored stones (which the Scottsdale De Beers and some other investment firms also offered). Since a good salesman could sell perhaps $2 to $3 million worth of stones a year, he might pocket $100,000 himself. Many soon saw the chance for even greater riches. Having observed for a few months how to play the game, they simply set up shop on their own. The Scottsdale De Beers ultimately spawned fourteen enterprises in Arizona alone.

Motivation was always important. One investment firm, feeling that its telephone salesmen were not aggressive enough, dressed them up in gorilla outfits and spacemen suits.

The unwary targets of such monkey business were usually selected at random from telephone directories. The art was to make sales only to people living in other states, first, to avoid liability for local state sales taxes, and second, to avoid the embarrassment of customers living just down the road beating on the door if things went wrong. Arizona provided an ideal base for such operations because of a long-standing frontier attitude frowning on any government interference or regulation of business.

The essential link between salesman and customer was, of course, the telephone. The boiler-room boys rented the 800 area code WATS lines that enabled a client to call them toll-free (but studiously avoided WATS lines from Alaska and Hawaii as the cost of calls was too high). De Beers in Scottsdale had as many as fifty WATS lines at one time, and its phone bill was reported at $40,000 a month. Another equally aggressive Phoenix company had twenty-three WATS lines. The initial approach was usually made by a "qualifier," a fledgling salesman who thumbed through the Yellow Pages looking for prospects among dentists, doctors, lawyers and other professional people likely to have ready cash to invest. John Dorschner, an enterprising reporter for the *Miami Herald*'s weekend magazine *Tropic*, who managed to get himself signed on as a "qualifier," noted, "My favorites were chiropractors, and

if they were in small enough towns, they rarely had reception-
ists, answered the telephone themselves (a big plus right there)
and seemed embarrassed to admit they would not have one
thousand dollars to invest in something that 'has a good potential profit.' " [21]

Anyone who did not have the wisdom to slam down the
phone instantly and could thus be lured by such tempting talk
as, "Now, doctor, did you see where the dollar has just taken
a ten percent devaluation against the Indian rupee?" was dispatched a brochure. A few days later a more aggressive salesman, often accorded the doubtful accolade of consultant, would
be on the line with his prepared "drive script" to clinch a sale.
Reporter John Dorschner picked up a few useful tips; never
call potential customers in the north on a stormy day as the
weather might sour their mood, and do not try doctors on a
Thursday—they are too busy.

The willingness of thousands of Americans to buy diamonds,
sight unseen, over the telephone from some stranger, who might
even be got up as a gorilla, is incredible. Yet it was sympto-
matic of the despair that the plight of the dollar has caused
among many small-town Americans in recent years. Although
sales figures are scarce (and have often been exaggerated), the
Scottsdale De Beers is estimated to have grossed at least $50 mil-
lion in just over four years. Another Phoenix outfit, also under
police investigation, made $7.5 million in just over three years,
with sales to more than 1,200 clients (an average of over $6,000
each).

The most unsuspecting investors have consistently been doctors. Indeed, the files of one firm investigated in Phoenix showed
that 50 percent of all clients were in the medical profession.
A physician in Connecticut paid $119,570 for diamonds and
precious stones from a Phoenix firm, only to find when he
sought insurance that the supposedly independent "appraisal
certificates" accompanying them vastly overrated the stones. A
New York doctor shelled out $32,640 for a 5.1-carat diamond
from the same outfit, only to be told bluntly by a certified
gemologist shortly afterwards that it was worth only around
$12,000. And a third doctor, an Iranian living in Newark, New

[21] *Ibid.*

Jersey, whose family in Tehran sent him $180,000 just before the Shah's fall, salted the money into seventeen diamonds that had all been graded flawless by an Antwerp laboratory but proved on further examination to be much inferior. Doctors were not the only people taken for a ride. A New Orleans insurance agent paid $22,000 for a 2.53-carat diamond, only to find when he had it independently appraised that its quality was misrepresented. A second stone, for which he paid $7,000 in advance, was never delivered at all. And an engineer in Overland Park, Kansas, who spent $14,000 on seven half-carat stones was staggered when he took them to a local jeweler who would pay him only $4,900 for them.

The complaints stem from buyers who have taken the trouble to get a second opinion on their diamonds once they receive them, either for insurance or because they later read articles warning of the pitfalls of such investments. Yet, curiously enough, complaints are relatively rare and may not be acted upon. The reasons are not hard to find. Some investors are just too embarrassed to admit that they have lost their shirt; they sit on their diamonds, Micawber-like, in the hope that something will turn up, believing that if they hang in there long enough they may finally get out even. But a more significant reason is that diamonds have often been bought with money that has not been declared to the tax authorities. "I had a doctor on the phone not long ago, complaining about paying thirty-five thousand dollars for a diamond that he did not get," said Joel Windman of the Jewelers' Vigilance Committee. "So the first question I asked him was, 'Did you declare that thirty-five thousand to the I.R.S.? If so, we can do this and this, but if not . . .' He was embarrassed and hung up."

Even more legitimate investment companies admit that many of their clients buy and sell diamonds under assumed names. "We've just sold some diamonds to a man who calls himself Charles Dickens," confided the chief salesman of a leading Phoenix firm. "A good percentage of our clients pay in greenbacks, and they often hide their identity—adopting an author's, a president's or a street name is a favorite gimmick." The attraction of diamonds as an investment is enhanced because they may be purchased anonymously, unlike stock or bond transactions which must be registered. "Many of our customers are wealthy right-wing people who are paranoid about government regulation and interference," the diamond salesman explained, "and diamonds offer them a nice way to get away with tax avoidance."

The hidden guilt of some buyers may also explain why they are tricked so easily; they are eager to launder their undeclared money, and diamonds offer a convenient haven. "What is fascinating," remarked a New York diamond expert, "is that a man, highly trained as a doctor or a dentist, throws all his natural intelligence aside when it comes to purchasing on the phone a diamond for twenty thousand dollars that is worth only five thousand dollars."

The Fifth "C"

The lack of discretion, however, is at least partly explained by an important piece of paper at the salesman's elbow—the diamond certificate. The trick of selling to people who cannot tell a real stone from a synthetic, let alone understand the caratage, cut, color and clarity of a true diamond, is to provide a laboratory certificate confirming certain specifications. And the diamond itself comes in a little sealed plastic package, the size of a match booklet, with a microfilmed copy of the certificate inside. "Certification," some investment wags like to say, "has become the fifth 'c' of the diamond game." The diamond investment boom has led to unprecedented pressure on existing gemological laboratories and the setting up of new ones. Previously, relatively few gem diamonds were certified by laboratories; the main demand was for insurance or estate-valuing purposes. "Now it's all the fad," said Robert Crowningshield, the crisp and courteous director of the Gemological Institute of America's New York laboratory. "We've got one hundred people in our laboratories grading a thousand diamonds a week. We keep running out of space." The certificates of the GIA's laboratories in New York and Los Angeles have won international recognition. Although it costs fifty dollars for certification, the resulting piece of paper confirming the shape and cut, the weight and measurements, the proportions, the finish and the clarity and color of a diamond can add literally thousands of dollars to a diamond's value.

The more astute diamond investment firms soon discovered how to turn that to advantage. They simply hired a GIA-trained grader to purchase stones from a cutter's display, backing his own judgment that they were of good quality and color. The stones could then be sent to the GIA laboratories for grading and with the resulting certificate immediately were worth much more. "If I buy without a certificate, I can probably get the stone ten percent cheaper in New York or twenty percent cheaper in Tel Aviv," said the buyer for a Phoenix investment house.

As the demand for certificates soon swamped the GIA's facilities, their experts ceased grading any stones weighing less than one carat. They also declined to test stones sent in to them by some of the shadier investment outfits. Unfortunately, this simply diverted the diamonds to new "laboratories" in the United States, Canada and Belgium. Several investment firms set up their own, which they claimed were staffed by GIA-trained personnel. That ploy at once opened the door to deceit; the worth of a certificate issued by an in-house laboratory is clearly questionable. The temptation to overgrade can be irresistible. After all, a simple declaration that a diamond is a top-grade D Flawless (the finest color and without any visible flaws under a ten-power loupe), when it is really just an E VVSI (the next color on the GIA scale with the speck of a flaw in it), can add $20,000 to its value.

The doubtful validity of certificates was not limited to in-house laboratories. Some "independent" laboratories set up in New York, Toronto and Antwerp were inclined to grade generously, especially in return for a little bribe. As a Belgian dealer remarked, "A lab man can say, 'What do you want me to write on the certificate? D Flawless? Okay, give me a hundred dollars.' " When the Federal Bureau of Investigation checked twenty-seven stones seized from a Phoenix firm, they found that all had a grading inferior to that listed on the monthly sales bulletin. And investigations by the Phoenix police department into another of the less reputable outfits selling diamonds there showed a consistent pattern of overgrading by a private Antwerp laboratory of stones destined for the Phoenix firm. When the police arranged for the stones to be regraded by the GIA in New York, they found that not a single stone submitted matched the specifications claimed on the original Antwerp certificate, on which the investment firm naturally based its price. "This company alone sold more than five hundred diamonds over one carat as flawless," alleged the investigating officer, "yet *none* of them were flawless." He searched through a filing cabinet and pulled out some comparative certificates. The original document accompanying a 1.17-carat stone from Antwerp showed it to be H Flawless, but under GIA scrutiny it was rated as I color VVSI, with a natural inclusion that could not possibly have escaped the laboratory grader's eye. Another 1.52-carat stone was certified originally as being J color and flawless but was proved at the GIA to be VVS2; it had what the trade called a "bearded girdle."

Such variations cause real concern to the directors of reliable laboratories. "I doubt if one diamond in ten given as flawless in Antwerp would get the same grading from the GIA or from us," said Caspar Beesley of the American Gemological Laboratory in New York. But the real trouble, Beesley argues, is that color grading is still a process of visual comparison between the stone under examination and a set of eight master stones. Even if the master sets of all laboratories were matched, the methods of studying the stones are not standardized. "Take lighting," he explained. "We use twenty-five watt north-day-light bulbs, others use fifty-watt bulbs, some use fluorescent lamps; inevitably color can look different. Then how do you hold the diamond in relation to the light? What we have to achieve is a consistent and uniform application of standards."

Meanwhile, the techniques of grading differ so much that discrepancies are inevitable and can always be explained away. Pinning down deliberate overgrading in a court of law is thus virtually impossible. The whole problem is compounded because the swift growth of certification has often led to the employment of graders with little experience.

The only satisfactory solution will be for independent non-commercial laboratories to be established by diamond industry trade associations in each country. Already the Diamond High Council (*Hoge raad voor diamant*, or HRD) in Antwerp has established its own laboratory, whose HRD certificates often warrant a diamond securing a slightly higher price than if the certificate was from a commercial laboratory. "Our laboratory was a response to the danger of commercial labs," said Leo Lismonde, secretary general of the High Council. "It is too easy for a cutter to say to a commercial laboratory, 'I'm such a good client that this stone *has* to be such and such a color.'" The intention is that the HRD laboratory be part of an international network, with all members operating to the same standards of certification. "Diamond investment is here to stay," said Sylvain Zucker, one of the High Council's directors and chairman of the Antwerp Diamond Club, "and it may take on proportions that we cannot foresee, so we have to do our utmost to keep it on a trustworthy basis, with certificates that people can believe in because they come from a nonprofit-making laboratory." Already CIBJO, the International Confederation of Jewelry, Silverware, Diamonds, Pearls and Stones, is trying to build up such a string of laboratories, modeled on the Antwerp HRD.

The scheme, however, is in its infancy, and meanwhile such reliable laboratories as the GIA in America and the High Council's HRD in Antwerp cannot cope with demand. So commercial laboratories proliferate, and the basic rule of diamond investment must remain *caveat emptor*—buyer beware. At least buyers cannot complain they have not been warned. Some first-rate investigative reporting by such newspapers as the *Arizona Republic*, the *Miami Herald*, *Forbes* magazine and the trade journal *Jewelers' Circular Keystone* (to name but a few), together with a CBS television news exposé on "Sixty Minutes," has highlighted the pitfalls. This reporting also spurred on investigations by the FBI and local police departments, so that the worst of the "boiler-room" era may be over. Several states issued orders banning specified firms from soliciting within their borders, while New York actually set up a diamond task force under the wing of the state attorney general's office to ferret out the worst of the swindlers. Attorney General Louis J. Lefkowitz warned New Yorkers against "succumbing to boiler-room, high-pressure promises of surefire, risk-free, inflation-hedging profit potentials." Over the border in Canada, the Royal Canadian Mounted Police rounded up over forty diamond investment salesmen, who had been cashing in on the American boom from a seemingly foreign safe haven. Meanwhile, in Arizona, the "Scottsdale De Beers" was forced into bankruptcy, much to the chagrin of several highly reputable New York dealers to whom it owed $1.3 million for stones delivered. The president and three senior officers, some of whom had prior criminal records, were indicted on fraud charges. But proving fraud is very difficult. Firms often stay ahead of the law by shutting up shop in one state and reopening under a different name in the next. Another Phoenix firm, faced with increasing police scrutiny, simply moved to Salt Lake City, Utah. And new firms start up almost weekly, especially in southern California, which by 1980 challenged Arizona as the favorite home of the investment operators.

Wooing the Neurosurgeons

The adverse publicity for diamond investment undoubtedly scared away a few would-be investors, but memories are short. The day of the telephone hard sell may be waning, but a newer generation of firms is picking up the reins with great success. The emphasis has shifted, however, to contacting potential customers by direct mail or by locating them at investment conferences and seminars. The soft sell has replaced the hard. At one "offshore" investment conference in Acapulco, Mexico, attended by 1,300 people who had each paid $350 to spend two days listening to speeches on how to invest wisely (including a half-hour lecture on the merits of buying diamonds), I found three leading diamond firms busy handing out glossy brochures with such exotic titles as *Diamonds Demystified*. All three had hospitality suites in which to woo potential clients. The sales patter was quiet. "I want you to feel comfortable," said a salesman, as he went over a price list with a prospective customer. The list offered a range of diamonds starting with an 0.45-carat G color VVS2 round-cut brilliant, with a certificate from an Antwerp laboratory, for $1,789 up to a 1.55-carat F color flawless, with a GIA certificate, for $29,063. The prices, the salesmen claimed, were "slightly above wholesale." But he was at pains to stress that profits were not instantaneous. "You should sit on a diamond for two years," he said, "but eventually, to enable you to realize your profit, I am able to rebroker the stone for you into our inventory at a seven-point-five percent commission."

The conference routine pays off. "Medical conferences are the best," the salesman confided later, "especially of orthodontists and neurosurgeons." What luck was he having in Acapulco? "We've made one firm sale for thirty thousand dollars and have three or four other good prospects, of which we'll probably close two," he allowed.

The most persistent worry that makes investors hesitate is how they can resell their diamonds. The investment firms have to be careful; they cannot guarantee to buy back the stones because they would then be making a market in a security. That would bring them under the strict regulations of the U. S. Securities and Exchange Commission in Washington. They get around this by saying they will make their "best efforts" to act as brokers in the sale of the stones. The real gamble, of course, is that most of their clients will sit on the stones for years. "If all the diamonds we had sold came back to us at once, we could do nothing, we'd be swamped," admitted Louis Steiner, the president of Gem Hedge International. "It would be just like a bank if everyone came in for their money on the same day."

In practice, profit taking is sparse, as I found in the dealing room of a leading New York investment house, Gemstone Trading Corporation. One whole wall was taken up with the status of their inventory. On the left were about sixty yellow slips, each representing one of the diamonds on the most recent price list circulated to clients; in the middle were a further one hundred and twenty blue slips, indicating new diamonds added to the inventory since the list went out; and finally on the right were a mere eight orange slips, indicating diamonds that clients wished to sell if a buyer could be found. "We do the best we can if a customer wants to sell," said Gemstone's president, Michael Freedman. "We will try to buy back at the selling price, less a ten percent commission. Several of our customers have gotten out at a profit in the last few years."

Such an offer gives the investor a chance of making a profit. The danger arises if the firm from which he purchased the stone goes out of business by the time he wishes to sell. Then he is at the mercy of the open market. And as the seller of a single stone, even with a certificate, he may have real difficulty in realizing any profit. The investment firms consistently tell clients that they eliminate the layers of middlemen in the diamond trade and sell at close to wholesale. But how close is close?

The evidence suggests that the markup over wholesale, even

of those firms which claim to have a direct link with Antwerp cutting firms, is usually between 80 and 100 percent. Since no two diamonds are alike, it is hard to make reliable comparisons. But in search of guidelines, I compared the price lists of three investment firms, two from New York and one from Phoenix, with a computer printout of the inventory of a leading Forty-seventh Street diamond broker whose prices could be regarded as genuine trade wholesale. All the diamonds compared weighed between 1 carat and 1.55 carats, and all were backed by GIA certificates. Ten diamonds could be reasonably well matched in terms of weight, color, clarity and cut; of these, the markup over wholesale by the investment firms was 125 percent in one example, 100 percent in another, over 80 percent in four more examples, over 60 percent in two others and 20 percent and 12 percent respectively in the remaining comparisons. The low markup on the last two stones is certainly explained by a note on the investment price list that they were not high-quality cuts (and for that reason to include them may hardly be accurate, for almost surely they were acquired cheaply).

The inference from this limited exercise is clear. The investor is often paying 80 and 100 percent over wholesale. He may indeed be able to win a profit if he can dispose of the stones back into the inventory of the firm that originally sold him the diamonds. But on the open market it will be a different story. He is likely to be offered the genuine wholesale price, or even a little below that. Therefore, if he tried to make a quick sale of a diamond he had purchased for $18,000, he might just get $10,000, but probably less, as the wholesaler would need his profit, too. If he was patient and waited for diamond prices to double, then he could get $20,000. But he might have to wait up to five years or more and then would show only a $2,000 profit on a five-year investment of $18,000.

This is the continuing hazard of diamond investment. As Michael Freedman of Gemstone Trading Corporation admits, "Diamonds are relatively illiquid. They are like stamps, art and antiques; they are not for the quick trade."

"If you want to get a good price, you must not be too urgent when it comes to selling," added John Wilkie, managing director of Diamond Selection Limited, an international investment firm based in London. "We tell our clients that small diamonds may be liquid in four to six weeks, but bigger diamonds can only be resold over six months or more. It's no good thinking you can get out like the stock exchange. The ideal diamond investor is the man who takes a five- or ten-year view and then is not in a hurry for his money."

The nightmare of some *diamantaires*, and also of De Beers, is that the investors may not always be so patient. Supposing they did dump? "Encouraging the sale of diamonds for purely speculative purposes exposes our entire industry to the dangers of a powerful time bomb which may ruin not only those directly involved but also inflict heavy damages upon our trade as a whole," warned Israel's Moshe Schnitzer, in his role as president of the World Federation of Diamond Bourses at their annual convention in May 1980. "It is one thing to emphasize the investment value of diamonds to jewelry buyers, and it is a completely different matter to renounce a long-established solid trade to enter the no-man's-land of ruthless international investment sharking."

Yet there is little sign of slowdown. The growing scale of investment in the United States, despite adverse publicity and prosecutions, is beginning to embrace the jewelry trade itself. Traditionally, jewelers have sold diamond jewelry for adornment and have shied away from selling loose diamonds for investment. The investment boom, however, has inevitably brought investors to their door, as publicity against boiler-room operators has stressed that the neighborhood jeweler is a more trustworthy source of diamonds than some persuasive voice on the phone. The ball has been passed to the jeweler's court. Rather reluctantly, some are grasping it. "One has to admit that the investment firms have merchandised diamonds fantastically," said Henry Harteveldt, a leading New York manufacturer. "They picked up the ball and ran with it. Jewelers have backed into it belatedly. But the investment concept is here to stay, and jewelers are beginning to realize they cannot always do their keystone [doubling] markup. They'll call us and say, 'We've got a doctor with twenty-five thousand dollars—can he have a good price?' " Another Fifth Avenue manufacturer confided that he had just concluded a $45,000 sale to a client in Kansas, who had bought a piece of land to put up a new jewelry store but had been asked to pay for the property in diamonds, not cash. "The retail jeweler has woken up and realizes this should be his business," added Glenn Nord, the diamond buyer for the GSI Corporation in Los Angeles.

The vogue for diamonds has been picked up even by some American banks, which have started offering to pay interest in diamonds on savings accounts. A new Los Angeles bank, American International, sought to win customers by prepaying interest in diamonds on certificates of deposit of more than $20,000 held for between one and ten years. On a three-year deposit of $50,000, for instance, the prepaid interest of $8,607 could be invested in a diamond bought by the bank for that amount. Another West Coast bank, First State Bank of Oregon in Milwaukie, Oregon, has accepted diamonds as part of investment portfolios for retirement plans since the beginning of 1979. The policy was adopted, according to a bank vice-president, in response to "many, many requests from our existing customers."

That is the nub. The awareness of diamonds as a medium for investment has grown apace. "The diamond investment boom has done a lot of harm but also a lot of good," concluded Joseph Schlussel of the Diamond Registry on Forty-seventh Street. "Harm because it has made some people think that everyone in diamonds is a charlatan, but beneficial, too, because all the publicity has educated the public about diamonds. When I started my business ten years ago, no one knew much about them. Now every magazine you look at—*Fortune, Forbes, Time, Newsweek* —is writing about diamonds, and in the end we all benefit. And it may make people realize that a diamond is a good investment if you buy it, let your wife wear it for ten or twenty years and then sell it. You may make a little profit, and at least your wife has enjoyed twenty years free wear."

3

Industrialists:
Some Like It Tough

A brainteaser for a quiz show might be, "Find the common link between the great Italian marble quarries of Carrara, a packet of frozen fish, an eye surgeon's scalpel, Hong Kong's Kai Tak airport, St. Paul's Cathedral, a North Sea oil rig, the Hollywood Freeway in California and a Venus space probe." The answer, of course, is a diamond.

In just the last forty years the diamond has come into its own as industry's best friend, cutting anything from marble to fish, grooving the concrete surface of runways and roads to prevent skidding, drilling out test cores from the masonry of ancient buildings or from the ocean floor, or simply resisting the great range of temperatures and pressures in space. Before each automobile rolls off the production line in Detroit, one and a half carats of industrial diamonds are consumed, polishing the pistons or rounding the window glass. Spectacle and contact lenses are ground with diamond abrasive. Even the humble plastic washing-up bowl is cheap because its mold can be honed so smooth by a diamond powder acting as a superior sandpaper that 10,000 bowls can be turned out before it has to be repolished. "It's simple, silly things like that, where nothing but a diamond will do," said Gordon Ferriman, director of De Beers Industrial Diamond Division. "The modern industrial world would almost come to a halt without diamonds. Life might not collapse totally, but many articles could not be produced so cheaply in mass quantity."

The diamond's toughness is its unique asset. "It is the hardest material known to man," stressed Horst Wapler, a German-born engineer who is a technical manager for De Beers. "With gem diamonds you look for the optical properties; the hardness is a welcome addition but is not essential. In ninety-nine percent of industrial applications, however, hardness is the outstanding property."

Surprisingly, this potential of the diamond was long overlooked. A few early applications were tried in the last century for drilling and wire drawing, and Carl Zeiss, the great German inventor of optical lenses, took out a patent in 1906 grinding optical glass, but for mining houses the industrial goods were almost an embarrassment. Gordon Ferriman recalls that when he joined De Beers just before World War II, no one was really sure what to do with the rough from Zaire, the main producer of industrial grade. "People used to joke about chartering a boat and taking it out to sea and dumping it over the side," he said. De Beers themselves had no in-house knowledge of the technical potential of diamonds; they disposed of industrials where they could to a few specialist dealers.

The diamond's industrial credentials were first really tapped following the invention in Germany in 1929 of tungsten carbide —the strongest of metal alloys. Tungsten carbide itself proved to be supremely tough and an excellent cutter, but it could be sharpened properly only with diamonds. Then the impetus for the mass production of weaponry in World War II finally established the diamond's reputation. The diamond's usefulness in wartime even inspired a poem, *The Brilliant Armament*, during the darkest days of 1941, which warbled:

With diamonds true up the wheels that grind,
Which have a part in rescuing Mankind;

> *Draw through the die a wire so delicate*
> *That no unaided eye can focus it;*
> *Send stones now needed in the furnaces*
> *Of all our metal-throated factories,*
> *And diamonds for the teeth of many a saw*
> *More richly dentured than the gods of yore.*

This epic was published with a foreword by the assistant secretary for raw materials at the ministry of supply, which itself waxed lyrical: ". . . the stones which the sorters once rejected demonstrate day by day in grinding, turning, wire-drawing and countless other engineering operations that adamantine durability and steadfastness which will lead us to Victory." [22]

Hyperbole aside, no one has since considered dumping industrial rough out at sea. In fact, demand has long since outstripped natural supply, and the gap has been filled only by synthetic diamonds. The creation of synthetics with exactly the same properties as the real thing, by crystalizing carbon under intense heat and pressure, has transformed the industrial scene. The original process was pioneered by the Swedish company ASEA (*Allmanna Svenska Elektriska Aktiebolaget*) in 1953 and patented by General Electric in the United States two years later. De Beers themselves, caught napping originally by this threat to their monopoly in diamonds, soon mastered the technique and eventually joined in the ASEA production.

Although the subtleties of the alchemy are jealously guarded, the basic recipe for making your own diamonds is now well known. Graphite (a common form of carbon) and a metal solvent are placed between tungsten carbide pistons and subjected to a sustained pressure of a million pounds per square inch, while being heated to temperatures of between 2500 degrees and 3500 degrees Fahrenheit. Slowly the graphite changes into minute diamond crystals. The longer the cooking goes on, the bigger the diamond created. That is the catch. It takes up to an hour to produce tiny industrial diamonds and close to a week to create a diamond of one carat. That time span makes it uneconomic, at the present time, to make gem diamonds.

Moreover, it is a very delicate task. "If a thunderstorm occurs

---

[22] Reginald Turnor, *The Brilliant Armament*, with a foreword by A. E. Lee (London, December 1941), p. 21.

during production, causing the electric voltage to drop even for a second [like lights flickering in a storm], the whole process is ruined," said Horst Wapler. Small synthetics, however, which are often like fine powder, carefully graded to sizes as tiny as one-hundredth of a human hair, can be produced cheaply. Low-cost synthetics have led to the real revolution. The price of the abrasive powder, known as grit, that makes up most of the industrial market is only on average two dollars a carat (compare that with up to fifty thousand a carat for the finest gemstone). The success of synthetic diamonds has enabled the demand for industrial diamonds to grow at around 10 percent a year since the late 1950s, without pushing up the price. The production of synthetics has also far outdistanced the natural industrial goods. Today the total market for industrial diamonds, worth around $300 million annually, is estimated at 110 million carats, of which 85 million carats are synthetics used as "grit." The remaining 25 million carats of natural industrials are split between 15 million carats of the lowest quality, *boart*, which is crushed into grit, and 10 million carats of near-gems.

De Beers, after a very belated start, is almost as firmly in the saddle of industrial diamonds as they are in that of gems. The natural industrial diamonds, of course, are already within their grasp. The output of Zaire, by far the largest source of industrial goods, is in the net of the Central Selling Organization, while the great Orapa mine, the next best source of industrials, is controlled by De Beers in partnership with the government of Botswana. The only significant industrial production that escapes the CSO is in Ghana, which has pursued an independent course for years, with China reputed to be its best client. The Russians, incidentally, use all their industrial goods themselves, refraining even from supplying their east European satellites, who are forced to buy their natural industrials in the West. The quality of diamonds the Russians use in industry, especially for drilling, is rated exceptionally high; much of it would be classed as gem elsewhere. De Beers sells the near-gem diamonds through the Diamond Trading Company in London to such leading industrial diamond houses as Van Moppes, the Henri Polak Diamond Corporation in New York, D. Drukker in Amsterdam and the ubiquitous Star Diamond, which is as deeply engaged in industrial goods as it is in gems. The *boart* and the synthetic, however, are marketed through De Beers

Industrial Diamonds, which has its sales offices at Shannon on the west coast of Ireland. At Shannon, De Beers has also established one of its three factories making synthetics. (The others are at Robertfors in northern Sweden and at Springs in South Africa.)

De Beers' grip on synthetics is almost as tenacious as it is on natural diamonds. Their only serious, and great, rival is General Electric, whose plant at Worthington, Ohio, is a major source of synthetic diamonds for the American market. The United States and Western Europe each consume about 30 million carats a year, and Japan around 20 million carats. De Beers, of course, cannot trade directly in the United States. World-wide General Electric and De Beers between them reckon to have close to 90 percent of the synthetics business, with each happy to claim the role of number one given the least excuse; the third runner, very far behind, is Tomei in Japan. The synthetic grit, along with the crushed *boart*, is all marketed on a day-to-day basis direct to industry through distributors (there are no "sights" for grit). De Beers Industrial Diamonds, for instance, has five main distributors to whom it ships grit at least twice a week.

The control that De Beers has won in industrial goods is not just pulling the supply strings. They are insiders on the technology, too. Back in 1946 Sir Ernest Oppenheimer, seeing how the industrial business had grown rapidly in the war, decided to establish a Diamond Research Laboratory in Johannesburg to study more varied peacetime applications. Since then De Beers has sought to initiate in the industrial field, rather than just sell goods into it. "We used to sell the material without any understanding of the technology," said Gordon Ferriman. "Now we lead the manufacturer by supplying him with more and more sophisticated products. We believe we've improved the quality of diamond tools so much that each carat does five times more work."

Certainly the chores, exotic and plebian, that can be simplified by the diamond are legion. Nor is industry just a useful dustbin for low-quality diamonds; it bids for some of the finest, too. The exceptionally rare-type 2a diamonds found at the Premier mine, for instance, are much sought after because their excellent thermal conductivity makes them indispensable in high-capacity miniature transmitters carrying television and telephone signals to and from satellites, where they absorb heat to prevent equipment burning up. "We must have high-grade stones free from inclusions," explained Horst Wapler, "because when the diamond heats up, any inclusion would expand at a different rate from the diamond, creating stresses which could result in the explosion of the stone."

One of the toughest assignments for a 2a stone was to serve as the window of the American space probe to Venus in 1978. The window had to be transparent, able to withstand the pressures of a four-month journey in outer space, the deceleration on the approach to Venus and the radical switch from the cold of space to the red-hot Venusian atmosphere. "Venus is an inhospitable place, and diamond was the only material that could meet all the requirements of strength, corrosion resistance and optical transparency set by one of the major analytic instruments, the Infrared Radiometer, which determined how temperatures varied there," explained Max Drukker, whose company in Amsterdam was assigned to make the window. Even finding a suitable diamond for this space porthole was not easy. Through the Diamond Trading Company in London, Drukker staked a claim for the next two large 2a diamonds (they needed a second for a backup window) mined at Premier. Fortuitously, an elongated 205.4-carat stone turned up, which Drukker ultimately honed into a miniature window three-quarters of an inch in diameter and one-eighth-inch thick, weighing just 13 carats (2.6 grams). "It was the largest piece of diamond ever shaped for scientific or industrial use," said Max Drukker proudly.

Some large stones, in fact, can cause as much excitement among industrialists as they did to a great gem salesman like Harry Winston. One day just before lunch at the Diamond Trading Company, Monty Charles, the managing director, came over and pulled from his pocket, like a conjuror producing an egg, a bulging blue-white diamond paper in which nested a 299.2-carat rough diamond. "It's a type 2b from the highest diamond mine in the world—Letseng-la-Terai in Lesotho," he said as a group of us admired it, "and I think I might sell it to the gentleman over there." He indicated one of the DTC's best industrial customers chatting nearby. The diamond itself was not very high quality; there was a large black flaw inside one end, but the 2b is prized for unrivaled quality in making thermistors that are acutely sensitive to temperature changes. (They can detect variations of ⅟₁₀₀₀th of a degree and are used, for instance, to measure the temperature of the stars.) The price penciled neatly on the diamond paper was $1,800 a carat—an asking price in all of over half a million dollars. Charles slipped the diamond back into his pocket and confidently went over to initiate a little business.

Industrialists do not get automatic priority; they must match the best offers of gem dealers, and they have resisted recent soaring prices. "My greatest enemies now are the gem dealers," lamented a manufacturer, "because I need high-grade stones, but I cannot afford to pay what some jeweler gets from an oil sheikh."

The large-scale needs of industry, fortunately, are not for buckets of gemstones, but for poor-quality near-gems or just for the mass of gray *boart*, which, before it is crushed to the texture of face powder, looks like a pile of peppercorns. The oil industry, for instance, devours tiny diamonds by the million. No less than 4,000 diamonds are set into the average drilling bit that bites down through the rock of Alaska, Mexico, the North Sea or the Arabian Gulf. Oil drillers do not use diamonds exclusively; much of the time tungsten carbide will suffice. "But if the rock is a problem for tungsten carbide, then we use diamonds," said an oil-drilling man, just in from three months' testing on North Sea rigs. "Maybe only three or four percent is drilled with diamonds, but it's the hardest part."

The advantage of diamond drills is not just the ability to penetrate the hardest rock but to make cuts as clean as a whistle. Oil men and miners employ diamond drills to dissect neat core samples of newly discovered reefs, while America's astronauts used them to cut out samples of the lunar surface. The same technique can be applied equally well to the renovation of an old building; when St. Paul's Cathedral in London underwent an extensive face-lifting, cores were extracted from the three-hundred-year-old masonry beneath the great dome to detect signs of stress.

The unsurpassed cutting edge of the diamond is ideal, too, for more delicate tasks. Engraving tools incorporating a diamond point of about one-tenth of a carat are used for stippling fine crystal with thousands of tiny chips or dots to make up an intricate design. Traditionally this was a craftsman's job, until an English company, Colin Mayers Ltd., got together with electronics experts at Southampton University to devise a computer-controlled glass-decorating machine with twin diamond-grinding wheels that can etch a range of patterns. And the economics of decorating crystal tableware may be altered drastically once this is perfected so that a computer can guide the etching of eight or ten glasses simultaneously.

The most sensitive cutting done with a diamond, however, is for eye surgery. Surgeons use a scalpel tipped with a one-twentieth-carat diamond blade to slice through the tissue of the eye without tearing it when they are removing cataracts.

Sharpness is combined with durability; a diamond blade or point does not blunt easily. A diamond "nib" is used, for instance, to write on stainless-steel tape in the "black-box" flight recorders in aircraft because of its long life. The same reliability recommends the diamond as the stylus for a record player. The positioning of that needle, however, is not as simple as one might imagine. "Each diamond has a 'hard' and a 'soft' direction," explained Horst Wapler, "so the diamond needle must be correctly orientated, because it makes the difference between two thousand hours' playing time and only six hundred hours." The average diamond for such a needle, incidentally, costs around twenty dollars.

Exotic jobs, which actually call for relatively few diamonds, naturally steal the limelight. The real bread-and-butter business is often less exciting, although the results can be almost as compelling. During the last twenty years perhaps no industry has been changed by diamonds more than that of the stonemason. Diamonds, or abrasive diamond grit set into the edge of saws, have enabled the stone industry to meet the bulk demands of modern construction and often saved quarries and stone yards from virtual extinction, because traditional cutting methods were simply too slow. A quarry near Bradford in the West Riding of Yorkshire, for instance, found that diamond-impregnated saw blades increased its output of sandstone by 900 percent. While at a stone yard in Aberdeen, Scotland, a new machine with fifteen diamond-impregnated blades cut the sawing time for blocks of granite from forty to four hours. Even the manufacture of clean-cut "curling" stones, for the ancient Scottish ice game, from granite hewn from the lonely island of Ailsa Craig has been able to continue economically after the introduction of diamond drills and saws to replace the traditional, but slow, hand shaping of stones.

The most unusual breakthrough, if that is the right word, occurred recently in the Carrara marble quarries in Italy, where sculptors from Michelangelo to Henry Moore have sought the finest stone. For generations the marble has been cut with heavy steel wires grinding into tons of abrasive sand sprinkled on the slabs; the constant gritty whining of the wires set teeth on edge for miles around. Then, in 1977, a local engineer, Luigi Madrigali, came up with a much simpler idea. He invented a machine that looks like an upgraded bicycle that rolls along the quarry floor on four small rubber wheels; it has a small power unit that drives a 60-foot-long cable studded with 1,000 electroplated diamond beads. The cable itself is threaded through holes drilled vertically and horizontally into the marble, and is then joined up and mounted over a flywheel on the "bicycle," which pulls it through the stone as it moves along. It slices through the marble like a piano wire cuts cheese. The Madrigali bicycle, as everyone quickly christened it, went into regular use in the Carrara quarries during 1980 to an astonished reception. In the Madriella di Massa quarry, which has the hardest marble, three diamond cables were joined to cut away a huge block over 60 feet high, 35 feet wide and 30 feet deep, weighing 6,000 tons. Enzo Dazzi at the Fanta Scritti Marmi quarry nearby found that, by installing three Madrigali bicycles, he stepped up output by 50 percent, and he promptly ordered two more. Luigi Madrigali himself calculates that his machine reduces marble-cutting costs from around twenty-five dollars per square meter to ten dollars. "It's the most revolutionary machine ever introduced in the quarries," said an Italian technical writer after going to see for himself.[23]

The value of diamonds as cutters is matched by their abrasiveness as groovers and planers of the concrete surfaces of roads, airport runways and even cattle pens. The technique was pioneered by a soft-spoken California road engineer, Cecil Hatcher, who devised what he calls a "jumbo-grooving train" with eighty diamond blades that can cut grooves one-eighth-inch deep every three-quarters of an inch along the surface of a highway. The grooves cut the risk of cars aquaplaning when either the concrete or asphalt surface is wet. Hatcher's groovers were first tested by California's division of highways with considerable success; skidding accidents were reduced by 75 percent. The improvement was even better on the Cahuenga Pass section of the Hollywood Freeway near Los Angeles, where 139 wet-roadway accidents in the year before grooving were followed by only 6 in the year after it was done. The initial improvement on roads prompted diamond grooving of airport runways, first tried out at Washington, D.C.'s, National Airport in 1967, and since adopted at the majority of U. S. airports and at many overseas. Hong Kong's Kai Tak airport, for instance, which is subject to flooding from tropical rainstorms (it also juts out right into the harbor, so it is essential planes do not overshoot), has been grooved, helping to maintain a very low accident record.

The benefits of diamond grooving have attracted some unexpected users. A California ranch owner, worried because at least two of his steers were injured or killed every month when they skidded on the slick concrete around the feeding pens, saw a freeway being grooved one day and decided that was just what he needed in his yards to give the cattle a better hoofhold.

Instead of diamond blades grooving a new concrete surface, they can also plane, or "bump-cut," an old and rutted one. Engineers, faced with the immense cost of ripping up worn roads, have found that alternatively a new surface can be shaved with a "bump cutter" that has 360 blades set with over 7,000 carats of natural and synthetic diamond grit.

The diamond's ability to groove, plane and cut concrete is rapidly extending its use throughout civil engineering. "Up to now the biggest success has been in the stone industry," said Horst Wapler of De Beers, "but I expect civil engineering to be our growth area in the 1980s, because the diamond can saw and drill even through concrete reinforced with steel." Diamond drills are already leading to new concepts of how to build factories, schools and hospitals. "When you plan a new factory you know the basic floor area," explained an engineer, "but you cannot gauge exactly where all the machines or installations will go. What we are now starting to do is build a solid concrete floor throughout; later on we can use a diamond drill to cut a one-inch hole for a waterpipe or a half-inch hole for a cable. Of course, you could always do that with a jackhammer, too, but it was slow, and a great deal of making good was necessary."

Diamond drilling is quicker and cheaper: when a leading West German cigarette manufacturer approved the technique on a new plant, it cut seven months off the building time. Diamond drilling is also being used exclusively in atomic-power stations to penetrate heavily reinforced concrete with the precision of a surgeon making an incision.

The diamond continues to advance as a cure for industrial headaches; the market is expected to double in the eighties. Since natural diamond production cannot keep pace, despite the development of the Jwaneng mine in Botswana and the prospect of good industrial yield from new discoveries in Australia, the real growth will continue to be in synthetics. The need for synthetic diamonds is spurred on not only by the wider market, but also by the rising cost of gems. The large synthetic may still be uneconomic, but alternatives to it are well advanced. De Beers has already succeeded in bonding together synthetic powder into little black pills which are called polycrystaline diamonds. "Diamond powder is bonded with cobalt and stuck on a disk of tungsten carbide," said Horst Wapler, spreading what looked like black aspirins on his desk. "You can put each of these in a tool holder and use it for milling, grooving, turning or drilling. By 1990 the polycrystaline diamond will have moved in."

Somehow that takes a little of the magic out of diamonds. Such high technology may have its benefits for industry, but what I really like to remember about the diamond is the resilient window of the Venus space probe, the incisive blade of the eye surgeon's scalpel and the diamond stylus of my record player the next time I put on Shirley Bassey's "Diamonds Are a Girl's Best Friend" or the Beatles' "Lucy in the Sky with Diamonds."

Bibliography

Bruton, Eric. *Diamonds*. London: N.A.G. Press Ltd., 1978.

Green, Timothy. *Precious Heritage, The Story of Mocatta & Goldsmid*. Circulated privately, 1978.

Green, Timothy. *The Smugglers*. London: Michael Joseph, 1969.

Gregory, Sir Theodore. *Ernest Oppenheimer and the Economic Development of Southern Africa*. London: Oxford University Press, 1962.

Hahn, Emily. *Diamond*. London: Weidenfeld and Nicolson, 1956.

Hocking, Anthony. *Oppenheimer and Son*. Johannesburg: McGraw-Hill Book Company, 1973.

Lenzen, Dr. Godehard. *The History of Diamond Production and the Diamond Trade*. London: Barrie and Jenkins Limited, 1970.

Patch, Susanne Steinem. *Blue Mystery, The Story of the Hope Diamond*. Washington, D.C.: Smithsonian Institution Press, 1976.

Roberts, Brian. *The Diamond Magnates*. London: Hamish Hamilton, 1972.

Ross, Lillian. *Reporting* (The Big Stone). London: Jonathan Cape, 1966.

Szenberg, Michael. *The Economics of the Israeli Diamond Industry*. New York: Basic Books, Inc., 1973.

Yogev, Gedalia. *Diamonds and Coral, Anglo-Dutch Jews and Eighteenth-Century Trade*. New York: Holmes and Meier, Inc., 1978.

Zucker, Benjamin. *How to Invest in Gems, Everyone's Guide to Buying Rubies, Sapphires, Emeralds & Diamonds*. New York: Quadrangle/The New York Times Book Co., 1976.

Index